Bread for the Journey:

Preaching to myself

Bread for the Journey:

Preaching to myself

Bill King

Pocahontas Press
Blacksburg, Virginia

Bread for the Journey:

Preaching to myself

ISBN 978-0-9967744-8-2

Cover art by Zac Neulieb
Interior design by Michael Abraham
Printed in the United States of America

Pocahontas Press
www.pocahontaspress.com

Dedication

There would have been no Bread for the Journey postings if the members of Luther Memorial Lutheran Church had not welcomed and supported me as their pastor. So this collection is dedicated to the members of that congregation who allowed me to share their lives. It is also dedicated to my wife, Gail, who has long given me what psychologists call "unconditional positive regard." Without her gentle support and honest suggestions my life would have been much poorer, my ministerial effectiveness diminished, and my tenure as a pastor probably much shorter.

Foreword

A wise teacher told me, "Preach to yourself and you can be pretty sure you will hit most of the congregation." I took that to mean that a good pastor and theologian looks at the events in the news, the witness of Scripture, and the best in religious traditions and then asks, "What question would I most like answered in this moment?" Much religious writing is an attempt to answer questions which few people are asking, in platitudes which, if the preacher is honest, satisfy neither the writer nor the audience.

For over 15 years part of my ministry as a pastor was regularly writing an online meditation. The series was called "Bread for the Journey," and these reflections were intended primarily for those who called me "pastor" and were an extension of my pastoral care for the students and parishioners whom I served. A number of people asked me to collect those reflections into a published form, hence this book.

These meditations were written over an extended period of time. I have organized them around the seasons of the Church Year and some themes which are often associated with those seasons. Since there was no systematic development of ideas I have made no effort to put them in chronological order. Some of these reflections were intended to bring the Gospel into conversation with events facing my congregation at the time I wrote them, but they were also intended to lift up truth which transcends the latest headline or social media post. Theological reflection is like fish, best served fresh. But sometimes there is value in looking back. I hope these meditations speak to the contours of your own life, even if the events which prompted some of them are no longer at the top of your news feed.

Contact

The author can be reached by email at:
luthercm@gmail.com

Table of Contents

Advent: Waiting

Advent in the Hospital

If you want to understand Advent, linger at a hospital. I have spent a lot of time in hospital and nursing home rooms over the past few months – though not nearly as much as some of our members and their families. Visiting with them you realize that it is all about waiting: Waiting for the doctor to make rounds. Waiting for the tests to come back. Waiting to see if the newest drug is going to work. Waiting for the physical therapist to work you in. Waiting for a broken bone, a ripped tendon, or a battered body to heal. Waiting, most of all, for time to pass in the midst of mind-numbing tedium. Forget about fire and brimstone, hell is being stuck in a sick room while Montel, soaps, and vacuous game shows drone on…and on…and on in the background.

You wait with a mixture of fear that the darkness will only get deeper and hope that today will be the one when the dawn breaks. You wait for the gears of the medical system to grind slowly to some resolution. You wait for the mysterious healing energy of your body to turn the tide against decay. You wait, wishing you could do something to speed up the process and in the realization that you are pretty much powerless to do much except cultivate patience. You wait.

The great virtue of the experience is that it strips away all the superfluous things of life. Beyond that room there is nothing. You discover how much energy is wasted in worrying about things which just do not matter--how many priceless moments you have failed to notice like diamonds scattered at your feet as you rush through life. But you also savor the beams of light that do pierce the darkness: the visit from a friend, the plant which shows up unexpectedly, the unfailing kindness of a CNA, the card which reminds you that you are not forgotten, a wise word from a book or the scriptures which feeds your soul.

Advent is the season of waiting, the season which reminds us that we are not in control. This season proclaims that God comes – seldom on our timeline – but God comes. We may not have the resolution for which we pray to God, but we will have God in the midst of whatever comes. Whatever we are waiting for we do not wait alone. This season reminds us that our longing for Emmanuel, "god with us" will finally be satisfied. The night may be so inky we cannot see the way forward, yet it is in the darkness that the faint light is most easily seen – if we open our eyes.—If you are waiting in the darkness this Advent, may your vision be attuned to the flickers of light on the horizon which herald God's coming.

Butterfly

In *Zorba the Greek*, Nikos Kazantzakis tells the story of a man watching a butterfly emerge from its cocoon. Eager to see a butterfly break free of the ugly sheath, he soon becomes impatient when the struggle continues without noticeable progress. Wanting to speed the process along and make the birthing easier he blows on the cocoon to warm it. The butterfly pushes through the hole it has made, but to the man's horror its wings are misshapen and unable to open. The butterfly writhes in pain and soon dies. Too late he realizes nature has a certain timeline which can not be hastened, and the struggle, while often difficult, is essential in forming wings which can take flight.

The Quaker author Parker Palmer uses this story to illustrate how we sometimes do violence to those we love when our intentions are the best. When family members, friends, or co-workers are doing things which we judge counterproductive, our instinct is to rush in and try to fix the situation. We offer our advice or perhaps even take charge of their struggle. We want to save them the heartache of bad choices and blind alleys. The danger is that we may take away something essential for their growth. The struggle which gives long-term health and confidence is usually more important than solving the short-term problem. I can think of many times when "all I was trying to do is help," but what I communicated was lack of confidence in my child, friend, or counselee. They did not need my wisdom, but my willingness to wait with them as they found their way.

Sometimes the hardest thing is sitting patiently and faithfully while another slowly discovers the truth she knows at a deep level but is not yet ready to acknowledge. In those times we do well to remember each person with whom we interact is wondrously created and perpetually loved by God. God is acting in every life. Our task is not to solve other's problems or spare them from hard questions; it is gently to nurture the life which is seeking maturity. We are neither the author nor custodian of another's life; we are midwife of the spirit. If we truly seek to serve another, as opposed to serving our need to be needed, we will not allow our impatience to do violence to the frail wings of a soul seeking to take flight.

Seed and Flower

The devotional resource I have been using quoted this brief saying from a Zen master, "The seed never sees the flower." Such brief observations are less about conveying information than inviting one into reflection, and on that day it worked.

The image of the seed is, of course, a familiar one in the

New Testament. Jesus told parables about seeds, soils, and the things which make for growth. Thinking of his impending passion, he observed that a seed must die if it is to give life. The image is familiar, but somehow I had never really pondered the relationship in time between seed and flower. What does it mean that the seed never sees the flower?

I am one of those people who likes to have the whole thing mapped out in advance. Before I start I like to have a pretty good idea of where I will end up. That is true whether I am taking a trip or writing a sermon. I have a hard time beginning unless I can see the conclusion. That makes me pretty focused for a sprint, but not so good in a marathon, where the goal is far removed from the starting point.

So I found this Zen saying to be an important reminder of how the really important transformations in the world take place. Imagine how many generations of Black grandmothers in the Jim Crow South kept planting the seed of dignity in their children until the soil was finally ready for it to sprout. How hard that must have been to keep planting when the evidence was so strong that there would never be a flowering.

Imagine how hard it must have been for the early Christians to keep the faith for several hundred years when it appeared that this little sect would be a tiny footnote in the historical narrative of Rome. Generations were born, grew old, and died without seeing much which looked like success as the world measures it.

Sometimes we are blessed to see the fruition of our efforts: a child grows up and makes us proud; we take a hard project to successful completion; the candidate for whom we labored wins the election. Yet just as often we feel more like a single drop of water in the stream pushing up against a granite wall – we can't see that we have made any immediate impact. It is hard to remember that billions of drops on that same spot will carve a gorge.

Advent is a season which prompts us to understand that planting seeds is just as important as seeing the flowers bloom, for absent patient planting, there will be no blossoms. We may never know how our words redeem another from despair; how a chance act of kindness prevented a suicide or a relapse. We fling the seeds and let the flowers take care of themselves. Our task is to faithfully plant and not despair when the fruits are delayed – and to give hearty thanks in those moments when the seed does see the fruit.

Acting in Trust

You need to take responsibility for your own health care. That's what all the literature says, and based on my observations in hospitals and nursing homes, it is certainly true. I yield to no one in my appreciation of doctors, nurses, and all the other people who serve in medical facilities. They meet people when they are in pain and at their most vulnerable and anxious. Most of the time they do an exemplary job in delivering fine care with great compassion. But they are stretched thin and overworked. They are balancing the needs of multiple people at the same time. You need to ask questions, understand your options, and follow up if something seems wrong with your own care or that of someone you love.

Still, there are limits to how much control you can have. I had sinus surgery last week and the experience made me keenly aware that at some point you are absolutely dependent on others. I can't read an MRI to know what it is saying about my internal orifices. I can click on sinus links on the internet until my eyes cross, but I will not know as much as one who has devoted his life to understanding them. I can weigh therapeutic options, but finally I have to trust experience and competence greater than my own. And as the anesthesia hits your system...your last thought is that, like it or not, your only choice is to trust.

Negotiating the health care system demands our best efforts and discernment. But it also brings us up against the limits of autonomy.

It occurs to me that this is not so different from cultivating a healthy spiritual life. A rich devotional life is not an accident. It takes a decision to block out time for prayer. It requires a choice to spend time in reading the Bible or devotional literature. It is opting to spend time in service rather than idleness. It is the result of seeking God in a world which is not always attuned to seeing the holy in the hubbub.

But after we have done all that, after we have worked hard to bring ourselves into the awareness of God's presence in our lives, we have to wait. God cannot be commanded to appear like a genie out of the lamp. The best we can do is open our hearts to receive what might come in a verse of scripture or the song of a bird on a hiking trail. After we have put forth our best effort we stand with open hands trusting that One who is wiser than we will fill them with what we need to be healed and empowered. The life of faith is never one of passivity, but it is often one of trust and patience. We cannot command grace to come to us; we can only give thanks when it does.

Exam Prayer

End of the semester. Last Lutheran Student Movement worship of the year. As we prayed around the circle, the petitions were heartfelt, sincere, and fairly predictable after twenty years in campus ministry. Predictable is not necessarily bad; some joys and needs endure from one generation of students to the next. The desire to rejoice or cry out for God's favor is not diminished because others before you have done the same. Several gave thanks for community which had been there for them during the tough times of the year. Others lifted up friends and family with special needs ranging from illness to anxiety over a weak job market. But because the end of the LSM year inevitably coincides with exams, there were many prayers on the order of, "Help us as we enter into exams to not let the stress get to us."

But then she prayed a petition I had never heard at the closing service. "Lord, we are really stressed, but help us to remember that the reason we are stressed is because we have opportunities that many people don't. We would not be here if we did not have the resources to be at college, so help us be thankful for these opportunities." I am not sure if that is a perfect quotation, but it reflects the Spirit – as I think her prayer did.

I confess that I did not track the rest of the prayers as we went around the circle; I was still back thinking about what she said. I thought about how much of my dissatisfaction is related to blessings I unthinkingly receive. Most of my problems are ones millions would love to have. I complain when my car needs a fuel pump, when the grass at my idyllic homestead needs mowing, and when I have a deadline to meet. Millions spend empty days dreaming of cars in front of shanty town shelters because there is no work for them to do.

Guilt is not the point; a spirit of thanksgiving is. The way we see the world determines how we respond to it. We are prone to receive the good as our divine right and regard the challenges as impositions. But if we remember that life is indeed a gift, we are less likely to squander it in resentment. When we focus on the symphony rather than the flat violin we begin to discover just how much joy is close at hand.

Today, take time to give thanks for whatever stresses you.

Hope Begins in the Dark

"Hope begins in the dark, the stubborn hope that if you just show up and try to do the right thing, the dawn will come. You wait and watch and work: You don't give up."

--Anne Lamott, from *Bird by Bird: Some Instructions on Writing and Life*

I ran across the above quotation last week. I am not positive, but I think it's from a chapter in which Anne Lamott describes the anguish of the writing process. You stare at the ceiling, desperately hoping that some idea – any idea – will present itself. You wonder what possessed you to think you have anything worth saying. You pace. You rearrange the pencils on the desk. Your gut fills with the sickening fear that several hours from now there will still be only a blank screen and a taunting cursor in front of you. You try to keep at bay the suspicion that all your efforts are a waste of time. The only way through that dark place, Lamott says, is to just show up, keeping vigil until inky despair gives way to a pinpoint of light, which becomes a hint of illumination, and finally something worth reading.

Her words brought to mind two groups of people for me. In this Advent season I am mindful of those I know whose lives are shrouded by darkness. For some it is the blackness of grief. For others it is the shadow of an uncertain job future. Still others confront each day from beneath a crushing depression which puts a grey shroud over even the most joyous events. The pain is different for each, but what unifies them is the sense that it is never going to end – that the night is their new normal. The word which comes to us in Advent is that even in the deepest darkness, there is a pinprick of light preparing to illumine our despair. Sometimes we feel like miners caught without a light in a cave-in; sometimes all we can do is wait until the light breaks through. If you are sitting in darkness as you read this, I hope the light comes quickly.

The other group I thought about was the volunteers who staffed Luther Memorial's hosting of "To Our House," the shelter for homeless men. Most of the hosting tasks were singularly unexciting. There was a lot of sitting around, a bit of washing (everyone's favorite task), a little chatting, and a few nights sleeping on a cot. It was not obvious that lives were changed by our efforts; folks were just fed and given a warm place to sleep. Yet these volunteers did it with good cheer. They did it willingly. In a word, they showed up – ready to be used as a small instrument of God's love.

Most of ministry is not spectacular, most of the work of the kingdom of God is done by folks willing to "wait, watch, and work." I am profoundly thankful for the ordinary saints who make To Our House and many other ministries possible because they show up ready to do whatever needs to be done. So if you are one of those folks who is wondering whether it is worth showing up to do a tedious or dull task – thank you – more often than not you are the reason the folks sitting in darkness finally get a glimpse of light.

Christmas: Incarnation

Grace Note

Bear with me. This Bread for the Journey may seem to start out like one of those insufferable Christmas brag letters ("Daughter Susie won the Indy 500 and was awarded a full ride to Oxford; son Roberto developed a cold fusion reactor over spring break after scaling Mt. Everest...") but I promise there is a nobler purpose.

Recently Gail and I received a note from our son's boss, Carolyn. Scott is marking ten years with his company and she wrote to tell us just how much she and the company appreciate him. You may think that is a bit unusual, sending the parents of a 36-year-old man a note about their child. And that is just my point. It was unusual. In the midst of a very busy time she took time to craft a beautiful note which affirmed both Scott and our parenting (yes, I blushed). She did not have to do it. Nobody was expecting it. It came as pure grace into our mailbox, and I suspect it may be the best present we get this holiday season.

I am not interested in ranting about the commercialization of Christmas; gifts as a sign of appreciation of those we love are fine. The fact remains that most of us have way more junk than we will ever need. We may think, in the moment, that our world will implode if we do not get the latest gadget, but in reality we will not give a second thought to that gadget two months from now. I can assure you that I will remember Carolyn's note long after our Christmas cactus is compost.

Few of us need more stuff, but everyone needs to know they are appreciated. All of us want to feel valued and no one likes to feel invisible or forgotten. We do not necessarily have the coin to buy lavish presents, but each of us has the power to bless by noticing another person and then speaking a word of kindness and affirmation.

So wrap up your beloved's heart's desire and stick it under the tree; accept my benediction on your generosity – go for it! But consider also telling a few folks in specific detail why you think they are special – especially those who have no reason to expect an affirming word from you. Drop them a note. Stop by on a cold day. Surprise them with a little piece of grace, a reflection of God's unmerited love given to all of us in this Nativity season.

How Many Blessings?

"How many blessings do we still have left?" She had used the phrase several times, but for some reason I heard it – I mean really heard it – this time. I was at the Valley Interfaith Child Care Center, helping to deliver the baked goods and tuition assistance Luther Memorial is giving, as a congregational Christmas Outreach ministry, to clients of the Center. A steady stream of parents had been coming through the doors, picking up their little ones, and leaving. So the director of the program was mentally taking inventory, "How many blessings do we still have left," that is, "How many children have not yet been picked up." Two observations about that choice of phrase:

First, in that moment I felt very good about supporting the work of this agency. It is great when folks do their work with competence and efficiency. It is even better when they begin that work with the assumption that the persons in front of them are not simply beggars at the feast but precious children of God, deserving of all the respect we can give them, and the means by which we may be enriched. Yes, little children are amazing; they melt your heart with a smile. But anyone who has spent much time in a day care or classroom will tell you that sometimes it takes an act of will to see anything in a little face except a cranky, demanding ball of mucus-dripping energy. I have to think those children at VICCC are better off when the folks caring for them start with the assumption that they are first and foremost a blessing. I suspect my most testy encounters would be much improved if I thought of the scowling face in front of me as a blessing.

That got me thinking about the great power of naming. If I call that piece of paper which is always on my desk a "to do" list, I think of those tasks very differently than if I call it my list of "ministry opportunities." I can have "appointments" or I can choose to have "chances to serve." I don't think this is just a cutesy word game. Remembering that every person is a blessing, every day a fresh opportunity to make Christ known, fundamentally changes how we live in the world and our openness to give and receive joy in the simplest of encounters.

Blue Christmas

The new pastor was making a call on a recently bereaved widow who had lost her husband of many years. Attempting to offer some solace the young cleric said, "Joan, his body is not in that grave, it's in heaven with his Lord." "I know," she replied, "but I wish it were in bed next to me keeping me warm."

I first heard that story as a cautionary tale from a pastoral care professor, a reminder that theological truth does not magically banish human pain. I write this about a week before Christmas. Amid the excitement of the season, hold

14

in your heart the many persons who are hurting this day. Christmas can be a brutal season when you find yourself swimming against a tide of happy-face muzak and idealized images of perfect families gathered in warm abundance.

Our days usually proceed with one blurring into the next. Christmas is a stark signpost which marks our life's journey from one year to next. As the day approaches we unavoidably ponder how our life has unfolded over the past twelve months. Sometimes there is cause for great celebration, but just as often the gay colors of the season make a painful contrast to the grayness in our soul. With "Silver Bells" and "Joy to the World" echoing in our ears we mark the death of a beloved parent, spouse, or son, the end of our marriage, the suddenly tenuousness of our job, the ongoing struggles of a daughter to find her way, the fear that illness inspires, or the despair of clinical depression.

This "bread" is not to minimize the profound power of celebrating "Emmanuel," God with us. In the midst of pain there is real consolation in knowing God is near. But it is a gentle word on behalf of all those who are crying as December 25th approaches. It is a reminder that one of the greatest gifts we can give at Christmas is the gift of sensitivity and compassion to those who are laboring under burdens we can scarcely understand. It is an invitation to be God's loving presence – Emmanuel – for someone whose sobs get muffled by the songs of the season.

…and if you are one of those reading this reflection through a glaze of tears, a few lines from an Advent hymn, words both honest and hopeful:

Each winter as the year grows older, we each grow older too.
The chill sets in a little colder,
the verities we knew seem shaken and untrue.

Yet I believe beyond believing that life can spring from death,
    That growth can flower from our grieving,
    that we can catch our breath and turn transfixed by faith.
    O Child of ecstasy and sorrows, O Prince of peace and pain,
    Brighten today's world by tomorrow's,
    Renew our lives again, Lord Jesus, come and reign.

Beep, Beep

Beep. Beep. Beep. Our cordless phone is getting old and cranky. The battery in the handset doesn't want to stay charged, so after you've been on the horn for any length of time it starts sounding like a garbage truck backing up. Beep. Beep. Beep. You know it's about to die and you better hang up or change to another phone.

I have written this before heading to South Carolina to visit family after Christmas. The holiday shopping crunch is over. The special services of Advent/Christmas are finished. Sitting in Aiken I have deliberately not brought a thing with me which I can use to prepare for next semester's work. This week I intend to be fully present to my brother, my parents, my children, and other special people. I am doing that because the week before Christmas I started hearing beeps.

I was getting short-tempered. Beep. I was eating too much of things I really don't like. Beep. I was having a hard time concentrating on important tasks – and did not particularly care. Beep, Beep. I do not know what yours are, but these are some of the things I've learned to see as warning signs that I am running on empty. When I start hearing those beeps I know that I'm about to have nothing much to offer other

16

people, and indeed that I'm about to do some harm with a harsh word or slip-shod work. So I start looking for time and activities which recharge the battery.

Think for a moment about what your beeps might be. What are the tip offs that you are fading fast? Maybe you don't have a whole week to recharge. That's okay. A phone works fine when you recharge it right after use, instead of running it to empty. Recharge daily. So what can you do to recharge your battery today? A long walk? A crossword puzzle? How about calling an old friend you've lost touch with? A trashy novel? You know better than I what puts a tiger in your tank. Just pay attention to your body and spirit and do what needs to be done.

… And please, for your own sake, don't say you haven't got have the time to recharge – after the beeping, my phone pretty quickly goes dead. That's not being overly dramatic, just the truth. Like it or not, the analogy applies to physical health, emotions, work quality, and our most important relationships. We recharge or we die.

Gift of You

"What do you give the person who has nothing? Comfort." The speaker is Heddy, a San Francisco flop house resident, talking about finding a birthday present for her long time companion, Monica, who is dying of ovarian cancer. Neither she nor her companion owns much and Monica already has little need for even those meager possessions. So Heddy gives the one thing she has, herself. She shows up. She sits by the bed. She shares memories. She makes sure Monica's last days will not be days alone.

As I listened to the podcast which contained the above

comment, several things came together in my mind. One was the holiday blitz which has begun, urging us to buy, buy, buy in order to prove to that special someone that he or she really is special to us. The thing she most wants in all the world is a diamond necklace, a silver Mercedes will make his life complete. That's the message which daily repetition of the same commercials hammers home. Deliver the right present, and you deliver bliss in a bottle.

Then I thought about all the lonely people littering the halls I see when I visit the nursing homes. I thought about the many people who tell me, "I don't know how you can stand to go there; it is so depressing, I just couldn't do it; I wouldn't know what to say." I thought about the cadre of people I know who do show up because they feel a genuine care for those who cannot come to them.

You do not need to be a Grinch to think that living a lie does no one any good. The lie is that if you don't have enough financial resources to do it up right, you don't have anything to give. The lie is that what people most want can be bought with a credit card. We need the material basics; there is no need to romanticize poverty. But the gift that most people want is the loving presence of another person who truly cares about them – cares enough to be present and share their joys and sorrows, cares enough to be with them when they are not terribly presentable or feeling very lovable.

The gift of care is not cheap; it can be emotionally expensive and time consuming. It's easier to give a trinket than to give yourself. But while we cannot all afford a new car, we can all give our attention, our patience, and our willingness to simply be with another person in their need. You do not have to have wise words, solutions to problems which have no answer, or explanations for suffering. You just have to show up.

To quote the jewelry ad, "This holiday season give the gift she [or he] really wants."

Scarred

I got one of those phone calls. You know the kind I mean, one that immediately refocuses your thoughts and priorities by inserting a new reality into your life. A call from the police at 2 a.m. concerning your child's accident is a call like that. So is one from your doctor the day after your tests. You pick up the telephone and five seconds later your life is radically different.

My call was from the director of campus ministry telling me that budget woes are going to mean some "reductions in force" and "reconfiguration" in the division of the ELCA for which I worked. Translation: Some colleagues are being laid off and my job description was changing a great deal.

In the midst of all that turmoil, I ran across a book by Joan Chittister, *Scarred by Struggle, Transformed by Hope*, which explores how our struggles are seldom sought but potentially life giving. As I wrestled with the grief of losing the familiar, the anxiety of the unknown, and the exhilaration of new challenges, the following section felt like a comforting word from God in a time of confusion. Change is not easy, but God is ever in the midst of even the most disorienting struggles we face as a necessary part of being human. I offer Chittister's words to all of you who are facing unbidden times of transition, a reminder that the wounds inflicted by change are often painful, but need not be mortal:

"The illusion of benign unchangeability is a seductive one. Each step along the way once accomplished, I have discovered, comes with a ring of permanence to it. But it isn't. It never is. It is always interrupted by an equally spectral series of obstacles and interruptions that make every next miracle seem impossible, every next point unreachable, every present situation unbearable…I have come to understand what the poet Arthur O'Shaughnessy meant when he wrote, 'Each age is a dream that is dying or one that is coming to birth.'… The regularity of small and irritating, great and debilitating losses that threaten the death of the heart, that interrupt the flow of life are, I have discovered, of the essence of living. But that does not make them welcome guests. Just when we feel that we have finally gotten it right, finally achieved what we set out to get, finally found what we have always wanted, the bubble bursts, the bauble breaks, the future is gone. The spiritual question becomes how to go about each dying without giving into the death of the soul."

Hurt and Hate

"I imagine one of the reasons people cling to their hates so stubbornly is because they sense, once hate is gone, they will be forced to deal with their pain."

These words from writer and social critic James Baldwin begin a chapter in Jonathan Sacks' wonderful book *Not in God's Name: Confronting Religious Violence* (perhaps the best theology I have read in the last five years). I have been reflecting on them a lot lately. Wherever I turn – whether to my Facebook feed, the morning paper, radio news as I drive around, or personal conversations – I am struck by how much anger and distrust is out there these days. You have to go back to the era of Viet Nam war protests and Civil Rights marches to find a time when there was such polarization. It seems to me that the task is two-fold, understanding what is going on and finding a way forward that moves us beyond a bunker mentality, where we view those with whom we disagree as malevolent.

It is incredibly hard to do, but as Baldwin implies, the first step may be to consider that those we perceive as haters are hurting – and then making an honest effort to understand their pain. Hate is at bottom a desperate effort to blame someone else for my misfortune, to bolster my sense of self by dismissing another as unworthy of concern. But when I sense that you are taking my pain seriously, that you want to see the world through my eyes, it is harder to see you as the enemy.

I am not saying we should gloss over injustice or excuse bad behavior simply because someone is hurting. We do not do that in parenting, and we should not do it in our life together. But can't we make an effort to understand the frustrations and fears which might prompt another to lash out? Can't we do that; particularly if the alternative is continuing to stoke a cauldron of bitterness which will bubble over and scald us all?

This Bread appears the week between Christmas Day and New Year's Day, between celebrating the Prince of Peace's birth and the festival of fresh beginnings. What better way to mark this week than to resolve to see others through eyes more interested in understanding than condemning.

Spirit of the Season

"Listen to this!" I had not even gotten in the door when the receptionist held up a compact disk and put it into the player. "The boss doesn't get into the spirit of the season, but he's not here today. So I'm playing it all day. Isn't this amazing?" In fact the music was rather nice, operatic settings of some traditional Christmas hymns and carols, but I was only half listening. I was still wondering what she meant by "the boss doesn't get into the spirit of the season."

I know nothing about her boss's religious convictions, but I would be surprised if he begrudges others a celebration of Christmas. Have endless repetitions of "The Little Drummer Boy" caused him to go screaming into the not so silent night, seeking relief from the little tyke's musical water torture? If so, I can relate. Is he trying to respect the religious convictions of the many non-Christians in our town who prefer that listening to wall-to-wall Christmas muzak not be a precondition for getting professional services? I'm not sure it's a major problem, but I'd give him credit for trying to be sensitive. Perhaps he takes the meaning of Christmas so seriously that he is troubled by the trivialization of the season wrought by dogs barking "Jingle Bells." Or maybe he just doesn't like Italian tenors. I don't know what was behind his receptionist's comment.

But I do know this man has always treated me with the utmost gentleness, attentiveness, honesty, and respect. I do know he gives a lot of time and money to agencies and organizations which benefit the poorest in our area. I do know it is a lot harder to be a person of peace and graciousness each day than it is to wear a piece of fake ivy on your lapel and max out the credit card on a buying binge in honor of Him who was born dirt poor. I do know honoring the spirit of the season is lot more than playing a compact disk of Bing's greatest holiday hits.

We get into the spirit of the season by making room for the transformation which the Christ child offers. The most profound way of getting into the spirit is letting God's Spirit get into us, so that every person we meet the rest of the year has a hint that we have pondered the babe in the manger and been changed by the experience. I like the parties, presents – and yes, the music – as much as the next guy. Still, as a sign of this holy season, I'll take one life characterized by compassion and justice over a hundred holiday songs.

O holy child of Bethlehem, Descend to us we pray;
Cast out our sin and enter in, Be born in us today.

Christmas Possibilities

Driving down to South Carolina to visit family for the holidays I was listening to the radio and heard an interesting thesis. We all know how excited children get about Christmas, much more than adults. One commentator suggested that the reason children love Christmas so much is not just because they like getting presents (though that should not be discounted), but because they see the world as filled with infinite possibilities. Before they go into the family room and see what Santa has brought, literally anything is possible. There are no limits to what they can imagine. The future is wide open and they can dream as boldly as they wish. That sense of limitlessness is itself a source of great joy.

In contrast, adult are more likely to come to Christmas looking back. Our thoughts often turn to a mythical, perfect day against which we measure every present Christmas – and of course it never quite measures up. Rather than focusing on possibilities we reflect on what has been lost: a loved one, our innocence, a simpler time. Instead of embracing an open future we attempt to freeze the past and desperately try to recreate it anew.

Can we learn from the children? Surely we would never deliberately squelch the wonder and hope which a child feels at Christmas; reality will intrude soon enough. There are already too many children whose innocence has been prematurely stolen by poverty, war, death, and abuse for us to go out of our way to deliberately add to their numbers. Much better to receive their gift.

If we are struggling with this season we might do well to borrow a little of their attitude. Yes, things are not going to ever be the way they used to be. There are some times and people whose loss we should and do mourn. Yet, as the children remind us, there are also new possibilities opening before us if we dare to be open to them: new relationships to be formed, new directions to be explored, new dreams to bring to fruition. Beyond all the commercial, sentimental accretions, isn't this what Christmas is all about: God was faithful in the past; give thanks. God has new possibilities waiting to be born out of divine love; welcome them.

Geza

With a twinkle in his eyes, Geza smiled and handed me the tennis balls as we changed sides after the first set, "Well, you're younger, but we have 157 years of experience." My doubles group is one of the increasingly few places where I am the youngster in the crowd. At a mere 55, I'm a child compared to most of the guys. But don't feel sorry for them. They can flat play the game. They are smart, and they don't yield to the youthful passions their clergy colleague too often gives free rein. I knew better than to give Geza any cheap pity; his sneaky, chopping strokes tie me in knots. For the record, my partner and I had to go to a tiebreaker before winning 7-6. I could learn a lot about tennis from those 157 years of experience.

And that got me thinking about the relative value we place on experience and novelty. This time of year we are bombarded by pleas to buy products simply because they are newer, hotter, or merely unusual. Watch the ads carefully and you will notice that they seldom bother to make the case that the product is actually better, just that it is new. The American presumption has always been that progress is inevitable, that newer must be better, that the old should yield to the next wave of innovation. But is that always true? Is the world really a better place because you can now watch the epic Lord of the Rings trilogy on a one inch mobile phone screen? Would anyone argue that the visual experience is actually better; isn't it merely novel – and inferior.

I am not arguing for the possibility or desirability of freezing innovation, but I do wonder if we fail to value experience enough, particularly when it comes to the hard won wisdom of a well-lived life. One of the things you notice about Jesus is that He was rooted in His tradition but never hamstrung by it. He drew on the best of Jewish faith and practice, which called the people to love justice, care for the poor, and give ultimate loyalty to nothing less than God. But He never followed a rule just because it had always been done that way. He preferred asking provocative, open-ended questions to giving safe answers. He valued thoughtful struggle over slavish, unthinking obedience. He was passionately committed to deep truth which had stood the test of time, but He knew that truth has to be articulated and embraced anew by each generation, through words and actions that fit the new context.

So what's your default? Do you almost always presume old

is better or do you tend to embrace novelty for the sake of novelty? How might God be inviting you to open up to new possibilities in the first case or to find enduring wisdom beyond the ephemeral in the second? It has been said that good parenting gives children both roots and wings; the same is true of mature faith.

One Spin

The roulette wheel whirls in a red and black blur. The ball clatters and jumps, finally settling into one of the slots. In that moment, just before you can read the winning number, time freezes. That is particularly true for the person who has piled all his chips on the table, investing his whole bankroll on a single spin. Ecstasy or despair? It all rides on something beyond his control, the bounce of a ball.

Most of us do not hang out in casinos wagering the milk money on games of chance, but we may do something similar with our emotional health during this Christmas week. Heart-warming television specials, a rose-tinged memory of holidays past, and a deep desire to turn the page on whatever disappointments and stresses linger at year's end tempt to us to invest too much emotional capital in the next few days. Don't get me wrong. I am looking forward to time with family, the quiet mystery of Christmas Eve worship, and the chance to disengage from familiar routines. But expecting Christmas to satisfy all our longings is like hoping two days at the gym can undo a whole year of overeating and riding the couch.

If we expect Christmas to "fix" all our broken relationships or give us joy when we have not cultivated the ability to find it in our daily existence, we will inevitably be disappointed. Tempers flare when the family gathers. Deep griefs intrude as we think of empty places at the table. Life can not measure up to a Hallmark card's fantasy world.

So, rather than expecting Christmas to supply a year's worth of hope, let it be what it was that first night in Bethlehem, a visible sign that, even in the midst of the darkness, there is light. Christ did not come fully formed into the world. The mystery had to mature; it was years before its implications were manifest. Christmas is not an oak, strong enough to bear the full weight of our human need; it is the acorn of hope planted in our lives to grow slowly, but dependably, each day of the coming year. Let Christmas teach you a new way of seeing the world, as a place where heaven touches even the most ordinary act, fills it with radiance, and calls you to celebrate God's drawing near.

This week, by all means, remember, but do it also during the other fifty one: "How silently, how silently, the wondrous gift is giv'n! So God impart to human hearts the blessings of His heav'n."

Letting Go of Hurt

Call it luck, coincidence, or providence, but it often seems that the word I need to hear comes to me when I least expect it. Before I went to bed last night I was mentally rehashing a particularly trying relationship. Just as you compulsively rub your tongue over an ulcer, I treated myself to the exquisite pain of remembering with righteous indignation all the wrongs another had done to me and mine. I succeeded in inflaming my resentment without doing anything to deal with it. All I did was give myself a case of spiritual heartburn.

When I arose this morning and opened the devotional

book I have been using I was greeted by these words from Henri Nouwen, "One of the hardest things to do in life is to let go of old hurts…Holding people's faults against them often creates an impenetrable wall. But listen to Paul: 'For anyone who is in Christ, there is a new creation; the old order is gone and a new being is there to see. It is all God's work.' Indeed we cannot let go of old hurts, but God can." [*Bread for the Journey*, December 30]

I write these words on the last day of the year. I look back with profound gratitude for the many ways I have been blessed, for the people who have eased my burdens this year. But I realize that once again I have carried resentments, like a backpack full of rocks, which have made my journey more difficult than it could have been. Any day is a great day to turn from pointless anger, but the turning of the year seems a particularly appropriate time to draw a line and begin again, to embrace the possibility that God can create something new in our lives if we do not insist on holding on to the petty, the resentful, and the hopeless.

I am not talking about being stupid – some relationships are abusive, need to be seen as such, and ended. I am not talking about denial which ignores what needs to be mended. I am suggesting that salvation is not an abstraction which deals with a distant heaven; it is God's gift to us right now when we refuse to be bound by own past – or the past deeds of those who have hurt us.

A new year. A new creation is waiting to be born when we allow God to free us from past rage and disappointment. When we break down old walls we can climb atop the rubble and perhaps see new possibilities on the horizon.

Two Funerals in Four Days

I went to two funerals in four days. As regular readers of Bread for the Journey know, my position with the ELCA Churchwide office was eliminated in late fall. In mid-December I made one last trip to Chicago to tie up loose ends, attend to transitions, and gather with colleagues to mark the official end of the unit in which we had all worked.

Because of the limited number of flights home, I spent several hours alone after all the official festivities were over, sitting and reading in our unit's offices. Those still employed had appointments elsewhere, and those who, like me, had been terminated, felt no need to linger. Many times over the years I had wondered how anyone got any work done in these offices – a beehive of cubicles with no doors and little sound baffling. That day it would have been no problem. Large banks of lights were dark because there were no people beneath them. The floor was quiet as a tomb. Empty cubicles still bore the nameplates of my friends who had hastily abandoned them, a ghostly reminder of what had been. Incongruously, the image that came to mind was a ballroom the morning after a party. Those eerie hours on the 7th floor brought home to me the reality of changes taking place in Christendom which I have been reading about for years.

While in Chicago I got word that my only uncle had died. So I flew home, repacked, and drove to Pickens, S.C. to be part of the funeral. He was 92, and though he had been in poor health, it was hard to imagine him gone. He was like a massive oak which has always been there and leaves an obvious hole in the canopy when it falls. I would not say we were particularly close; we just did not spend that much time together. But he had been a constant in my fam-

29

ily since I took my first breath, and his death was like seeing a piece of my life's mosaic come unglued and fall to the floor.

You will read this during the Christmas season and a few days after New Year's. This season prompts us to reflect on what has happened over the past year. There are usually joys to celebrate, but inevitably there have been deaths. Sometimes the death has been literal, the loss of a dear friend or family member; sometimes it is a job, a dream, a relationship, or some element of innocence which has died.

Staring out over the dark 7th floor of the ELCA offices and down into my Uncle Lawrence's casket I remembered some words from the "Order for the Burial of the Dead," "God, the generations rise and pass away before You. You are the strength of those who labor; You are the rest of the blessed. We rejoice in the company of Your saints." Like tides at the beach, our institutions and families arise, break forth in a flurry of activity, and then ebb away. Nothing is constant, save God's care. It is good to remember that in the midst of whatever changes and transitions we face, we are not alone. The loss of the past does not mean there is no future – it will just be very different.

Cell Phone Ban

NPR recently carried a story about a recommendation of the National Transportation Safety Board that texting and talking on cell phones while driving be prohibited by law. The story included several reactions, including one from a guy who said, "Well, if they pass that I will just ignore it, I can't do my business without talking and texting while I'm driving."

For the moment, let's leave aside the monumental selfishness which says I have right to endanger the lives of others in order to make a buck. Leave aside also the fact that his work got done (I believe the man was a contractor who was bidding jobs) before it was possible to talk and text while driving, so his statement is empirically false. No, the point is neither the morality nor the absolute truth of his statement. What fascinates me is this as an example of "need creep," the process by which we convince ourselves that more and more things are essential for our happiness.

At this time of year my wife's kindergarten class does a unit on "wants" and "needs." The class talks about a number of things and discusses whether each item is a "want" or a "need." Despite the occasional outlier who thinks a 52-inch plasma TV really is a need, the vast majority of the kids do a pretty good job of distinguishing the two. Unfortunately we, their parents, are not so discerning. The phone we thought of as an extravagant luxury a year ago is now a "need." When the adequate job becomes a little tedious or our stable marriage less than a thrill a minute, we decide we "need" a change. For one the next need is a new shotgun, for another it's a daily "grande espresso machiatto with an extra shot" from Starbucks.

In this week following Christmas I have no desire to be Scrooge; there are times when we appropriately desire something new. But let's be clear, what we are longing for is almost always a want and not a need. Let's also recognize that burdening ourselves with "needs" which really are not sets us up for a lot of needless dissatisfaction. Need creep skews our view of the world and blinds us to the suffering of others. We lose the capacity to distinguish between lack of something we desire and true deprivation. We forget that the pain of not having enough to eat and the pain of a poor Wi-

Fi coverage are not equivalent. The ultimate consequence is that we take for granted the precious gifts we have – health, family, enough for food and shelter – in pursuit of the next "need."

The apostle Paul was a master of traveling light, he knew that, finally, very few things apart from the assurance of God's love and the support of a community are essential for happiness. In Philippians he writes, "I have learned to be content with whatever I have. I know what it is to have little, and I know what it is to have plenty. In any and all circumstances I have learned the secret of being well-fed and of going hungry, of having plenty and of being in need. I can do all things through Him who strengthens me [4:11-13]." I confess that most days I cannot match Paul's light backpack; I carry a lot of "needs" which load me down. Today, take a look at the "needs" you are carrying. Are there some things you could drop to lighten your load?

Death and Life

It was a very solemn group. Pastors from all over the synod were vested and gathered in a large meeting room, waiting to process in the funeral of our dear friend and colleague, Chip Gunsten. Each of us had been in many hospital rooms; each had tried to help numerous families through the process of grieving. We were no strangers to the dynamics of death. But this brought home the reality of mortality in an intimate way; a clerical stole, we realized, is no totem against untimely and absurd death. Steve was no less sad than the rest of us, but he also seemed a little preoccupied. Finally, he sidled up to me and confessed, "It is just going to kill me to turn off my phone in a few minutes; my first grandson is in the process of being born in North Carolina." There, in a nutshell, you have it: the juxtaposition of death and life, brutal ending and hopeful beginning – the nature of human existence.

I write this on New Year's Day. As you flip the calendar to a new year it is all but impossible to avoid taking inventory – what (or who) was lost in the past twelve months, what was gained, at which checkpoint are you on that mental road which you imagine as your life's trajectory? Sitting in the quiet of my office with no one else around I think back to all the students I have known over the years, the Lutheran Student Ministry worship and programs I have led, the campus ministry events I have planned, attended – and driven many miles to. I will know more students in the future, of course; you can-not minister in a college town and not be part of the academic world. But I know that the new duties I assume today as the senior pastor of Luther Memorial will mean a big change in how I relate to that world; after over 30 years as a campus pastor I am again primarily focused on a parish. It is as though the star by which I have navigated my professional life has suddenly shifted in the sky. There is sadness in letting go, poignancy in a little death.

But there is also excitement in new possibilities, freedom to explore fresh challenges, the opportunity to do more of things I love, rediscovery of elements of pastoral ministry which I have not often exercised. And this is the point, for both you and me: Not only does death often abut life, sometimes it is the necessary precondition for it.

If you read this reflection more aware of what has died in your life than what is being born, I would not presume to minimize your pain. Sometimes suffering and loss seem more than we can bear. Yet I hope you will not equate pain with abandonment. One of the touchstones of this Christmas season is "Emmanuel," "God with us" – in both times of joy and loss. To a despairing people Isaiah wrote,

Zion has said, "The LORD has forsaken me,
my Lord has forgotten me."
[God replies] "Can a woman forget her sucking child,
that she should have no compassion on the son of her womb?
Even these may forget you, yet I will not forget you… "

At the dawn of this new year, may you discern what is waiting to be born in your life.

Epiphany:
Revelation and Light

Flag

The wise men are still hanging out. On the front of our house we have one of those small flag poles which allows you to display decorative flags. Right now the wise men adorn our porch. I am sure that some people driving by think we are a little lazy, like folks who keep the Christmas lights up until 4th of July. If the truth be told there have been times when we have forgotten to change the flag, so that we had summery images flapping in the wind as the air grew crisp. But in this case, it is not about inertia, it is because we are in the season of Epiphany. This is a very low key effort to bear witness to a different way of marking time than the culture at large. It is a simple reminder to Gail and me that January is not just snow and sleds; it is also the season to remember how Christ is proclaimed to the whole world.

Our flag is hardly a bold confession of the gospel; it is just a small way to remember who we are in a world which often could not care less. Too often when we talk about evangelism, the choice seems to be a false one: between an aggressive in-your-face attitude which ultimately turns people off and a fear of standing out which makes us simply conform to the culture around us. Part of our task as disciples is to find ways to bear witness to the hope which is within us, not necessarily in bold gestures (though there are occasions when those are required) as in many small actions and attitudes.

Most people will not notice our Epiphany flag, and that is okay. But I do hope others notice an attitude of care when I speak to them. I do hope they sense that my actions and beliefs are different because I confess Christ as my Lord. Think about what simple, subtle ways you can confess Christ in the week to come.

Sacrament of Notice

On NPR's *Morning Edition*, Chef Nigella Lawson was making the case for doing your special Valentine's Day meal at home, "Anything is better, I think, than going to one of those restaurants where there are couples who have dinner with each other only on Valentine's Day, and there are about twenty tables of silent couples."

If you went to a nice restaurant for VD, please do not take this Bread for Journey as a critique of your romantic or culinary tastes. There is a lot to be said for a great meal with your beloved, free of the need to prepare the food or clean up the dishes. But I found Lawson's image very familiar. I have been in that restaurant, so many bucks being dropped for so little joy. You can see in the strained expressions and tight smiles of the awkward duos that this one night is supposed to make up for a year of relational neglect – and it isn't working. Instead of love they are discovering how very little they actually have in common.

Valentine's Day is over for another year. Yet we have daily opportunities to offer the "sacrament of notice." A sacrament is a tangible sign which conveys the grace of God, and in our often harried lives there are few things for which people long more than simply being noticed, to sense that they are known and valued. I wonder if the popularity of Facebook isn't a gigantic corporate scream, "Pay attention to me!" A smile at the right moment conveys God's love as surely as chalice and paten. One of the great gifts we can offer another is to simply notice him or her.

Surely that is the case concerning your spouse or significant other. If you want to improve your marriage, make it a point to notice your beloved's hopes and hurts each day – not once a year. But noticing need not be confined to your romantic interest. The sacrament of notice is important for all of us, whether we are widowed, divorced, single, or married. When I notice your pain I begin to heal you. In asking how life is for you, I take you seriously and show that God values you too. Do a quick study of Jesus' ministry, and you will see that many of His most significant encounters take place when He pauses to notice someone whom everyone else is ignoring or dismissing. His healing miracles begin with noticing the ones lost in the crowd.

Look around your workplace – or your home – to whom can you offer the sacrament of notice today?

Flannery Transfiguration

If I could claim credit for just one piece of writing it would probably be Flannery O'Connor's short story, "Revelation." It is a perfectly cut literary gem which reveals the offense and beauty of grace. Mrs. Turpin is a priggish, self-righteous woman when a minor miracle happens. Looking out at a Deep South sunset...

"A visionary light settled in her eyes. She saw the streak as a vast swinging bridge extending upward from the earth through a field of living fire. Upon it a vast hoard of souls were rumbling toward heaven. There were whole companies of white-trash, clean for the first time in their lives, and a band of black niggers in white robes, and battalions of freaks and lunatics shouting and clapping and leaping like frogs. And bringing up the end of the procession was a tribe of people, whom she recognized at once as those who, like herself and Claud [her husband], had always had a little of everything and the God-given wit to use it right. She leaned forward to observe them closer. They were marching behind the others with great dignity, accountable as they had always been for good order and common sense and respectable behavior. They alone were on key. Yet she could see by their shocked and altered faces that even their virtues were being burned away."

We are left to wonder whether she will be transformed, but there is no doubt that for a brief moment she has seen in a new way. For one instant her pig pen has become the throne of a God drawing near to save her from herself. This is a moment of what the Bible calls transfiguration, the ordinary giving way to wonder, both fleeting and undeniable.

Sometimes I end my Bread for the Journey with an exhortation. But the thing about transfiguration is that you cannot compel it. You can't exhort, "Now go out there and experience the holy in a jaw-dropping way." Revelation is not a matter of gritting your teeth and trying hard to have an epiphany. Moments of transfiguration come to us as pure gift.

Although we cannot compel transfiguration moments, we can be open when they come. So maybe I have an exhortation for you after all: be attuned to the fact that the ordinary may suddenly blaze with wonder – maybe even expect it. In the laugh of your child, in the touch of your friend, amid the tension and chaos of the work day, be assured that God comes if you have eyes to see. And when God comes, filling the mundane with a glimpse of eternity, something can change in how we see the world and the people in it.

Weight

It's not so much what I eat as what's eating me that gets me in trouble. The New Year has come, and that has many of us thinking about how the battle of the bulge is going. If you are like me, an extended holiday season of Thanksgiving dinners, baked gifts, fatty dips, and televised football has left your angles a little more rounded than they were two months ago. But I do not intend to write the clichéd "10 handy dandy tips to lose weight" column – you can find that on the Web or in last Sunday's Parade section. Besides that, my fantasies of a magic bullet not withstanding, it all comes down to two things anyway: eat less and exercise more.

I would, however, invite you to think a little bit about why you eat what you eat. To be sure there is solid fitness value in attending to your weight – you just feel better if you don't look like Jabba the Hutt from Star Wars. But that is a conversation for you and your doctor. My concern here is different. Beyond wanting a healthy body, I pay attention to my weight because it is usually telling me something about my spiritual state. For me extra tonnage suggests that I am habitually anxious, depressed, angry, or somehow unfulfilled.

Put another way, our eating habits may be markers for what is going on in our souls. We talk about "comfort food," dishes which conjure up fond memories of childhood or have chemical properties that give us a sense of well-being. Nothing wrong with those in moderation. But when we find ourselves eating just to feel good, because we are not getting joy from the rest of life, we ought to ask ourselves what is going on. Is there a change I need to make in my relationships? Am I spending time in ways that are really fulfilling? What is going on in my life that I am ceasing to care about my body? Of course, not all the solutions are spiritual; one response we may need to make to the extra pounds is slowly putting down the brownie and stepping away from the plate. Sometimes the issue is genetic (and my heart goes out to those who have to play with a stacked deck). Nor is the symptom always too much weight; obsessive concern with being thin also suggests that something is spiritually amiss. Still too much weight is often a sign of a starving soul.

Jesus described following Him as eating the bread of life. He knew that we are hungry people – hungry for meaning, purpose, joy, and security – we will eat something to fill that void we feel in our souls. It may be sex. It may be work. It may be food. But we will eat something to fill the hole. So do pay attention to what you're eating – calories count. But it may be that the real issue is less what you are putting into your mouth than what you are not finding in your life. Maybe what you need is not just a new exercise program in your day, but also a renewed sense of God's love and priorities in your soul.

Being Ananias

"I see campus ministry as being like Ananias, to be there when the scales fall away." If you do not get that allusion, you might read the ninth chapter of Acts. At a meeting I was at last week, our opening devotions reminded us of the key role played by this man who shows up only once in Scripture. If the conversion of Saul were a Hollywood blockbuster called Damascus Road Turnaround, Paul would be the clear star, but there would no story worth telling without Ananias.

Saul, a confident, even arrogant man, comes to a moment of crisis when he is struck blind. He who has inspired fear in the hearts of many is reduced to being led about by the hand and huddling in the dark, awaiting direction. Acts 9 could have been simply a story of God's judgment on those who oppose the gospel, but, in fact, it is more than that. It

41

is a story of transformation and redemption because Ananias is there at a pivotal moment to embody God's love to a broken man, bring healing to him, and show him a new way forward for his life. Because of Ananias, Saul the persecutor becomes Paul the apostle.

I like to think my daily work is in the tradition of Ananias. The nature of the college experience is that there are a lot of crises: relationships bud, flower, and wilt, long held occupational dreams become impossible, simple answers to life's deepest questions seem hopelessly naïve in the glare of new knowledge and experience. I try to be there when the old is dying, and the new is struggling to be born.

But in this Bread I want to affirm that you have a chance and a calling to be Ananias to someone else. Most of life proceeds in rather routine fashion; the drone of daily life makes it very hard for someone to hear and embrace the radical call of Christ. Like a Great Plains interstate, one mile of our life looks pretty much like the last and the next. But in every life there are pivot points when, for a brief moment, the defenses are down and the eyes are open to new ways of seeing and being. Perhaps it's an illness. Maybe it is a particularly vivid image on the evening news. It could be the morning you wake up from an all night bender and think that there just has to be more to life than this. Or maybe it is the day you are overcome by the wonder of being incredibly blessed and wonder what to do with all the joy. Whatever the specifics, there are moments when another might have his or her life radically altered if we are there to speak as did Ananias, "Brother Saul...the Lord Jesus has sent me..."

I am not talking about "death bed evangelism" or exploiting human suffering in order to unload our agenda – there is something ghoulish about taking a perverse pleasure in another's suffering so that we can recite a formula. The most important thing that Ananias does is simply go to Saul's side. Afraid, unsure, feeling decidedly unprepared Ananias summons his courage and shows up at Saul's side to BE God's love to a broken man.

Dehydrated H20

When I was in college I had a gag gift on my bookshelf. It looked like a normal soup can, but it was labeled "Dehydrated H2O." The directions for use? "Just add water."

I thought about that can as I prepared to teach a Sunday School class last week. We are reading Ron Sider's *Rich Christians in an Age of Hunger* and one chapter opened with these words, "Social Scientists who examined the factors that shape American attitudes on matters related to the development of the poorest nations discovered that religion plays no significant role at all [my emphasis]. Those with deep religious beliefs are no more concerned about assistance and development for the poor than are persons with little or no religious commitment." (Sider, p.39)

Leave aside for a moment the question of what the difference ought to be – religious faith made no difference! Think about that: Knowing that a person claims Jesus Christ as Lord and Savior gives little to no insight into how he or she will respond to human suffering. Religion as dehydrated morality; just add the values you got somewhere else. Faith becomes a hollow vessel conveniently containing convictions which may have little to do with Christ.

But that is not quite what Jesus had in mind. "You are the light of the world." "You are the salt of the earth." Jesus clearly imagined that following Him would make a difference in how we view life and respond to its challenges. More than that, He envisioned his community leading, not following; molding the world, not conforming to its flaws.

This week you will have many choices to make. I invite you to consider how your decisions are different from those made by those who do not claim the Way of Jesus as their norm. Does the witness of Jesus imprint your actions? As the old bumper sticker puts it, "If you were accused of being a Christian, would there be enough evidence to convict you?"

Thirty Seconds

This week I've been writing a thirty second radio spot which will air on a Christian rock radio station. My job is to say something in thirty seconds which will make high school seniors want to be part of the ELCA's campus ministries. It would be easy to write a short essay, but just thirty seconds to grab attention, make the pitch, and seal the deal? That's hard. It's given me new appreciation for folks who write advertising copy.

It got me thinking about what I would say to someone to convince them to consider following Jesus. If I only had thirty seconds, what would I say to them? Suppose you had that job? In fact you do. In our fast paced world we seldom get the chance to spin out a detailed theology; we just get unexpected moments when someone crosses our path, a quick opportunity to, as the writer of 1 Peter says, speak of "the hope that is within you." So, you've got thirty seconds to say it. What is it about your faith which makes the Christian way worth commending to someone else? If we have trouble with evangelism I suspect that at least part of the problem is that we have never reflected on why we choose to confess Christ.

I'm not going to give you my answer because what compels me may not excite you, and that is the key: You need to find that piece of the Gospel which lifts your heart, satisfies your mind, and challenges your spirit. Think about it, why are you a Christian? You've got thirty seconds.

Carl

"So where do you preach?" she asked. She was a very sick lady, and I was the volunteer chaplain at the hospital. After I introduced myself she wanted to know just what species of preacher had appeared at her bedside. When I told her I was the Lutheran campus pastor at Tech, she lay back in her bed, closed her eyes as though in deep thought, and finally said, "I think I've only known one Lutheran. Do you happen to know Carl Jones?" In fact I did know Carl, an incredibly gracious individual, whose gentleness, enthusiasm, and joy in the gospel were obvious two minutes after you met him. I told her how much I appreciated Carl; she expressed similar feelings. We had a nice visit, and I left.

Walking down the hall to my next visit I had several thoughts about that brief encounter. If she were only going to meet one Lutheran Christian in her life, I was glad Carl was the one. He embodied the accepting love at the heart of what it means to follow Jesus. And then I wondered what somebody, somewhere else, in some other bed would be thinking if she said, "Hmm, I've only known one Lutheran, Bill King." If I were someone's religious sample of one, what would she think of Lutherans – or Christians in general?

I also thought about what the writer of Hebrews calls the "cloud of witnesses" which surrounds us, that legion of saints

45

who have gone before us in the faith. Even from the grave Carl brought a hint of joy to that sickroom. Like a flower whose beauty has faded but whose fragrance lingers in the air, the simple remembrance of his life sweetened the medicinal odor of the room. The moment we remembered Carl, the room became a little brighter, a little less frightening. His quietly faithful life created a bridge between a critically ill woman and a pastor she'd never met. We smiled as we talked of Carl, and I think I felt his gentle hug enfolding us when I took her frail hand in prayer.

Today, give thanks for all the saints who have shown you what joyful life in Christ looks like – and resolve to be such a sign for someone else.

Bethlehem Church

"You have to understand, when you live in the Diaspora, every homecoming of the prodigal is something you have to celebrate." That was the explanation the pastor gave for interrupting his announcements in mid-sentence, running to the elderly woman behind me, and giving her a big hug. It had already been a memorable worship experience for all concerned. Four vans of college students, in Louisiana for a spring break week of Katrina response service, had made their way to this historically black ELCA congregation in a poor section of New Orleans. Past piles of flood damage heaped on the sidewalks, we filed into the little church, increasing their normal attendance over a hundred percent. Surprised by the invasion, they were unabashed; their welcome was warm and genuine. I sensed this is a place of joy and stability amidst chaos.

It turns out that the woman behind me was typical.

Though the church building was minimally damaged by Katrina, many of the members were sent into exile by the broken levees. This was the first week she had been in church since September, and it was cause for rejoicing. The lost was found. The community was a bit more whole. It was occasion for rejoicing.

Surely no one would wish for the catastrophe which hit Bethlehem Lutheran Church, but how good it would be if we cultivated the kind of Christian community which knows when others are missing, mourns the struggles of our brothers and sisters in Christ, and actively rejoices in their small victories. It all begins in seeing the person next to us on the pew through the eyes of Christ, not as a fellow spectator at a religious event, but as one with whom we share a deep bond and investment because we confess the same Lord. This week make sure somebody knows you are glad he or she is with you in the community where you worship.

Promise

Moses had a revelation at Mount Sinai; I had one in front of the refrigerator. As in many homes, the King's fridge is equal parts appliance and billboard. Two sides are covered with pizza coupons, schedules, cartoons, phone numbers, and pictures--lots of pictures. We also have an assortment of single words on magnets which you arrange to make sentences. Most of the time I don't notice the door as I groggily open it in search of the 2% for my morning Go Lean Crunch. But today something caught my eye. Right in front of me was one of our daughter's elementary school pictures (she is now 21), held to the door with the word "promise." I do not know how it got there. I suspect Gail was going through that box of old photos we all have stashed in a closet, saw a particularly cute picture, and grabbed one of the largest words to hold it to the door. However it happened, the juxtaposition got me thinking.

How would our behavior toward those around us change if we all wore a little tag saying "promise"? Would we be more patient if we remembered that God created those we meet and values their lives as much as our own? Would we treat them with more respect if we kept before our eyes that whatever the present state of their lives, we serve the God who proclaims, "Behold, I am doing a new thing"? Would we be kinder if we believed each person embodies amazing potential awaiting proper nurture, perhaps from someone like us?

Stewardship is more than how we spend our money; it is also about caring for the human capital which God entrusts to our care and responsibility: our children, our friends, our acquaintances who can be hurt or healed by the way we treat them. Paul wrote, "Finally, beloved, whatever is true, whatever is honorable, whatever is just, whatever is pure, whatever is pleasing, whatever is commendable, if there is any excellence and if there is anything worthy of praise, think about these things." (Philippians 4:8) In other words, imagine everyone you meet wearing a reminder, "Great Promise – God's work zone."

Ladder

"It's better to be at the bottom of a ladder you want to climb than half way up one you don't." So observes a character on the BBC comedy, *The Office*, after realizing he hates what he is doing and needs to make a change. I am thinking of putting his words on little cards to give to folks who come into my office for counseling. It would not solve every problem, but it would go a long way toward resolving about 50 per cent of the cases. Whether it is a student trying to decide on a major, a spouse wondering if she should get out of an abusive relationship, or someone, like the employee in The Office, wrestling with a job choice, many of us are burdened by both a persistent sense of doing that which gives little joy and the fear of starting over from scratch.

Even when we have a vague sense of having made a mistake, we are loath to begin again. Though the knots in our stomach harden with each step, we continue moving ahead. Like someone lost in the woods, we think if we just thrash about for long enough we will be okay. But as any ranger will tell you, it's more likely that you end up exhausted and farther from home.

Take your pick of metaphor, ladder or woods; the point is the same. Success consists less in how much effort we expend than in directing our efforts to the right thing. If we are climbing the wrong ladder or stumbling along a dead end path, we ultimately have a moment of reckoning when we realize our life is not what we want. Wisdom is having that heart to heart conversation with ourselves sooner rather than later. What gives me delight? What are my abilities? What does the world need from me? Is this how I want to spend the next 20 years? How can I best serve God? These are questions worthy of attention this summer, on a leisurely stroll around Pandapas Pond or over an afternoon staring out at the breaking waves.

Chalice in the Earthquake

On the day that the news was breaking about the devastation in Haiti, I happen to be browsing through a magazine article. The story told about an earthquake some years ago, not in Haiti, but in northern Italy. Because there had already been several shocks, the worshiping community was gathered outdoors to celebrate the Mass. The elderly priest gathered some rubble into a makeshift altar and was guiding the people through the ancient ritual. Just as he was elevating the chalice, the moment when Christ is understood to become present in a special way, another shock rippled through the crowd. The priest staggered but kept the chalice aloft. He was reeling but Christ was lifted up high for all to see.

I find that image of a chalice raised like a beacon to be a powerful symbol of what it means to follow Christ in the world. There are precious few days when I do not experience some little shock – and there have been a few when I reeled from a full scale quake. I have not seen all my possessions washed away by a Katrina, or choked on the dust of Twin Towers in my lungs, or felt a whole city crumbling beneath my feet and on top of my head. But I remember 4/16 and its aftermath. I have looked into the face of my mother's imminent death. I have wondered, as have all of you, where God is when the rich crush the poor and the innocent pay the price for the recklessness of the stupid and callous.

In those moments, when the quakes come, we reach out for something solid. In that instant we look for some sign that God is indeed present in the midst of the chaos. So, next time you are at worship – before a quake hits – take time to notice what is given to you at the altar, a tangible sign that Christ is present. To take the sacrament is to remember that the body and blood of Christ is not safely watching the world's suffering from a distant heaven, but is with those who mourn in Porte-au-Prince or struggle to find meaning in Blacksburg. Take time to be sustained by the promise of God with us.

Then....remember that, having been so strengthened, you are now called to be the sign of Christ's presence in the world. You can be the chalice which another sees lifted up. Your acts of compassion are the gentle defiance which proclaims God's care when another's world is reeling. What a holy calling indeed!

Huckleberry Epiphany

One minute I was bicycling home from the office on the Huckleberry Trail; the next moment – and it was for just a moment – I was at the foot of Paris Mountain, in South Carolina. Perhaps it was the amber light filtering through the first golden leaves of autumn or the hint of wood smoke in the air. Maybe it was the totally oblivious couple, holding hands as they slowly strolled down the path toward me, so eager to make their walk last as long as possible. It could have been the exhilaration of my muscles pleasantly straining after a long day in front of the computer screen, a straining which filled me with a sense of freedom, release, and deep wellbeing.

Whatever the cause, something clicked, and memories of my first date with my wife, Gail, hiking on a glorious fall day 32 years ago, flooded in. Yet more than that, distilled into an instant as fleeting as the beat of a hummingbird's wing and as exquisite as a perfectly cut diamond, I felt all the joy and unmerited grace I've experienced with Gail since that day. With no warning, the veil of the ordinary that deadens our senses slipped, and I glimpsed the profound love which undergirds daily existence. So overwhelmed by gratitude, I could hardly breathe. I stopped in the middle of the trail to analyze the experience, but it was gone like a doe at dusk. Moses before the burning bush. Jacob dreaming under the stars. Isaiah awed by a smoky seraphim in the temple. God comes in unexpected ways and places. I will remember a day on the bike path when I saw a flash of the holy next to the German Club.

I do not share this incident to exhort you. How do you exhort someone to experience a gift which comes unbidden and unexpected? I certainly do not share it to impress you with my spiritual sensitivity; most of the time all I notice on that trail are my leaden legs and the cracks in the pavement. I share this snapshot to bear witness to you that grace is all around us – pure, precious, and potent. In the midst of divorce, depression, disappointment, unemployment – whatever the paralyzing pain which might be seeping into your soul as you read these words – accept my fervent hope that this day you will glimpse the love which never lets us go. May a simple sight or sound, be for you a sacrament, the holy wrapped in the ordinary "given for you."

Squeezing Life

One of my best friends has a laugh like a mountain steam and a smile which warms up a cold room ten degrees. Sit with her and it's as though God turned up the dimmer on the sun, making the world a bit brighter. The other day I watched her leave a string of happy faces behind as she worked a room. Knowing she has her fair complement of stresses, sorrows, and sadness, I commented, "You always seem to be filled with joy, no matter what's going on." She looked a little quizzical, genuinely unaware of how unusual her electric spirit is or of the impact she has on other people. Then she reflected, "I guess I just want to squeeze every bit of life out of life."

"I guess I just want to squeeze every bit of life out of life." There is more than one way to mean those words. For adrenaline junkies it reflects the ever escalating desire to experience a thrill – any thrill – bigger than the last one, to manufacture meaning out of the mundane. For such folks boredom is the greatest evil and personal indulgence the chosen path. Much called "going for the gusto" in our culture is simply a frenetic desire to fill a hole where purpose is supposed to be. But that is not what drives my friend.

For her it's not about creating excitement where there is none; it's about noticing that each day is inherently exciting and each moment precious. It's about cultivating a sense of wonder, so that each fragile flower, each child's song, each gentle hug is received with profound thanksgiving. She sees her life, not as a reservoir to be jealously hoarded, but as a resource to be lavished on the parched ground of another's need. She assumes that every person is a treasure and every experience has sweetness to be savored and shared – if she opens her eyes.

How about you? Are you squeezing every bit of life out of life? Have you learned to see miracles in the minute? Do you need to create faux fulfillment or does joy and peace well up within you from being well used by God to bring healing and hope to a broken world?

Russian Madonna

Last week two of our members gave Luther Memorial an icon. These generous folks are downsizing so they offered this work of art to the church. They bought it some years ago from a vendor on the streets of Moscow. No claims were made regarding its origin, so it is almost impossible to know its provenance. It was purchased simply because of its inherent beauty.

I do not know where this icon will ultimately "live" but right now it is sitting on the altar in our chapel. I put it in there so that anyone who visits the chapel might be able to use this icon for the purpose for which it was created, as a means to enter into holy reflection and prayer.

I am no expert on iconography, but the central figure of this icon appears to be the Virgin Mary. The picture is primarily written (you write icons rather than painting them) in rich browns and reds. But the figure is outlined by brass with an aged patina, so the icon has a soft glow when light strikes it. A slight vertical crack in the wood runs through the Virgin's face. To her side is a smaller figure, which would normally be the infant Jesus (at least in my limited experience). But this is no Gerber baby; this is more of an older child, even an adolescent. He stares out at you with what seems to me like a slightly quizzical look.

As I stared at that icon I began to ponder where it had come from and how it came to be in our chapel. Perhaps it had a place of honor in some small chapel in the countryside. Perhaps it nurtured generations of worshipers, who, like Christians in most times and places, ceased to notice its beauty and began to treat it like the wallpaper of their church. Perhaps that Madonna and child looked out in mute sadness as the community of faith they inspired dwindled during the Communist years, and the church's vestments, sacramental vessels, and icons were plundered for a quick buck, relics of a distant day. I imagine that quizzical Jesus asking, "What the heck is this….." as he looks around our small chapel, so distant and so different from the Russian Orthodox houses of worship half way around the world.

I look at the crack through the Madonna's face and the green vestiges of metal polish in the cracks and crevices of her brass adornment and think what a hard, long road she has traveled to invite us into contemplation of the mystery of God among us. Across the miles, perhaps across centuries, she bears witness that generations rise and fall, once fearsome governments ultimately fall into the dust, and simple saints offer their prayers in the silence of quiet places – through it all God has promised to come if we but pause to open our hearts in welcome.

It would be hard to name music more different from the world of this icon than the 19th Century gospel songs of America, yet there are lines from one which come to my mind as I look at this Russian Madonna:

Take time to be holy, speak oft with thy Lord.

Abide in Him always, and feed on His Word.

In our chapel in the company of the Madonna, in your favorite chair, on a mountain path…take time to be holy this week.

Seasons of Life

As I write this, it is Spring Break week at Virginia Tech – and it makes precious little difference to me. For most of my professional life, serving as a campus pastor, the world pivoted around the academic calendar. This was the week when most of my "congregation" was absent from Blacksburg, and so I spent this time catching up, decompressing, or, more often in recent years, going on a service trip. Sitting in a different chair (as pastor of Luther Memorial) I am now much more aware of Lent's demands than the ebb and flow of students from campus. This is just one small sign that I am in a different season of my life.

A piece of us wants to freeze time, to find the familiar and settle into its routines as into a cozy rocker before a raging fire. It is not to be. The variables of life keep changing all around us. Old friends move. Career demands change. Our bodies cannot do all that we once took for granted. Family dynamics get shuffled by death and birth, marriage and divorce, the aging of parents and our children's coming of age. New knowledge brings fresh perspective and hard won wisdom breeds discontent with ideas now become too small.

Perhaps we focus on what is lost and deeply mourn that which we loved. Sitting here I am slightly envious of my colleague, Joanna, and the adventure she and our campus ministry folks are enjoying this week on their break trip to Philadelphia. As natural as it is to miss what is gone, it is ultimately as futile as trying to hold back the tides from our sandcastles.

Far better to receive the gifts of each season. It will be nice have this week with my wife – and not to spend it in a sleeping bag on a church floor or living out of a backpack. More than that, I will probably spend some time with an elderly member who always fills me up by her graciousness. I'll sit with some men in Bible study who inspire me by their intuitive sense of the holy. Each season has it fruits which we can pluck and savor if we do not waste too much time mourning that which was both beautiful and bountiful but now past. Memories are precious; we can and should value them. A deep sigh naturally arises as we think of past joys. Yet life awaits…

The crocuses are peeping up; winter is slowing giving way to the season of tender possibility. May your new spiritual season be filled with something beautiful – and may you have eyes to see it.

Everybody Talks About the Weather

"Everybody talks about the weather, but nobody does anything about it." So goes the old aphorism. But I recently saw an exception to the rule. It had been a bitterly cold day when I sat down to eat with one of our members. All day everyone had been making the usual observations, speculations, and exclamations as they came into a warm room: "Water in my birdbath was frozen solid this morning…wonder if my pipes will freeze tonight…Gol-lee! It's colder'n a coal miner's belt buckle."

When our meal was set on the table my host offered an earnest prayer: "Lord, on this cold day, as we sit in warmth, we remember those who are cold. As we feast on this abundance, we remember those who wonder where their next meal will come from. As we share the joy of fellowship at this table, we remember those who are lonely tonight. Accept our thanks for these blessings we savor and open our eyes and hearts to share them with those who are in need."

It was a prayer made beautiful by its thoughtful weaving of the holy and the mundane. I admired the way my host took our common experience and brought it into the presence of God. Something as ordinary as the weather became an occasion to reflect on both blessedness and opportunity.

I began to think about ways I could transform my daily annoyances into prayer:

- In the midst of this traffic jam outside the Kroger, Lord, I give you thanks that I do not have to walk ten miles for a bag of grain to feed my family.

- Cooling my heels in this doctor's waiting room, I give you thanks, my God, for access to good health care and money to pay for it. Give me grace to remember those who have neither.

- Waiting for the plumber to come and fix my busted pipes, I give thanks that the water which he will restore is safe and clean. Forgive my callousness to the plight of those who will die this day of dysentery because their drinking water's source and their sewer are the same muddy ditch.

You see where I am going. Most of what we complain about are decidedly "first world" problems. Each experience can be an opportunity to see, not with eyes blinded by aggravation and complacency, but with eyes filled with thankfulness. We can not necessarily change the weather, but we can change how we respond to it. Each moment can be the beginning of a spiritual awakening.

Grasping Our Experiences

During the Christmas season, Gail and I started watching back episodes of *This Is Us*, a television show I now highly recommend. It has a lot of heart and captures the complexities of how our childhood experiences profoundly affect our adult identity.

One scene which has stuck with me involves a beautiful young woman and an old man sitting on the front porch after a family holiday blowup. She is a gifted and successful actress, but also emotionally cold and stunted. He is dying of pancreatic cancer. They do not really know each other but she still asks him, "What's it like to be dying?" He stares into the middle distance and replies, "It's like seeing all these experiences flashing by and you reach out and try to capture them, trying to make them as real as possible. You want to hold them and savor them, all those special moments. But they keep going by faster and faster." (This is a paraphrase of a much more eloquent speech.)

I suppose it's human nature to grow dull to the beauty and blessing which surrounds us. When your spouse's laugh is as dependable as the rising sun, you stop noticing how it warms up a room. When you bound out of bed with little pain, you forget that there are many for whom each step is a victory. If you've never been on a battlefield, never heard gunshots in the night outside your bedroom, never had to run from a wildfire or hurricane, you may not appreciate a day without fear that it will be your last.

Classical theology distinguishes sins of commission (what we do) and sins of omission (what we don't do). Perhaps our greatest sin of omission is failing to notice, savor, and give thanks for all the little things which are remarkable for their ordinariness – the touch of your child, food on the table, the cycle of the seasons, the courtesy of a stranger in traffic. This is sin because it fails to discern the holy embedded in the stuff of life and thus cuts us off from the One who called us into being and sustains us in each moment. Noticing – reaching out to grasp those precious moments – is a way to draw refreshment from the pool which surrounds around us.

I seldom make New Year's resolutions, but I am resolved to do a better job of reaching out and capturing some of those experiences as they flash by. How about you?

Lent: Darkness

Intimate Ash Wednesday

The wintry weather made road conditions a bit iffy and so our Ash Wednesday services were very intimate this year, less than 20 at two services. Let me emphasize that I am not using Bread for the Journey as an opportunity to chastise those who felt it unsafe to be out. Nor am I using "intimate" as a euphemism for sparsely attended. I say our services were intimate solely to lift up the blessings of the small service.

Too often we judge events and initiatives based on how big, how popular, how well-attended they are. I would certainly have wished for ideal weather and 100% participation in the solemn worship which sets the tone for Lent. But that was not to be. What did happen was that that we gathered in our chapel, looking out into a snowy courtyard which was the visual embodiment of Lent's message of life out of death. What did happen was a sense of community in our worship which is not always as easy to feel in a larger space. What did happen is that Christ came into our midst just as surely as if the sanctuary had been filled to overflowing.

I share this simple experience for two reasons. First, our chapel is a wonderful place for prayer and reflection. I invite you to treat yourself to a little time apart in this space during Lent – or whenever you could use some Sabbath time from the crush of life. But more broadly I share this story of an intimate Ash Wednesday to remind us that much of life is about finding blessing in what is second best. Sometimes, in life or in liturgy, things do not go as planned. We can bemoan what was lost or we can be ready to receive the blessings made available precisely because our preferred path was closed.

4/16 Anniversary

One of the best novels I've read in the last year is Geraldine Brooks' *March*. Those of you who know Little Women will remember that the father is absent for most of Louisa May Alcott's classic story, off fighting in the Civil War. Brooks has filled in the narrative gap, telling us about his life while Meg, Jo, Beth, and Amy are maturing in Concord.

March serves as a chaplain in the Union army. Early in the novel he looks out across a river where bodies are floating from the last battle and turkey vultures roost in nearby trees, waiting to feast on the carnage of war. He reflects to himself, "No wonder simple men have always had their gods dwell in high places. For as soon as a man lets his eye drop from the heavens to the horizon, he risks setting it on some scene of desolation."

As I write this the Blacksburg community is one week away from observing the first anniversary of 4/16. We prepare ourselves for the great plague, not of locusts, but of jackleg preachers and ravenous news trucks, which will soon descend. For some the pain is fresh as a razor's slash. For others it is like an arthritic knee, dully aching and only occasionally – and surprisingly – debilitating. We come to that day in many emotional and spiritual places.

But surely all of us here a year ago will come to that day with a greater sense of being part of the fellowship of human suffering than we had on 4/15/07. Sudden, violent, devastating loss is no longer something that happens to someone else – in a far country or ghetto – perhaps deserved or at least explicable. We now know how easily one's eye can fall on a scene of desolation. March's observation reminds us of the temptation some religion offers to simply turn away from the pain, to avert our gaze to a more idyllic place: "God is in heaven. We struggle in a vale of tears. Think on heaven."

Yet that is not the word of consolation and hope which the Bible offers us. God is not in some high place beckoning us there; God is in the midst of our pain right here. As the psalmist puts it, "Where can I go from Your spirit? Or where can I flee fromYour presence? If I ascend to heaven, You are there; if I make my bed in Sheol, You are there. If I take the wings of the morning and settle at the farthest limits of the sea, even there Your hand shall lead me, and Your right hand shall hold me fast. If I say, 'Surely the darkness shall cover me, and the light around me become night,' even the darkness is not dark to You; the night is as bright as the day, for darkness is as light to You." (Psalms 139:7-12).

All of us go through times of darkness, whether in the aftermath of 4/16, the breakup of a marriage, or struggling to find direction as graduation approaches. In those times it is good to remember that God is not far from the desolation, but cradling us in loving arms.

Blood and Ash Wednesday

My agenda for this day includes two items; I need to proof the worship folder for Ash Wednesday and schedule a blood test as part of my annual physical. It occurs to me that the two items have something in common; both involve pausing to consider what I would prefer to ignore.

Most of the time I give little thought to the blood coursing through my veins and the amazing physical processes it enables. Nutrients get delivered. Waste is filtered and carried away. Thousands of chemical reactions go on automatically without an ounce of conscious oversight on my part. But an aging body is more like my '89 Volvo than a brand new

BMW; there is a high probability that something is going to get out of whack. So, on the theory that with both bodies and cars it is better to monitor problems than to wait until they stop you dead, I am going to have blood drawn. I would love to entertain the fantasy that my lifestyle requires no change from when I was 18. That is just not true and my long-term health depends on facing that fact.

Reading the Ash Wednesday liturgy line by line is pretty brutal. It includes an uncompromising recitation of all the ways we fail ourselves, our neighbor, and God. Then comes the ashen smear on your forehead with an ominous invitation, "Remember you are dust, to dust you shall return." Why do we immerse ourselves in the experience of Ash Wednesday and Lent? Denial is a much more pleasant option.

We do Lent for the same reason that I have blood drawn. If we are going to be healthy we need to face the reality of our existence. Relationships do get broken, so they need some attention. Life is short, so we don't want to sleepwalk through it. We are sometimes callous or greedy, so we need to apologize and make amends.

Lent is not about self-hate or gratuitously dwelling on the dreary. Lent is a gift, an opportunity to take our lives off of autopilot and reflect on whether we are as spiritually healthy as we would like to be. Embraced it gives us time out from the incessant demands of daily existence to take our bearings and be sure we are on the path that leads to life. Most of all, Lent is thinking deeply about the divine love, revealed most fully in Holy Week, which does not want us broken, drifting, or filled with regret – and giving thanks for it.

Blood test and Lent – think of each as a diagnostic tool which leads to health.

Weight Club

I joined the Weight Club a few weeks ago. For a long time I've tried to get some daily exercise, but I decided I needed to add strength training to my routine. Given the loss of muscle mass which accompanies aging, I did the math and realized that I cannot walk enough miles to keep my weight down. If I do not want to look like Jabba the Hutt (or destroy my joints) I either have to start eating a super model's diet of sprouts and water for dinner (a non-starter for one who loves cooking) or do some strength training,

The reason I resisted doing this earlier is more psychologically complex than I care to ponder in depth, but I've gotten a bit of insight. I notice that amid the planks, pushings, pullings, and puffing I have two main feelings which alternate like a strobe light: shame and superiority.

The shame is easy to understand. Surrounded by buff college bodies and guys older than me who have way more discipline, I am painfully aware of how I fail to measure up. My body in the gym is like Ramen Noodles at a Five Star restaurant. Knowing it was going to feel like that I put off the day of reckoning as long as I could. Few folks seek out the places where their flaws are obvious.

Why I sometimes feel superior is harder for me to understand; maybe it is a compensating shadow side of the shame. But when I look at those buff bodies I think about all the time that has gone into sculpting those layered muscular forms. I may think, "Is this really what we are put on earth to do? Isn't this exhibit A of the American obsession with physical beauty, our denial of death, and the way we make sports and fitness our idols? Wouldn't some moderation be better?" Since I did not want to be one "those" people with their skewed priorities, I resisted joining the club.

I am not proud of either of these feelings. Neither shame nor a judgmental attitude is the least bit helpful in moving us to a healthy place. All of us have things of which we are ashamed, places where we do not measure up in our own eyes. The appropriate response is not to obsess about the past, but to take positive steps in the present. By the same token, it is petty and futile to think you can lift yourself up by deprecating another's choices.

You do not have to read the gospels closely to see that Jesus does not shame people. He simply invites them to make a change, to believe a new future is possible. However, He does have harsh words for those who look down on others – primarily because it blinds them to the work they need to be doing on themselves.

So let me invite you: Today, lose the shame and be a bit more gracious toward those who make choices which are not your own. I am trying to do that when I go to the gym, remembering that I am loved even if my gut drags the mat and that the hours I spend reading novels to feed my imagination probably look pretty wasteful and self-indulgent to those who prefer lifting weights. To the degree that we can let go of shame and the desperate need to feel superior we are healthier in spirit and body.

Veni Sancte Spiritus

"Veni Sancte Spiritus" (Come, Holy Spirit) is the beginning of one of the great hymns of the church. Called the "golden sequence," you will find it in liturgies spanning from the Medieval Church to the modern Taize Community. It speaks the longing of a worshiper for God. But when you think about it, the words don't exactly make sense, do they?

Is God in some distant celestial realm, awaiting a prayerful summons? Is there a place where God is not already present? Paul asserts that God exists mystically within every heart. "Likewise the Spirit helps us in our weakness; for we do not know how to pray as we ought, but that very Spirit intercedes with sighs too deep for words [Romans 8:26]."

Praying "veni sancte spiritus" might seem akin to saying "come oxygen come" just before taking a big breath. Do you need to invoke that which engulfs you in every second of every day?

No – and yes. God is indeed present in all times and places. God is eagerly drawing near to us, hoping to pull us into a holy embrace. Paul is right; we constantly carry God's Spirit within us. But the invitation is still important. In *The Screwtape Letters*, C. S. Lewis notes that one of the distinctive things about God is that the Holy One cannot ravish, but only woo. We often define God in terms of power, but, in fact, love is the defining characteristic of the God revealed in Jesus – and lovers do not barge in where they are not invited.

The Lenten season is about offering that invitation. Just as we have good friends whom we somehow never get around to inviting over for dinner because our schedules are so crazy, so it is easy for us to get so busy that we never actually block out time to invite God into our hectic lives.

For the rest of Lent, let me suggest a simple spiritual discipline. When your alarm goes off in the morning, before you get out of bed, repeat three times, "Veni Sancte Spiritus." (Or mouth whatever invitation seems most natural to you) With the hosts of saints who have gone before you, open your heart to the One who longs to comfort, guide, challenge, and sustain you in all that your day will bring.

67

Restore Yesterday or Redeem Tomorrow

Last week on the eve of Holy Week observances columnist Leonard Pitts observed how the proclamation of Easter Sunday had become the touchstone for the world's largest religious faith. Then he continued, "But that faith has in turn been a source of ongoing friction between those adherents who feel it compels them to redeem tomorrow and those who feel it obligates them to restore yesterday."

I cannot think of a more succinct statement of the tension which runs through the contemporary church. Throughout its history the Christian faith has served two sometimes contradictory functions. The church has been the custodian of morality and a rich tradition. In times of chaos, faith has often been an anchor for both individuals and societies. When our world mistakes novelty for truth, religion has often been conservative in the best sense of the word, conserving that which ought to be valued even if it is not fashionable.

Unfortunately that has sometimes meant defending the indefensible merely because it was familiar – think, for example, about the church's persecution of Galileo, anti-Semitism through the centuries, and the Southern church's silence regarding Jim Crow laws. Yet that is not the whole story. Christians have passionately labored, in Jesus' name, to envision a new future. The university, hospitals, the push for universal education, and ongoing concern for the marginalized in society – all of these are part of the church's legacy too.

The art in being a faithful disciple of Jesus is knowing when the critical need is to conserve and when God's call is to innovate. If you pause for just a second I suspect you can readily decide whether your default mode is to see Christian faith in terms of conservation of the past or innovation going forward. All of us have a preference, and, if the truth be told, it is probably more a function of our personality than our carefully developed theology.

In this week after we have observed the ultimate sign of God's desire for reconciliation (Holy Week) I offer two observations. First, the world and the church need both conservers and innovators. Without the first we become slaves of the trivial and the tawdry; without the other we are in bondage to our prejudices and doomed to irrelevance when the world inevitably changes around us.

Second, being part of the body of Christ means that we need to work hard to receive the gifts of those who see the priorities of faith differently than we do. It takes no great exercise of will or spirit to get along with those who share our preference for conservation or innovation. But putting the best construction on the words and deeds of those with whom we disagree – ah, that is a challenge worthy of people who have understood the implications of a cross and empty tomb.

Bloomin' Onion

Revelation comes in many forms. This week it came to me in a "bloomin' onion." Like many of you, I have made a resolution to lose some weight in the coming months. But there I was at the Outback Steakhouse...the menu before me...someone else paying...the onion there for the ordering. And yes, my brothers and sisters in Christ, I confess that my resolve did not stand a chance; I had to have that fried antithesis of all that is nutritionally wise. At the risk of seeming to trivialize a serious subject, a few observations on what a bloomin' onion has to do with Christian discipleship:

69

• Discipleship is about small choices. Most of us want to follow our Lord more faithfully, but, like losing weight, that does not happen because of an abstract wish. Discipleship means forgiving that particular pain who works in the next cubicle, blocking out a specific five or ten minutes for prayer and devotional reading, choosing to react with patience rather than passion to a specific slight. It would be much easier if following Jesus involved a one-and-done grand gesture. Consistent faithfulness in little things is a lot harder.

• Discipleship lets us start anew each day. I most assuredly blew my diet as I popped greasy petal after succulent petal of that onion into my mouth. It was discouraging to face just how lacking in seriousness I had been in that moment. But at least for today I am back on salad, the stationary bike, and smaller portions – one failure is not decisive. Luther said that the life of the baptized is a daily dying and rising in Christ. We do lapse. We do disappoint ourselves. We do fail to live up to our ideal image of ourselves. Life in Christ is not about beating ourselves up when we fail; it is about being willing to start again. It is about being as aware of God's grace as of our own fragility.

• Discipleship is about the long haul. I shared that bloomin' onion with two guys who had run a marathon in the past month. For them the extra calories were a tiny blip in a fundamentally healthy lifestyle. Of course we do not deliberately plan to abandon the way of Christ for something we know is destructive. Still, if we are fundamentally centered on Christ and what He desires of us, our lapses will be fewer and of less consequence.

Jesus once asked a man, "Do you want to be healed?" We will soon be in the Lenten season of self-reflection. It is worth asking ourselves whether we really do want our Lord to make a difference in our lives – and what we are willing to do to follow Him over the long haul in the daily choices of life.

Lady in the Van

Last week I went to see *The Lady in the Van*, a movie about a homeless woman who parks herself in a playwright's driveway for fifteen years. This is one of those movies which could easily send you into sugar shock – curmudgeonly old woman and hapless young man slowly discover one another as violins swell in the background. But, for the most part, Maggie Smith, in the title role, and a good script keep the treacle in check; there is cayenne in the chocolate. Some in the neighborhood see Mary Shepherd through rosy glasses, an odd but endearing old soul. Alan Bennett, the playwright whose driveway is filled with garbage, bags of human waste, and Shepherd's hand-painted yellow van, has no such illusions. At one point he describes his squatter as smelly, rude, racist, and ungrateful – yet he invests himself in her welfare for fifteen years.

I write this during Holy Week, a time when television is filled with sentimental costume dramas featuring longing stares and chiseled bodies. I don't have any real problem with these dramatizations of the Passion. In a culture where colored eggs are more likely than the empty tomb to be seen as the defining symbol of Easter, we can celebrate anything which gets the basic story in front of people. I have only one request, let's not get too quickly to Easter morn. Passion Week is not a sentimental tale which ends "and they all lived happily ever after." This story invites us to confront all the darkness which we inflict on one another and to marvel at God's amazing willingness to see us with no illusions – and still stay invested in our welfare.

We need not indulge in self-flagellation, but let's get beyond the illusion that we are such swell guys and gals. The wonder of Easter is that we are not always – or even often – so swell, but God loves us anyway. St. Paul cuts to the heart of the matter: "For while we were still weak, at the right time Christ died for the ungodly. Indeed, rarely will anyone die for a righteous person – though perhaps for a good person someone might actually dare to die. But God proves His love for us in that while we still were sinners Christ died for us." (Romans 5:6-8).

Love sees clearly and still gives. Holy Week shows us what that looks like in painful detail. May we see, give thanks, and follow where Jesus has led.

Maintenance and Innovation

This morning as I was puffing my way through squats, curls, and step-ups at the gym I listened to a *Freakonomics* podcast entitled "In Praise of Maintenance." Apropos, I thought, given that I was there trying to hold back the ravages of aging. The piece's central thesis was that as a society we value innovation and entrepreneurship over maintaining what we already have. We reward the bright new idea, but devalue older systems which are essential to our well-being.

So, we get ever more exotic phones but drive on roads and bridges crumbling from neglect. We write libraries of books and papers on new approaches to education, even as we allow class sizes to balloon from lack of funding. We laud the inventor of a new medicine, but hardly acknowledge the guy who maintains our plumbing and sewer systems (and thus does much more than the inventor to prevent disease and keep us healthy).

What particularly caught my attention about this thesis was its implications for how we treat one another. When we make innovation and entrepreneurship a fetish, we not so subtly devalue the contributions of folks who do the unglamorous but essential tasks of fixing, making, and maintaining the stuff of our lives. When we give outsized reward to a few we create resentment among the many who know their work is indeed valuable. As a side note, that insight is worth considering as a lens through which to view the recent election.

Yet my point is closer to home. The church is often guilty of looking for the next big thing, the next sparkling program which can bring in the hoards and balance the books. We want a breakthrough idea and the charismatic leader to implement it. We neglect to proclaim loud and clear the unconditional love of God. More than that, we too often forget to celebrate the silent saints who plod along mowing the grass, serving the meals, turning on the heat, showing up at the food bank, contributing to the relief of the poor, and calling on the sick and shut-in. So this week's Bread is for all of you who seldom hear your name called for recognition, but just happen to be the foundation on which God builds a holy presence in the world – thank you.

Innovation and maintenance are not opposites; we need both. Let's celebrate those who show us a better way, while never forgetting to value the teachers, engineers, policemen, craftsman, and countless others who, by attending the basics of our life together, literally ensure that our world does not fall in around us.

Moment of Clarity

Maybe I was just too tired to care. Last week I was visiting my family in Louisiana. As they say, "You can't get there from here." On the best of days it takes pretty much a whole day to fly from Lake Charles to Roanoke. This was not the best of days. We landed in Charlotte, sat on the tarmac for twenty minutes, ran like scared rabbits to make our very tight connection (you literally could not have a longer walk than the one we had from our incoming to outgoing gates) – and discovered that our flight had been canceled. No more planes that night and the three flying the next day were totally full. The solution? American Airlines put us on a bus from Charlotte to Roanoke.

I am not a patient person. I certainly was not excited about a midnight bus ride. Yet somehow it did not seem so bad. I think it was because in my head I kept seeing that iconic picture of a little Syrian boy on the beach, drowned trying to escape the hell in his home country. As we rode through the night up I-77 I was thinking, "I am warm and fed. In a few hours I will be safely in my bed. This delay is the worst thing which has happened to me in a week; how many millions of people would love to say that? The most onerous consequence of all this is that I will be a little sleepy when I go back to work in the morning."

Please do not read this reflection as a pious proclamation that I have achieved some sort of Zen state of equanimity in the face of adversity. On the contrary, I am pretty sure I will be irritable and cranky the next time I face a small sling or arrow of outrageous fortune. This Bread is more a thanksgiving for being given a moment of clarity. Much of our unhappiness can be traced to a loss of perspective. As I write this a bunch of Vikings and Redskins fans are in agony – but last

74

time I looked the sun was still coming up. Finally, much of what steals our peace of mind just doesn't matter in the long term. My hope for you is a life-giving moment of clarity and perspective next time you confront a challenge, great or small.

Oak Tree

Some years ago I read an article by a church consultant entitled something like "Get Rid of the Oak Tree." His topic was not landscaping but better meetings. He told of a congregational council which had "oak tree" on its monthly agenda for a year. A very old tree stood in the front of the church yard and there was much debate concerning what to do about it. Some said it had been there for years and had caused no problems, so they favored leaving it alone. Others lobbied to cut it down before it fell on the church, reasoning that was just a matter of time before it caused a problem. Still others suggested that it be trimmed, but that option prompted further discussion about whether trimming should be done by the property committee or a professional team. Round and round they went, taking up valuable time every month – and never reaching a decision.

The author said that every church has an oak tree, and it is important to identify the things which suck energy from the group, act thoughtfully on them, and then move on to what is most important. In my experience that author was right on; most groups do tend to get sidetracked by niggling issues which take up way more time and energy than they deserve.

The insight applies to more than church meetings. Think about your daily mental agenda. Is there a conversation you really need to have with someone, but you keep putting off because it is likely to be awkward or unpleasant? There it sits in the back of your mind, taking up space on your agenda but getting no closer to resolution. Unresolved problems in relationships are emotionally draining; more than that, they block us from more constructive ways of spending our time. Like a car stuck in the mud, we just churn our mental wheels without getting anywhere.

Better to forthrightly seek reconciliation. Paul offers some good counsel, "Be angry but do not sin; do not let the sun go down on your anger [Ephesians 4:26]." Note, he does not say we should pretend that everything is okay when it is not. Rather, we admit our anger, but then move toward reconciliation as quickly as possible.

What is the oak tree you need to check off your agenda?

Quietism and Acrimony

"A plague o' both your houses! I am sped."

So speaks a bleeding Mercutio in *Romeo and Juliet*, his wound the result of getting in the middle of the feud between the Montagues and the Capulets. In that moment he does not care a whole lot about who is right or wrong, who started the cycle of recrimination and revenge. He is literally sick unto death of the whole mess. He is sped, done, finished.

Maybe that is how you are feeling after the political conventions, with three long months of presidential politics still in the offing. "A plague on both your houses; just make it all go away." I feel it too. Whatever your leanings, following politics these days is like hiking next to a ruptured sewer line – the path has interesting sights, but the smell is always there.

Let me assure you that this Bread is not about urging you

76

to support one candidate or the other. Rather, in these trying times, I invite you to avoid the extremes of quietism and acrimony.

Quietism puts up its hands in despair. Faced with momentous choices, it emotionally checks out and refuses to believe that anything really matters. "Wake me when it's over." Tempting, but this amounts to rational people ceding the field to the rabid. Instead of thoughtfulness we have a society driven by mere passion.

At the other end of the spectrum is acrimony and demonization. We are fully engaged but assume others are stupid, ignoble, and utterly devoid of integrity. Nuanced answers to complex problems are way too much work, so we opt for simplistic slogans. Trying to understand the pain of others takes a lot of effort, so we just dismiss their concerns without a second thought.

Quietism and acrimony are entirely understandable responses to our toxic political climate. Indeed they are the most basic animal responses to unpleasant stimuli – flight or fight. But don't we need more than our most primitive reactions in these troubled times? We need the "new creation" of which Paul speaks; hearts and wills transformed. We need the hard way of Jesus, committed to loving justice and mercy while reaching out to those who care little for such things.

One wit said, "He who can keep his head when all others are losing theirs – obviously doesn't understand the situation." We dare not pretend that our political choices do not matter, because the way we live together matters. A fractured society needs followers of Jesus to make a distinctive witness. We might modify that whimsical comment: "Those who seek both righteousness and reconciliation when neither seems near – are obviously trying to walk the way of Jesus."

Parker's Vet Trip

Whenever I talk with my son, Scott, at some point the conversation usually turns to Parker. Parker is his dog and a lucky dog she is – when I die I want to come back as Scott's dog, because Scott is wonderfully attentive to Parker's needs. Most of the time Scott's tales of her exploits are pretty light, but this week was a little different. In a freak accident, Parker face-planted and broke her jaw. Telling us the gory details of the trip to doggy ER, anesthesia, operations, and splints Scott said, "As I was taking her to the vet I was feeling so bad for her; I knew she was hurting." Then he added with a wry laugh, "And I was wondering just how much this was going to cost me!"

As we hung up the phone Gail and I looked at each other and smiled. "I guess our boy just discovered what it's like to be a parent." Anyone who has ever had a child can relate; there is nothing you would not do for your beloved, but, sentimentality aside, kids (or dogs) can be an expensive proposition.

The more I thought about Scott's comment the more I realized it has an application far beyond dogs and children. When we understand what it means to be a follower of Jesus we inevitably find our hearts torn by the suffering around us. Life is a lot easier when you don't have that pesky voice of Jesus murmuring in your ear about "caring for the least of these." When we see the pictures of need or hear the tales of woe, like Scott, we feel bad and long to alleviate the pain. It would be simpler indeed to have as a credo, "Go for the gusto; look out for number one." But that is not the sort of person we want to be.

Still, there is a cost, and we need to realize that if our awakened feelings are not to be merely stillborn intention.

Jesus was honest about the cost of following Him. There is always a cost – it may be paid in fewer hours to go running, passing up a phone upgrade to give money to the food pantry, lost sleep as we ponder another's need, or missing a party to volunteer – but there is always a cost. Discipleship involves understanding that our call is more than feeling bad, but responding in love by paying the tab.

The thing is…it's worth it. That's what Jesus dares us to believe. Scott's wallet is going to be a little lighter by the time Parker is fully healed, but I think he will count the cost as worth it because giving love has a way of enriching us in subtle ways. Scott will get to play with his crazy dog, that's the immediate payoff. But beyond that he will have practiced compassion in a concrete way which opens him up to receiving beauty and love from those around him. The tit-for-tat payoff of investing ourselves in others is not always obvious, but the impact is like a thousand small brushstrokes which over time build up to form a beautiful picture in our lives and in our world.

No Simple Template

"But if everyone did like him, who would grow the food and cook the meals?" I love it when people refuse to simply go along. Our Thursday morning faith group was in the middle of a session on Francis of Assisi, and we were suitably impressed by the saint. There is no way you can dislike St. Francis. He is justly one of the most admired figures in church history – gentle, humble, a model of simplicity, magnificent in his ability to discern the holy in the ordinary, his life an eloquent testimony to the graciousness of Jesus. But all those virtues meant he lived as a beggar, absolutely dependent upon others for the basics of existence. So she gently asked whether he really is the model for all Christians. Should St. Francis be the template for Christians in the 21st Century?

Maybe a better question is whether there is any template at all. A few years ago it was popular to wear a wristband bearing the letters "WWJD" for "What Would Jesus Do." While that is surely a better ethical guideline than asking "What would Pastor King do," I don't think it is the right question. The question suggests that we are all the same, that we have the same gifts, opportunities, responsibilities, and challenges. Asking what Jesus would do assumes that God needs me to do the exactly the same thing that Jesus needed to do. Certainly we try to follow in the way of Jesus, listen as he speaks, and attempt to let his spirit guide our decisions. But that is different from assuming that every Christian has the same calling. Part of the challenge of faithfulness is discerning what God needs from me in this particular time and place, which may be different from what God needs from you.

Some years ago I read a brief piece of fiction in a magazine called *The Other Side.* The author imagined arriving at heaven's gates and very proudly telling God how he had turned his back on the fame, money, and prestige of writing for a major magazine. Instead he had spent his life writing for a small religious newspaper. Much to his surprise and chagrin God castigated him, "I gave you a great mind, a bold heart, and incredible writing skills. Every week you were in a position to lift up the need for justice and mercy to millions of people and you squandered the chance to do great good." That parable has haunted me for 35 years, a reminder that calling is complex.

Discipleship is not a one-size-fits-all garment. Part of the hard work of following Jesus is asking exactly where He wants me to go. It goes without saying that there is an ever present temptation to evade the harsh demands of faith by making our preferences the preferences of God. But there is also the temptation to ease the tension of living in a broken world by aspiring to a faux spiritual purity far above the muck of daily life. There is no simple way of discerning our call; perhaps the best we can do is seek to align our hearts with the prayer of another great saint, Ignatius of Loyola:

O my God, teach me to be generous,
to serve You as You deserve to be served,
to give without counting the cost,
to fight without fear of being wounded,
to work without seeking rest,
and to spend myself without expecting any reward,
but the knowledge that I am doing Your holy will.

Joy on the Way

"I used to think I did this to help people, but then one day I realized that I did this because it gave me so much joy." The speaker was Harold, a man who has, for many years, been gathering a group of volunteers each Tuesday to harvest, transport, split, and stack firewood for low-income families. I met him last week during our spring break service trip to the Boone, N.C. area. For three of our work days, thirteen of us worked on a Habitat for Humanity house. That was a great experience; it was satisfying to see the flooring, paint, and trim we applied bring the project a little closer to completion. But, based on the debriefing our group did at the end of the week, working in the wood lot was the high point for many of us – and Harold's offhand comment helped me see why.

Despite the plain biblical teaching that those who take up the cross and follow in the way of Jesus will find life at its most fulfilling, we tend to think either/or: Either we can hunker down and do what we think we ought to do – grudgingly and perhaps guiltily sparing a little time, money, and energy for the less fortunate – or we can do something which gives us pleasure. But I can assure you that there was precious little guilt or grudging in the folks I met that day. It was bone-wearying work (particularly dragging logs and brush on a mountain hillside), but you would never have guessed it from the jokes and camaraderie which permeated the atmosphere. There was no sense of either/or around that wood lot.

I think Harold is being a little modest. He and his friends are deeply motivated by a sense of having been blessed and wanting to share out of their abundance. But they have discovered that deep joy in serving is what folks in south Louisiana call "lagniappe" – an unexpected gift, a little something extra – which comes free to those who stop measuring out compassion with an eyedropper.

We sometimes think of Lent as a rather dour season, but as Harold taught me, the way of the cross is paradoxically the way of deepest happiness.

Long Loneliness

"We have all known the long loneliness and we have learned that the only solution is love and that love comes with community." (Roman Catholic social reformer Dorothy Day, in *The Long Loneliness*)

Sometimes it's pretty obvious: the scruffy guy hunched over on a park bench, a little girl looking hopefully around the playground for someone to invite her into the game, the painfully shy guy at the party intently studying his beer – to keep from looking at anyone. Sometimes it is easy to spot loneliness. But not always.

Loneliness can look like the gregarious guy, constantly telling jokes to mask how few true friends he has. Loneliness can look like a woman slowly, but very deliberately, leaving worship and sliding out the side door because nobody greeted her. Most of the time, of course, we do not see the deepest loneliness because it hidden away behind closed doors. Loneliness in our culture is like an iceberg, only the smallest part visible.

In the first chapter of Genesis, God says, "It is not good for the man to be alone." We usually read those verses as the warrant of marriage, but the words also say something fundamental about what it means to be human. They remind us that we are not fully human when we are totally isolated. In order to live with verve and joy we need other people to challenge us, support us, and share the wonder of life with us. Only a dead person, either literally or figuratively, does not need others.

Loneliness is more intense for some than for others, but we have all felt the spiritual chill of feeling isolated and vulnerable. A byproduct of our mobile culture is that we are often far from the friends and family which once bundled us in care. It is, therefore, all the more important for us to be the community of care which Jesus calls his followers to be. As Dorothy Day notes, love is the flame which holds the dark shadows at bay. That flame springs to life when people rub their hearts together in a Christian community which sees with the concerned eyes of Jesus.

Open your eyes today; see if there is a lonely person at hand who would be blessed by your smile and genuine interest.

Love Like the Movies

So you want to be in love like the movies,
But in the movies they're not in love at all.
And with a twinkle in their eyes,
They're just saying their lines.
So we can't be in love like the movies.
Now in the movies they make it look so perfect,
And in the background they're always playing the right song.
And in the ending there's always a resolution,
But real life is more than just two hours long.
--"Love Like the Movies"--

I went to a concert by the Avett Brothers last night. After the music stopped, the clapping was over, and my ears stopped ringing, the above lyrics echoed in my head. I find them as succinct a comment on our national malaise as I have heard in long time. It seems that I increasingly encounter folks who are grumpy, depressed, vaguely discontented; you could use a lot of descriptors. But the unifying theme is that things just are not what they should be – and somebody has got to pay. To be sure, the economy does stink, the prospects if you are a young adult are far grimmer than when I graduated from college, and the politics of gridlock are enough to bring any person of good will to despair. Still, I wonder if part of the problem is not that so much of our lives is built on illusion that reality is inevitably deflating.

Relationships are messier than in the movies: We don't always find the right words to say which make things right. Our children break our hearts and continue down destructive paths, despite our best efforts. The morning's first glimpse of our beloved is not always accompanied by a sound track of lush violins. Sometimes the pain just keeps going on… and on… and on. It's not that we could not cope with reality; it's that we have a false image of what goes into this mixed bag of joys and sorrows we call life.

Addressing his disciples in the shadow of the cross, preparing them for life without him physically by their side, Jesus gave it to them straight, "In this world you will have trouble, but take heart, I have overcome the world." There is no illusion, no chick flick sentimentality, no macho bravado – just honesty and the promise that he will not abandon them.

Sometimes life is very painful, and it's hard to see an easy resolution to our struggles. Finally, we do not really want love like in the movies; we want sometime more, something real and enduring when our personal film is a horror story and the plot line is heartbreaking. God does not promise us an easy way, just Christ's sustaining presence in the hardest of times and the assurance of victory at the end.

Jaws

Last week I was clicking through the channels and happened upon Jaws. Yes, in these days of computer generated graphics, the shark sometimes looks comical; you can almost hear the gears creaking in its mechanical mouth. Still, I was reminded of what makes this such a great movie. Director

Stephen Spielberg has an incredible capacity to keep you off guard. That signature music builds, the shot comes in tight and ... nothing happens. Then, just when you settle in to take a deep breath and relax, the savagery begins. The unpredictable timing keeps you on edge for the whole film, vaguely anxious, even when things seem normal.

I give you this mini movie review because Jaws can teach us something about the dynamics of grief. Following a death or other great loss, most of us are pretty good at girding up our loins, marshaling our resources, and getting through the immediate crisis. When we are bystanders to another's pain, we usually pick up the sound of that tense music and rush in to give whatever support is necessary. That's wonderful; by no means do I want to minimize the necessity of doing all we can to support those in crisis or being there when folks are too numb to think for themselves.

Yet, in my experience, the really devastating attack comes a little later. The obvious crisis has passed, you think the worst is over, and you are finally settling into what passes as the new normal, after coming to terms with your loss. Then, like that shark in Jaws, a wave of despair hits you. The attack is doubly devastating because you thought you were all done with the agony and now you are facing it without the support of those who rallied to your side in the immediate aftermath of your loss.

Grief is not a one and done sort of thing. It is a series of pulsating pains, often excruciatingly unexpected and triggered by a sound, a smell, or a memory. If you are struggling with profound loss, be gentle with yourself and don't expect to be perpetually in control. And if you care for someone who is dealing with a death, the loss of a dream, or debilitating injury, remember that long after the Jaws theme has stopped sounding in their lives, there is a lot of pain lurking. Make a point to be there after the immediate drama is over and the unexpected attack hits their heart.

Ash Wednesday

We've all had it happen: You open an e-mail or pick up the phone, and suddenly you have a major task plopped on your plate. You had a pretty good handle on the week – there were challenges, but you had a manageable plan for keeping the balls in the air – now you wonder how it all gets done. Sometimes it's work. Sometimes it's a family crisis. Your blood pressure spikes and the muscles in the back of your neck get a little tighter. I got blindsided like that last week.

There are a number of ways to respond. One is petulant refusal to change a thing. A sign in a local business informs the reader, "Failure to plan on your part does not constitute an emergency on my part." That was my initial response to the fateful e-mail demanding that I reorient my week; I'd ignore the imperative and get to it if and when I could. But the task really was important, and the person asking had had the load dropped on her desk without warning – and I do like my job. I might rant and rage over the unfairness and poor planning, but in the end the task still had to get done.

There are time management strategies which we can employ to categorize, prioritize, and reorganize our days to, in some measure, get done what we must. You probably know and use some of them. I am trying to work a little smarter.

But on this Ash Wednesday two themes growing out of the heart of our Lenten discipline come to mind, which are worth remembering all year when we confront unexpected pressures. The first is the transitory nature of life. This day and the whole season remind us that life is a divine gift with a limit; we do not have an infinite number of days. "Remember you are ashes and to ashes you will return." It, therefore, behooves us to not waste a second in futile resentment. Yes, sometimes others put unreasonable demands on us, but that can only happen because we are enjoying the precious gift of life. The nature of life is coping with the unexpected. Our attitude can be a lot better if, rather than burdens, we see demands as opportunities to exercise our gifts during the moments we are given.

Lent is also a time of fasting and discerning what is most important. For a season we may give up something to remind ourselves how very little is truly essential. As we walk with Jesus during Lent we will notice how focused He is on His mission, how little energy He wastes on things which do not make much difference. When we feel pressure from unexpected demands it is often because our lives are already too filled up. Like a backpack filled to the brim, there is no place to put anything else. But if we take some things out of the pack we discover that new weight is perfectly manageable.

Life is precious and ought to be spent on what is most important. This is worth remembering when we get blindsided by unexpected challenges.

Till, Ignore, or Mulch

"Once more into the breach dear friends" – or maybe not. It's spring, which means I am once again looking at the large, brown spot surrounding a small tree in my front yard. This year it is bigger than ever. I do not know if it is the deer stomping and munching during the winter, shallow roots of that small tree sucking up all the good stuff, or some sort of systemic deterioration of the soil. All I know is that every year about this time I have to decide whether to reseed, fertilize, and water this little patch of desolation in a seemly vain effort to keep it from turning into a mud hole. It has been a long time since I had visions of my front yard looking like something on the garden tour. Mowing grass is my definition of futility, so if it is green and stops erosion, that's good enough. But I can't even grow dandelions, moss, or chickweed on this corner of creation. So do I join the battle once again?

The only reason I mention this little gardening poser is because it illustrates a more basic truth – much of life is deciding just how passionate we want to be about making changes to the status quo. Some causes are worth all the effort we can muster. Even if we fail, it is better to go down fighting than to silently acquiesce to evil. These are the parts of life where we refuse to be defeated because something essential is at stake; we till, seed, water, and labor until ugliness becomes beauty. On the other hand, a lot of things just don't matter, and we do well to invest little or no energy in getting upset. These are the parts of life which are like my back yard – unseen, unimportant, unfertilized – you take what you get. Then there are those spheres – most of life's challenges in fact – which are candidates for mulching. They are neither critical nor unimportant. You can find a way to deal with them without getting too agitated. The wisest and happiest people have learned when to till, ignore, or mulch.

Of course we all have to do our own prioritization. I know some reading this meditation would tell me to just let the whole yard go au naturel (believe me, I have considered that) – and some of you would put a lush, well-nurtured lawn up there with the Mona Lisa as an artistic triumph. My values are not necessarily going to be your values in deciding what is worth great effort. In landscaping, as in many things, I hope we can be at peace with those who hold slightly different values from our own.

Yet during this Holy Week I invite you to ponder the passion which took Jesus into Jerusalem. There are things worth dying for; Jesus and the martyrs who followed him in discipleship bear witness to that fact. If you have never found such a passion, you are probably mulching too much. If Jesus is our Lord, this week will make us ponder anew what He devoted those 33 years of his life to saying and doing. As we try to discern what to sow, what to ignore, and what to mulch in our own lives, at least one question ought to be, "What kind of world was Jesus trying to grow; what fruits was He hoping to grow from His tree on Golgotha?"

Working in Black and White

I was recently listening to an interview with a famous cinematographer. He observed that he loves to work in black and white. "There is a certain simple elegance with black and white. Color can be very difficult, very distracting, cluttering the screen with nonessentials. With black and white you are forced to focus on what is important, conveying emotion with a bare palette of grays."

That is an important insight as we enter Lent. Our culture makes it hard for us to enter into a Lenten mindset. Gone is the world where the whole society dances to the rhythm of the church year, celebrating on holy days (hence the word "holiday") and observing restraint during seasons of reflection. We fear boredom above all else and push ourselves to keep the stimulation coming: music mainlined through an iPod, surfing 100 television options, breathless trivial tweets and texts. If our real lives run out of drama we buy a pig for our online virtual farm.

Lent is a season of black and white, but if we think it is dreary for the sake of being dreary we have missed the point. To be sure there is a somber element; after all, Lent traces our Lord's journey to crucifixion. Still, the point is not to wallow in misery or Lenten deprivation of our favorite treat. Lent pulls the color out of the palette, tones down the volume, and slows down the beat of our lives so that we can focus on the bare essentials. If we receive the gift of Lent we will take it as a chance to ask where we are headed and whether that is really where we want to go.

After 4/16

This is not the Bread for the Journey you were supposed to be reading. I was supposed to be in South Carolina on Wednesday, so I wrote my Bread last week and gave it to our secretary to send out today. Maybe you'll read that one some other time, but it seemed a little inappropriate after Monday's events. [The death of 33 students on the Virginia Tech campus on 4/16/17]

The book of Job is the Bible's most extended wrestling with the mystery of incomprehensible, pointless, "how-can-a-loving God-who-cares-one-iota-about-humanity-allow-such-absurdity" pain. It spills oceans of ink in trying to come to terms with the inexplicable. I remember reading the comments of a great Old Testament scholar who noted that after Job's life falls apart, his three friends came "and they sat with him on the ground seven days and seven nights, and no one spoke a word to him, for they saw that his suffering was very great." [2:13] The scholar notes, "And that is the last thing they do right in the whole book." The rest of the way they offer long-winded explanations of Job's agony. They blame Job. They defend God. They try to tie up the loose ends that make no sense. They leave Job hurting.

Over the past few days I have been struck by the temptation to frenzy, the compulsion we feel to do something – anything – just so we don't feel so impotent. We babble. We organize. We probe the minutia of the timeline. But the really hard thing to do is to simply sit with people who suffer. I would love to have brilliant answers to why this absurdity has visited our campus. I wish I had glib words about divine care and providence which would pull the poison paralyzing us right now. But pat answers are the stuff of Job's comforters not the Biblical witness. The Bible does not give us answers, it gives us a witness. God deals with suffering, not by making it reasonable, but by sharing it and asking us to be willing to sit with those whose agony is almost too much to bear.

One panel of Matthias Grunewald's magnificent Isenheim altarpiece depicts the crucifixion. John the Baptist stands at the foot of the cross and points at one of the most excruciatingly detailed pictures of human suffering you will ever see. No words. No explanations. But it seems to say, "This is God's answer to suffering, to all the evil we do to one another – Emmanuel, God with us."

Brothers and sisters, recovery is not going to be a sprint; the road to healing for our community is a marathon. There will be many opportunities to sit in silence with those who suffer. Resist the temptation to explain. Just...listen...and wait on the healing which God will provide in due season.

Memorial for the Unknown

What do you say at the memorial service of someone you've never met? I'm sitting here pondering that question. Pastors are periodically asked to conduct a service for a person with whom they have no prior relationship. You are glad to offer what help you can, but you always feel inadequate. You want to do justice to this life, render it proper respect and reverence as you mark its passing, yet, without any recollections to incarnate the name in the obituary, it is hard to do.

As I stare out the window, I wonder what Gunter was like. Did he fish? Where did he grow up? Was he a pillar of some community far from here or hero only to his family? Did his eyes twinkle when he laughed? How loud did he snore when he fell asleep in front of the TV? Would his musical tastes run more to Bach or the Beach Boys? What memories did he buy with the days of his life?

Gunter was coming up on one hundred years old. Living as long as that is bittersweet. Few would wish for a short life, but for him it meant outliving most of the people who gave his life meaning and texture, existing long past the time of healthy vitality, ending his days in a facility which was a poor imitation of his home and being memorialized by a pastor who never met him. There is inescapable pathos to such an ending.

So what do you say? I suspect I will lift up the truth that anchors the Christian life every step along the way: Whether we are famous or anonymous, powerful or plebeian, appreciated by many or only by a few, we are at every moment known to God. The accomplishments for which we strive so mightily may fade, but the love of God continues to shine upon us. Whether the world remembers us or not, we are never outside the thoughts of the One who called us into being and welcomes us home.

The Lenten season is, among other things, a time for reflecting on our mortality. Still, such contemplation need not end in bleak despair; there is reason for joy, even when the transience of life is inescapable. Paul reminds us why Christians have courage in the shadow of mortality, "If we live, we live to the Lord, if we die we die to the Lord; so then, whether we live or whether we die, we are the Lord's." Maybe that's what I'll say.

Cruel

I was cruel. He said he had felt belittled for years. I'd like to say he was overly sensitive, but in truth I think he was right. I could quibble that he should not have suffered in silence and allowed the tension between us to build, that he could have let me know how my words and actions felt to him. That's the counsel I give someone at least once a week, "Maybe he does not know how you are feeling; let him know and you might be able to work things out." But that would just be a feeble effort at self-justification. The truth: I was habitually condescending and cruel.

As he spoke about his pain I realized four things. First, he had probably been doing the best that he could under burdens which I did not understand. Second, my tendency to belittle him was rooted in attitudes and motives which I imputed to him at least as much as it was in what he actually said or did. Third, I was acting as though he had some obligation to meet my expectations. Fourth, it should have been different between us.

The first three insights are straight out of any introductory course on counseling or building better communication skills. That does not mean they are unimportant, just that there is nothing particularly Christian about trying to understand the issues another faces, see the world as she does, and be aware when our expectations are inappropriate. But it should have been different, not because I am a pastor, but because I am a Christian.

The point is not whether my judgments were objectively accurate. Jesus calls me to a higher standard than being right; He invites me be His disciple. Jesus sometimes spoke hard words. But those words were not wrecking balls bluntly demolishing all in their path, but precise scalpels wielded, not to hurt but to heal. If Jesus is my Lord, healing and reconciliation are supposed to be my priorities.

I offer this reflection as a reminder that our greatest spiritual failings are often the perversions of our gifts. If you find these words a little self-indulgent I hope you will forgive me; I can best illustrate with the perversions I know best. I like to think my strengths include honesty, an incisive intellect, and a willingness to say hard things. But those gifts easily became callousness, arrogance, and cruelty. How has God gifted you? Are you using them to serve Christ's reconciliation and justice in the world?

One final thing – the most important reality of all is that each day God offers us forgiveness when our lives do not match our confession, invites us to turn from destructive patterns, and bids us leave our failings in the past. If I did not believe that, I could not write this meditation.

Winter Olympics

I have a shocking confession to make: The winter Olympics bore me to tears. I would rather eat cold grits than watch an hour of people skiing down cold slopes. I'm sure part of my reaction comes from growing up in a state (SC) where basketball is the main winter sport and the only time you get on ice is unwillingly, when a sleet storm coats the sidewalks. Participating in a sport gives you the ability to identify and appreciate excellence, which I never got with winter Olympic events. Yes, I enjoy a few minutes of the figure skating, but that's because the music and dance choreography make it feel as much like fine art as sport.

I recognize the incredible skill it takes to do these sports, but as I was watching snowboard racing the other night I found myself thinking, "What an incredible waste of time getting to this level of excellence!" How many hours did that guy devote to what is finally a pretty useless skill – riding a surfboard down a mountain? But, of course, he could have asked me if lying in bed, eating a bowl of pudding and watching him do his thing were any better use of the minute it took to complete the race.

And that is the point of this little reflection. All of us have different interests which energize us. There is no absolute standard which makes some ways of spending time inherently better than others. Still, we should be mindful that time is a gift from God, not to be squandered. The issue is whether the choices we make in how we use our time reflect a balance of pursuits which feed our souls and contribute to the healing of the world. Notice the rhythm of life which Jesus models in the gospels – investing Himself totally in those around Him, and then giving Himself to both prayer and partying, activities which recharge His battery. Lent is a great time to focus on discerning how best we can cultivate this healthy rhythm in our own lives.

This week reflect on how you spend your time. What is the balance between delight and duty? When we honor God's gift of life, we give time to each.

Close to You

"Just like me, they long to be – close to you." Karen Carpenter's sweet honey voice oozing out of the iPod speaker on the table took me back to my college days. I thought of lazy days studying – and dozing – by a placid lake. I recalled lonely dorm nights, wondering if I would ever find someone who'd sing me that song. I remembered the exhilaration of walking back from my first date with the woman who became my wife. Most of all I remembered the kaleidoscope of possibilities that song evokes for me, those days when the world was laid out at my feet with infinite possibilities.

But this was nothing like the carefree days of college. This was a vigil. His infinite possibilities were rapidly narrowing to one. He was dying and there was nothing anybody could do about it. The sighs filling the room were not romantic sweet nothings but his gentle gasps for breath. The words of love gently spoken to him were probably unheard – and if heard, not long remembered. This was far from the boisterous football tailgates he loved.

At first the juxtaposition of the song and the sparse hospital room seemed vaguely absurd. The longer I sat there the more I saw something beautiful and powerful, something which moved me to tears. It's wonderful to celebrate the bloom of new love, to passionately confess that all you want from life is to be near your beloved. I've known that feeling and can attest it is intoxicating ecstasy. Still, love is easy when limbs are strong, minds are clear, the future is bright, and the road wide open. It's a lot harder when all that is left are memories. If you want to see mature love, sit by the bed of the dying and see care poured out with little hope of reciprocation. "Close to you." He had nothing left to give, but his beloved still wanted nothing more than the privilege of being close to the very end.

I preach a lot of sermons; most of them at some point talk about love. Some of the most powerful sermons need very few words because they are preached by long, excruciatingly tedious hours of faithfulness. Sometimes we preachers do well to shut up and let those who really know something about love teach us.

Harmless Cross

My friend Marty was recently making her way through airport security when she heard that beeping sound, dreaded by all travelers, which means you are in for detailed scrutiny by the staff. A very serious young woman pulled her out of line and told her to assume the position: legs spread, arms out like a scarecrow, and face forward. As soon as the alarm went off Marty knew what had happened. She had forgotten to remove the small cross she carries in her pocket as a reminder, when she digs for her change, that she is a beloved child of God. "Oh it's just a cross," she assured the unsmiling screener, "it's harmless." She started to reach down to show her, and the security guard jumped back like Marty had pulled a copperhead out of her pocket and barked, "Arms out!" She was not at all sure whatever was in that pocket was harmless.

98

I laughed when she told the story, but it got me thinking. That little metal cross was indeed harmless, as the security personnel soon agreed, but is the cross on my forehead also harmless? Does it make any difference that I have been baptized. Does the invisible mark I carry as one claimed and called by God have the potential to shake things up, or is it so inconsequential that the world does not notice I carry it all the time?

Jesus once said that He came not to bring peace, but a sword. Jesus never gratuitously sought conflict, but neither did He shy away from letting folks know that faithfulness to God demands some changes in business as usual. If our baptismal cross never sets off an alarm, never makes the world step back and give us some extra scrutiny, maybe it has become a little too harmless.

Homeless Picture

Some might call it a coincidence. Those of a more New Age mindset would call it a harmonic convergence. For me it was an exquisite epiphany. Gary has a painting in his office I have long wanted to include in our Good Friday service which uses slides of art, music, and John's passion story. In this painting, entitled "Homeless," clothes are arranged across cracks in the sidewalk to give an impression of crucifixion. This year I finally got the picture taken.

Since the slide does not illustrate a particular moment in the passion narrative I inserted it rather arbitrarily into a section where I had fewer images. There was no plan, but as I clicked on that slide the choir was singing poignant words from My Song is Love Unknown, "In life no house, no home/ My Lord on earth might have;/ In death, no friendly tomb/ But what a stranger gave." I was so moved I almost forgot to advance the slides.

It is terribly easy to think of the passion as something that happened in a distant time and place. Yes, we think, it had major significance, but it is at best holy history. Media critics thrash out whether Mel Gibson's movie blames the Jews for the crucifixion, as though our Lord does not still suffer daily at the hands of apathy, greed, and the desire to maintain the status quo.

Meditation on icons is an old devotional practice. So I offer you an icon of sorts. With a little luck (and patience if you have slow computer) you have an attachment of "Homeless" with this reflection. Open it and take a moment to think about how Christ suffers still. What can you do this day to stand against the scourging?

Took Bread

"… took bread, gave thanks, broke it, and gave it to His disciples saying, 'take and eat, this is my body given for you.'" If the words of institution can never be ordinary, they were at least very familiar as we pastors of the Virginia synod gathered at our meeting's closing worship. The days had been long. I was more than ready to be on the road, and only half present to the liturgy's well worn words. Then it happened. I suppose it was some sort of feedback from the celebrant's microphone; I'm not really sure. But into that brief, dramatic silence between the consecration of the bread and the consecration of the wine came a deep, "tha-THUMP, tha-THUMP, tha-THUMP," like a heartbeat heard through a stethoscope.

In an instant the words ceased to be merely a recitation

of long ago events. From a ball room at the retreat center I was transported back to a dim space which smelled of sweat, roasted lamb, and cheap wine. The people sharing that meal in Jerusalem were no longer abstractions from a Leonardo daVinci mural, but flesh and blood humans whose hearts must have raced as Jesus spoke. Which heartbeat was I hearing? The resolute but burdened heart of our Lord? The anxious heart of Judas, fluttering wildly in anticipation of his betrayal? The confused heart of a disciple trying to make sense of Jesus' strange departure from the Passover liturgy? The dull heart of one groggy from too much wine, and thus oblivious to the unfolding drama? I don't know whose heart I was hearing. Yet I was intensely aware that whatever abstract theology we spin about the significance of the Sacrament, the meal is rooted in history and comes to us reeking of the real emotions, and struggles, and confusions, and only half-expressible hopes of those who long ago received food and drink from the Lord's hand.

When the script becomes overly familiar it is easy for us to forget that the drama of our liturgy is designed to evoke remembrance, to create a connection to actual people across the centuries who, facing the same questions about meaning and mortality which are the lot of all generations, found strength in, with, and under simple gifts of bread and wine. We easily become passive spectators of the mystery rather than participants in its reincarnation. Those first disciples did not have the benefit of generations of erudite reflection to make sense of that meal; they knew only that somehow God's love was present for them in the eating and drinking. They were not super-Christians. They were like us: imperfect, often clueless, and faithful only in fits and starts. Yet, with hearts trembling like ours, they tasted and dimly knew that the Lord is indeed good.

Next time you come to the altar, squint a little and see if you can discern the cloud of witnesses which have been at many such tables before you. Before you take the wine, sniff long enough to let its sweet smell remind you how God's care comes in ordinary ways. And as you stand or kneel in silence, attend to your heartbeat – with each pumping cycle feel it reminding you of the supper's central promise: "I'm-LOVED, I'm-LOVED, I'm-LOVED."

Daily Blessing

There is no way to know whether she heard me. Standing over her bed I thought that she was the embodiment of Paul's words, "I have fought the good fight, I have finished the race, I have kept the faith. From now on there is reserved for me the crown of righteousness, which the Lord, the righteous judge, will give to me on that day…" She had been one of those amazing marathoners of the faith, a woman of both gentleness and grit. Now she was wearing down, her remaining earthly life measured in hours not days, deep in a coma from which all agreed she would never emerge.

Yet you never know how much those in their last hours can hear. So I took her parchment hand in mine, stooped and put my lips close to her ear, and offered her the only gifts I had, my presence and a prayer. I gave thanks to God for her life. I prayed that God's gentle presence might draw near to her in an undeniably intimate way on this last leg of her pilgrimage. I assured her that she was not alone, that she was surrounded by those who love her.

Please do not think I tell you this story so that you will think I am a wonderful pastor who brings incredible sensitivity to his calling. I did nothing extraordinary. It would be both absurd and tacky to brag about the sublime privilege of being with such a saint at her end. I share this brief moment for precisely the opposite reason, to remind you that each of us has the capacity to give something precious to another. You can bring light into the deepest darkness.

At the deepest level we all want to know we are loved, appreciated, and not alone in the midst of adversity. At a deathbed it is easy to see this most fundamental need; everything else fades into the background. But tell me, is there ever a second when you do not long to feel connected to others, ever a time when you would not value a word of support and kindness, ever a moment when it would not thrill you to know that another person counts you a treasure beyond price?

Now think, is there someone to whom you might say, "I thank God for your life?" Can you imagine what a lift hearing that might give someone? There is no reason to wait until you are standing at a bedside in the shadow of death. Give this beautiful flower to the living.

Facebook Profile

Writing your own obituary is a classic exercise to promote self-awareness. We spend so much time moving from deadline to deadline, from one urgency to the next that we seldom reflect on the relationships, priorities, and accomplishments which are our life. Writing our obituary invites us to reflect on how we are spending the coin of our days.

Last week I did something comparable to writing your own obituary, filling in my Facebook profile. According to a recent survey, it is one of the top places where teens and young adults prefer to get information about their world. It is a computer community where you can go to check out people and organizations. Being a rather private person by temperament, I had not put much information on my profile (the quick description of who you are and what you like), but I decided that more details might provide conversation starters with students. So I pulled up the form and started filling it in.

I won't bore you with the epiphanies I had as I filled in my favorite books, movies, and activities. Nor will I give you my dime store shrink's assessment of what those lists suggest about the mystery that is Bill. But I will tell you that I was surprised by how revelatory and evocative it was to make those lists. As I typed the titles of beloved books and movies I remembered critical moments in my emotional and intellectual development. I brought to mind people who had touched me at pivotal points, and pinpointed the moment a certain big idea expanded my universe. In those books and movies I could chart the geography of my life, the places and pursuits which give me joy, orient my steps, and haunt my nights.

Out of this Facebook experience I offer you two observations. First, it is well worth the time to make your own lists of favorite books, movies, TV shows, art, and pastimes. You will be amazed at the map of your life which such lists yield. Look at your lists. What do they say about what you love and value?

Second, it matters what is on those lists. Most people love Cheetos, but if that is all you are eating, malnutrition is inevitable. The things we read, view, and do are our soul's food. Everybody loves a Twinkie every once in awhile, but we need more. Be sure you are eating what nourishes for the long haul. Paul put it well, "Finally, beloved, whatever is true, whatever is honorable, whatever is just, whatever is pure, whatever is pleasing, whatever is commendable, if there is any excellence and if there is anything worthy of praise, think about these things."

Amour

Last week I saw the much acclaimed French film, *Amour*. The movie follows an elderly couple, both retired music teachers, as they deal with the wife's stroke and slow decline. Because the director has a reputation for making bleak movies, some critics have suggested that the title is bitterly ironic, that the movie's vision is that "love" may seem beautiful but finally comes to no more than deterioration, death, and adult diapers. The film is decidedly hard to watch; anyone who has sat helplessly by such a bedside will immediately recognize this painful territory. But on balance I found the movie bracing and beautiful in a dark way.

Think about how love is usually portrayed on screen: A quirky and always beautiful, young couple bicker and snipe at each other with sparkling repartee until they fall into each other's arms – and usually into a nearby bed. Most movies end just when the easy part is over, when the couple might actually begin discovering how hard and wonderful it is to love another person with all your heart over the long haul. *Amour* suggests how deep love can be and the nobility of caring long after there is a quick payoff.

It is easy to "love" another when he or she is beautiful, kind, appreciative, interesting, dutiful, reasonable, patient, and healthy. That kind of love is like pedaling a bicycle downhill, fun but not terribly taxing. Love starts when it is hard. Love, and here I am not just talking about couples, demands a great deal from those who claim to practice it. Yet nothing is as deeply fulfilling.

Most will read this meditation during Holy Week. In the passion narrative we see that love is about much more than sex and romance. It is finally about a choice to care even when those we love cannot – or will not – return our care. Love is choosing to hear the pain behind the angry word rather than the pettiness or bile it expresses. Love is about choosing to be people of peace when violence of word and deed comes more naturally. Love is becoming part of the world's transformation for which we long. Holy Week is about more than this kind of love, but it is not about less.

Blind Persons Don't Know Who to Hate

Revelation comes in the most unexpected ways. The student group which went to Clemson last week for our campus ministry's spring break trip had finished a satisfying day of work. We were on our way to get some ice cream when I glanced toward a parked car and saw a bumper sticker: "If everyone were blind we wouldn't know who to hate." I've been chewing on those words for a few days now because they suggest some important – and rather disturbing – truths about our species.

It is uncomfortable to be reminded how superficial we are. We make sweeping judgments based on the barest sliver of data. Any dark-skinned person can give you chapter and verse on the profiling which takes place every day: the way you clutch your purse when he walks behind you on the sidewalk, the suspicious looks she gets when she walks into the convenience store, the odd coincidence that he gets pulled out of the line half the time by the TSA – and his non-Arab traveling friend, almost never. But our presumptions are more than racial. If we know someone's politics, hobbies, educational level, or civic club affiliation we immediately impute all sorts of moral characteristics to him or her, which is to say we relate to our image of that person, rather than the complex human being behind the labels.

More disturbing to me than our superficial judgments is the bumper sticker's subtle, yet true, assertion that there is a part of us that needs and wants to find someone to hate. Sound too harsh? I invite you to study any good history of immigration in the United States – or rent *The Gangs of New York*. Lou Dobbs may be the highest profile hatemonger these days, but the first generations of Irish, Italian, Polish, German, and Asian immigrants from multiple countries would attest that he is only the latest in a very long line.

There is something within us which is threatened by those who are different. In order to feel good about myself I find reasons to demean you. I buttress my fragile ego by creating something lower than myself: "I may be less than I want to be but at least I'm not a ...."

In this Lenten season we do well to remember that the one reason the gospel is so radical and so often at odds with the powers that be is that it rests on a vision of humanity with no divisions. In a world where Political Action Committees tell you the first thing they have to do is create an enemy to mobilize the faithful, following the way of Jesus – and renouncing the creation of an enemies list – is a bold choice.

"For He is our peace, who has made us both one, and has broken down the dividing wall of hostility, by abolishing in His flesh the law of commandments and ordinances, that He might create in himself one new man in place of the two, so making peace, and might reconcile us both to God in one body through the cross, thereby bringing the hostility to an end." (Ephesians 2:14-16)

Diverse Art

I've been doing some interior decorating. For the past two years the long office wall which my desk faces has been blank. Now four pieces hang there: a bright impressionistic painting of Maasai men which I bought in Tanzania, a reproduction of Andrei Rublev's icon "The Trinity," a black and white rendering of Paris' Notre Dame Cathedral, sketched by a friend and given to me as a gift; and a cross-stitch of a favorite poem by Elizabeth Barrett Browning which my wife made for me.

I don't know what one with a more polished eye than mine would say about this grouping or the way I have them hung; they have little in common in style or subject. What unifies them is my life; each calls to mind a special person, a place, a turning in my journey. Each represents a brushstroke in the painting which is me. I have been formed by the diverse experiences, people, and ideas which put these particular artistic expressions on my wall.

Earlier in my life I felt a much greater need to like some types of art and dislike others, to think in terms of either/or. That had more to do with my ignorance than the merit of the art; I disliked what I did not understand. I hope I have grown. One sign of aesthetic maturity is greater appreciation of different styles and themes, a more comprehensive vision.

What is true in art is often true of religion. We limit what we can appreciate. We seldom say it so explicitly, but we may act as though granting the beauty or truth of a "non-Christian" perspective is somehow being disloyal to our core convictions. In a misplaced effort to honor our faith we choose to be willfully blind to richness which also comes from God, but is not explicitly Lutheran or even Christian.

One reason Jesus inspired such devotion was His way of blurring the distinctions between holy and profane, religious and secular. When communicating the most sublime truth He preferred images as ordinary as seed, weeds, and sheep. He could look at a Samaritan, a centurion, or leper and see something precious to affirm. In a world which loves to divide us, it is smart – indeed crucial for our survival – to cultivate a broad vision of the holy. But more than that, we cheat ourselves when we refuse to receive an unfamiliar or challenging perspective.

I will always have a special place in my heart for Monet or Rembrandt, but I've learned to appreciate the passion and insight of Jackson Pollock or Salvador Dali. So, too, we can find delight in the parables of Jesus and still be moved by the poetry of Rumi or benefit from pondering a Buddhist koan. The first words of that cross-stitch hanging on my wall say it well, "Earth's crammed with heaven and every common bush afire with God…" Open your eyes to today. Cultivate the ability to appreciate beauty and truth wherever it may present itself for your delight and edification.

Open Our Eyes

During Lent Luther Memorial offers an opportunity for worship each Wednesday at noon in the chapel. This year the overarching theme of these services is "Open My Life." As we come together this week we will pray these words as part of a litany:

> When we cannot see the beauty of Your creation, open
> our eyes, that all living things thrive and grow.
> When we neglect the poor, the sick, and the grieving,
> open our hands to do Your work in the world.
> When we ignore the cries of injustice in our midst, open
> our ears, that all will know Your love.

Preparing for this service I realized that we will pray those words the day before the House is scheduled to debate and vote on a healthcare proposal which will radically affect the health of millions. I happen to think the proposed legislation is very bad, but the specifics of this proposal are not this Bread's focus.

Rather, I am struck by how the debate has focused on whether the policy will or will not save money – as though saving money is in and of itself virtuous. If that is true, then miser Ebenezer Scrooge, rather than Jesus, is the exemplar of morality. Cost cutting seems to be the only thing we can see. We do not see those who will be affected; they do not matter if we can create a smaller bottom line. Yet Lent is a season in which we are particularly encouraged to see that to which we have been blind, to allow our eyes to view that which we would rather ignore because it is so disconcerting.

Reasonable people can disagree over how best to respond to suffering in our society, but if we don't think seeing that suffering is important, and that responding to it is a priority, then let's retire the phrase "Christian nation" once and for all, for clearly the priorities of Jesus have no standing when we make hard decisions.

Do we dare to open our eyes and see the pain beyond our comfortable decks? Will we allow the cries of the outcast to penetrate through our ear buds and the drone of ESPN?

"Open our lives Lord, that all will know Your love."

The Agony of Isolation

This week the church observes Palm/Passion Sunday, the beginning of Holy Week. Beginning with Jesus' entry into Jerusalem we mark the suffering and death of our Lord. This is the time of the year when the popular press runs stories about the excruciating nature of crucifixion and flagellation. We are treated to all the gory details of the events which the gospel writers relate.

Sacred art has often rendered the physical suffering of Jesus with exquisite detail. (See, for example, Matthias Grünewald's Isenheim altarpiece.) But as we enter this week my thoughts are more on the agony of isolation. I would not for a minute minimize what it must feel like to have a crown of thorns thrust deep into your scalp or your skin flailed to ribbons. Yet, I suspect even worse for our Lord was going through such torture feeling abandoned and forgotten. We can endure a great deal of pain if we have those who rally around us; without such support the suffering is magnified a hundredfold.

I guess my thoughts are on the pain of isolation because lately I have talked with a lot of folks who have mentioned it. "Since X died, it is as though I have dropped off everyone's radar."…"I just sit here all day watching TV; nobody comes to visit."… "I feel like I am in this deep, black hole and I have no way to climb out – and the world just keeps on going without me."

To visit a nursing home is to weave your way down a hall filled with plaintive eyes, to walk by an army of sad souls who, whether accurately or not, feel that they have been cast aside. That is why we resist visits to such places isn't it, because it reminds us that our worst nightmare might become reality?

In the Garden of Gethsemane, Jesus did not ask His disciples to bear His cross. He asked them to stay awake and be with Him as He struggled. It is most assuredly not easy to do that, to sit with another's pain. Yet sometimes that is all we can do and sometimes it means more than we can guess. As you observe Holy Week I invite you to think about how you can "watch and pray" with someone who is feeling forgotten – and then take time from your busy schedule to ease their isolation. I can assure you that it is not what you say, but that you show up, which is most important.

Easter: Joy and Rebirth

I Believe

"I believe...." When we come to the confession of faith in the liturgy, we often go on autopilot. It is easy for the confession to become the equivalent of the old sofa in our family room – ever present and hardly noticed. We unconsciously sink into the comfort of familiar words, seldom actually thinking about what they mean or how they might be different. But what do we believe?

I thought about this as I was looking ahead to the words we will be using during the Easter season. At Luther Memorial we make a point to use more than the traditional creeds in our corporate worship. We use those great confessions, of course, but we also use others during the year. We do that because faith is not static; it is an ongoing enterprise which demands that the church ever strive to communicate its central hope in words which both reflect the confession of the church and are honest to what the community actually understands and believes. There are good reasons for using multiple confessions but we need to realize that in doing so we are always walking a liturgical tightrope.

If we simply use the historical confessions of the church (Apostles, Nicene, Athanasian) we place ourselves solidly within the tradition which has been honed and tested over the centuries. Each word was parsed and examined with a care and thoughtfulness seldom given a text. The historic creeds are marvels of precision and depth. But they are also historical, that is, they are products of a particular time and place. They pointedly address issues which the church was facing in the first centuries – which may be different from the challenges we face. There are two dangers when we use those Creeds exclusively: They may seem to be addressing questions our world is not asking. They easily become so familiar that we cease to experience them as bold and energizing.

So we look for fresh language which speaks to a new context. And that brings us to the other side of the tightrope. It is easy for so-called "contemporary confessions" to be theologically shallow, linguistically awkward, and every bit as culture bound as anything written in the first centuries. There is profound arrogance in thinking that just because something is "new," "scientific," or "boldly relevant," it is an improvement; sometimes it is just naïve, fainthearted, and ugly. At its best a confession expresses timeless truth in words which a community claims and recognizes as its own. It both reflects and guides that which we embrace with our heart.

Which is why I am agonizing over the words we will use in worship this Easter. How do we keep faith with those who have come before, drawing on resources which have sustained them through all manner of circumstance, while also finding our own voice to speak of the unspeakable mystery of God in our world?

All of this is an admittedly lengthy prologue to offering you a little spiritual exercise: Sit down with a piece of paper and write "I believe _____." Then fill in that blank. If you were asked to write the confession for worship, based on what you are willing to go to the wall for, what would you put in there? What do you believe about Jesus? Why is He important? Where is God in our world and how do we experience the Holy One in a way which makes a difference in how we live? I will make only one prediction. If you take this exercise seriously, you will come away with a new appreciation for the historic creeds, even if you feel the need to speak them in new words.

Icon

Every time I see a religious icon my stomach flips a little. You know the feeling you get when you remember an embarrassing moment – like the night you called the girl you were sure had been flirting with you in class and she said, "Bill, who?"…I'll just crawl in my hole now…

Several years ago a good friend brought me back an icon from his travels. During a public presentation a few weeks later I remarked, "I've never really gotten into icons." I did not realize what I had done until I saw his eyebrow arch; then it hit me how that comment must have felt to him. But in addition to regretting the subtle slight of a very thoughtful gesture, I am embarrassed by the sheer cloddishness of the statement. Like going to the symphony and complaining because there are no kazoos, my words said more about the speaker than the art.

So I've been trying to increase my appreciation of icons, which are so important in the Eastern Orthodox tradition. I've learned that in contrast to Western art since the Renaissance, which creates perspective by locating the vanishing point within a picture, icons typically locate the vanishing point in front of the picture. Western art invites us to see the piece from a certain critical distance, as an observer; icons have the art observing us, suggesting the movement of God into the world.

If that seems a little esoteric, take a look out your window this spring day. You will probably see a world flush with new life: grass greening up, trees and flowers budding, birds scrounging for twigs to make a nest. In short, you see a day aglow with Divine vitality. In a world besotted with suffering it is easy to assume God is fundamentally absent from creation and only makes guest appearances. The Orthodox

116

tradition and its iconic art invite us to presume the world is saturated with the holy – if we allow ourselves to notice. God does not regard us from a critical distance, but like a well-written icon, closes the gap and fills each moment with exquisite beauty. You are surrounded by holiness, be attuned to it today.

Personal Brand Statement

It's the end of May and that means it's retreat time. For many years the pastors of Luther Memorial have blocked out some time at the end of the program year to think back over the past months and reflect on what went well, what could have gone better, what furthered the mission and ministry of LMLC, and what was a not so good a use of time, energy, and resources. Then we begin to think about what new initiatives might be worth trying.

One result of that time is sometimes a pithy statement which summarizes our anticipated focus for the coming months. Some of you may remember the banner which hung at the front of the narthex: "Disciples Under Construction." That was the year we decided to make Christian education and formation a high priority. The focus we set for ourselves may or may not be expressed in a banner, but we try to have one – if only for ourselves. It's like a ship's captain focusing on an island on the far horizon; it keeps her from drifting aimlessly about in the sea.

Along with reflecting on the ministry of LMLC I usually take the occasion to do some personal reflection: What has given me joy over the past year? How has God used me and how have I perhaps refused to go where I was called? Am I using the gifts with which I have been entrusted well? What do I need to change if I am to be the person God calls me to be? And, amid all the hard questions related to what I ought to be doing, how can I learn to savor and receive the gift of life in Christ.

One exercise I employ is to ask, "If I were branding myself, trying to summarize my driving attitudes, priorities, and goals in just a few words, what would they be?" So, for example, I might decide that "Blessed to be a Blessing" summarizes my belief that God showers love on us so that we can do the same for others.

What would you say? If some folks were honest their branding statement might be

- Get all you can – the grave comes soon.
- Body, Babes, and Beer: the Holy Trinity.
- I got mine – sorry you're a wimp.

I offer some extreme examples to keep from biasing your own reflection, but I invite you to take an honest look at what you really value – and how it meshes with your professed identity as a follower of Jesus. In ten words or less, what drives your life, what's your slogan?

Vase of Lavender

A vase of lavender. You could have easily missed it amidst the clutter of his apartment, unobtrusively sitting above the books and DVDs which are his other loves. Dried flowers. Dried dreams. She'd gathered them along a French country road on the trip which was their final, defiant celebration of joy before the ravages of cancer robbed him of her touch forever. A lonely sentinel it stood as a mute reminder of the grace given him late in life – then absurdly snatched away. Not a shrine, but a quiet link to their life together, a portal to memories both precious and excruciating.

Four years to the day since she died. Tomorrow he would marry again. So with the reverence of a priest elevating the host he took up the vase with its sacred treasure and drove to the beach. The ebb tide lapping at his ankles, he stared across the waves as though he could see that French roadside and be there one last time. He thought of the journey distilled in the now faint fragrance rising from his hands. Salt spray mixed with tears as he offered prayers of remembrance, remembrance of smiles shared and agonizing lessons learned. His shoulders warmed by the evening sun, he dropped the lavender into the gentle surf and murmured a benediction from the treasury of the saints: For all that has been, "thanks;" for all that will be, "yes."

The writer of Ecclesiastes reminds us that there is a season for all things: a time to hold, cherish, and heal; a time to let go, cherish anew, and embrace the future. A dear friend has shown me how to live both times with courage and faith. I share this story, hoping it will give you patience if you are in a dark place and boldness if it is time to venture toward a new horizon.

Relax and Live

"Brother G--, a postulate who has come to the end of his rope and wants to leave... stands in the novitiate library leafing through a book called Relax and Live. Sooner or later it comes to that."

--Thomas Merton, *Conjectures of a Guilty Bystander*

I've had *Conjectures of a Guilty Bystander* next to my desk for several years. Like fudge, it's too rich to appreciate in big gulps, so I periodically treat myself to a small serving from this collection of long essays and short reflections from Merton's monastic life. He often uses simple experiences to lift up deep truth, such as in the quotation above, "Relax and Live. Sooner or later it comes to that."

Relaxing does not mean ceasing to strive for excellence. Relaxing is not the same as laziness or sloth. Relaxing, as Merton uses the term, is not the opposite of working. Rather, it is adopting an attitude of gentle trust, confidence, and hope as we confront our daily challenges. The opposite of relaxing is spending our days in a state of constant alert and anxiety. Think for a moment how much time and energy you have wasted in mentally confronting challenges which never materialized, passionately pursuing ill-conceived goals, obsessing about events over which you had no control, or allowing anger at another to drive your life. Jesus often counseled his disciples to live without anxiety, not because life is without hardship, but because God's love is a secure foundation beneath the shaking floor. Jesus constantly noted that anxiety is futile, in that it adds nothing to our ability to confront life, and unnecessary, because God cares for us. Jesus knew anxiety is the great thief of life.

What most interests me in Merton's reflection is his matter of fact confidence that sooner or later – either by deep reflection or brutal experience – we will discover the richest life comes in letting go of our fears and allowing God's love to hold us up like water beneath a swimmer. Sometimes the lesson comes hard; we only learn the futility of anxiety when our own resources prove pitifully inadequate for the challenge, leaving us no choice but to trust God's care. How much better it is to cultivate, through daily prayer and practice, the ability to rest in God. When we cease dissipating our energy in futile flailing, it is amazing how much more strength we have for savoring life's many blessing and pursuing challenges which matter.

Deli Lama

Last week I was listening to a talk radio show when a caller mentioned the Dalai Lama, except she pronounced it "Deli Lama." Her pronunciation may be correct, but my imagination immediately began firing off all sorts of strange images and concepts: a bratwurst Buddha, serenity through kosher salami, learning to be totally present to the Dijon mustard, a saffron robed monk serving up bagels and lox. Like a series of firecrackers the pictures popped in my head, and what started as a little chuckle grew into laugh out loud hooting as I cruised down the interstate. By the time I reached my destination I felt noticeably more relaxed than when I started.

Looking back I realize that I was looking for an excuse to laugh. It had been a long week, several deadlines falling together in a way that spiked my stress and lowered my patience. It was good to let go of the grim seriousness of life and play within the confines of my mind, to allow myself to remember that the fate of the earth does not depend on my eternal vigilance against the forces of darkness (whatever those might be).

One writer observed that most Christians treat life as though it were a tragedy, when in fact the gospel says it is ultimately a comedy – a comedy, not in the sense of jokes, but in the sense that a joyful future is guaranteed by our loving God. Christians need to strike a delicate balance between being fully engaged in our world and learning to commend the future to God in hope.

121

So laugh a little today. Instead of being filled with anger, dare to see the absurdity in the pompous posturings of others – or yourself. When we can see the comedy in life we are less likely to create tragedies in our homes and world by uncompromising seriousness.

Welch, WV

Welch, West Virginia, is not a place where it's easy to hope. Like the rest of McDowell County, it bears the burden of devastating floods, corrupt politicians, ongoing racism, and absentee landlords which suck the wealth from the land and throw it away like a squeezed orange. Even the majestic terrain which evokes awed admiration makes it hard to see beyond the next hollow, much less to see possibilities beyond the mountains. So I was deeply moved by the mural.

I came to Welch serving on the staff of the Bishop's School, a program which invites high school students from the Evangelical Lutheran Church in America's Region 9 to spend a week in study at the seminary and in experiencing a cultural context with which most are unfamiliar. This year the program went to the coal country. One stop was an amazing battered women's shelter. As we toured the facility I saw the wall painting left behind by a college group's week of service in Welch. They painted a mural of a breaking day with words from St. Francis de Sales written across the red and orange rising sun: "Have patience with all things. But chiefly have patience with yourself. Do not lose courage considering your own imperfections. But instantly set about remedying them – every day begins the task anew."

What a word of grace that must be to those women who see it each time they go to the dining room! The average woman leaves her abuser eight times before she leaves for good. Most are beaten down by illiteracy, failure, terror of the future, and a lifetime of being told they are ugly and unloveable. Someone knew exactly the right word to speak to their unspoken anxiety.

Consider de Sales' words in your prayer time today. God speaks them to each of us in those moments when we wonder if we have a future, when we are keenly aware of our limitations, when it is hard to feel that we have much to offer anyone. Have patience. That is different from being complacent. Hopeful patience believes God is never finished with us, that if we raise our eyes to Him we will see the faint glimpse of a new day dawning from God's love. God is bringing hope to Welch; may the sun rise in your shadowed places this day.

Child's Annotation

I opened the red *Revised Standard Version* which has been my study Bible since Dad gave it to me in college. I sometimes read other translations to get a different perspective on a text, but this is the one I start with. Its binding is patched together with layers of yellowing tape. The multi-colored underlines and notes in the margin from successive readings of passages chart how my understanding has changed over the years.

This day I was preparing for a Sunday School class on John 17, and the annotations there are unlike any others in my Bible. Long ago little hands (I can't remember which of my children it was) took a pen and scribbled all over the page. I hope I was not too harsh with Scott or Laura when I discovered the additions to the holy text because now I find that every time I come back to these pages I smile and see those scribbles as a gracious witness to the gospel's basic simplicity.

John 17 is usually called Jesus' High Priestly Prayer. It is a very beautiful – and in places very dense – passage. The language soars and turns back in on itself, complex as a well crafted sonata. To read this prayer is to be pulled to the edge of eternity as Jesus and the gospel writer speak of the mystical union of God, Christ, and the community which gathers in Jesus' name. I appreciate the complexity and depth of the words. Yet, for a reason I cannot really explain, when I see all those scribbles juxtaposed atop the text I imagine a little two-year-old commentator saying, "This means God loves you more than you can imagine."

The quest to make the way of Jesus intellectually credible is a worthy one, particularly in a community devoted to learning such as Blacksburg. I yield to no one in appreciation of fine writing and rejoice when truth and exquisite eloquence kiss in a way that takes us deep into mystery. Yet, as I write this devotion I am keenly aware of the many people who have crossed my path this week, persons who need to hear the good news straight up, no embellishments – folks whose jobs are on the line, folks who are watching loved ones waste away, folks whose kids are struggling to find a way forward, folks whose depression dimmed vision is as dark as a coal mine at midnight. So for you:

God loves you more than you can imagine; don't be afraid.

Grace Under Fire

I would have been spitting nails. Not too long ago I got

into a conversation with someone who had just had a close encounter of the worst kind with our healthcare system. Lola (not her real name) went in for a routine procedure and was the victim of lousy luck and what sounded to me like incompetence. As a result she experienced aggravation, anxiety, and severe pain. If I had been on the receiving end of this medical fiasco I would have milked it for a lot of sympathy at the very least – and probably thundered about the idiocy of a few select people and systems. In fact, she was all smiles.

She gave me the bare bones facts which I have just given you, but she quickly left that behind to talk about how blessed she felt to have everything turn out well. She emphasized how wonderfully attentive most of the staff had been to her needs. While perfectly willing to talk about her recent trials, she was much more eager to ask about how I was doing and about how a mutual friend was coping with a challenge. I left that conversation with my heart strangely warmed and her laugh echoing in my ears. My world was a little brighter for having been in her presence.

Since then I have reflected on why Lola was not tied in knots by her experience, why she was able to be light in the midst of darkness. You could say it came partially from her temperament; that would be true but inadequate. I know plenty of usually pleasant people who turn into snarky terrors when given a little physical pain – I think specifically of one VT campus pastor I know intimately. I know her faith is important to her, so I suspect that part of Lola's secret is that she gets what Paul means when he writes in Philippians, "Rejoice in the Lord always, again, I will say rejoice."

Neither Paul nor Lola denied the adversity in the situation (he in prison, she in pain) but both lived convinced that despite it all they were incredibly blessed. Like someone who looks over the junkyard in the foreground to savor magnificent mountains at the horizon, Paul and Lola put adversity into perspective by focusing on the Love which sustained them.

Rejoicing is not merely, or even primarily, a response to positive circumstances; it is a choice we make, a decision thankfully to focus on God's care for us, most clearly revealed in Christ. Rejoicing in the Lord means remembering that we swim in a sea of divine love, and thus we find ourselves noticing its warm currents, even when life's buffeting waves are cold and choppy.

Dive in today and feel yourself carried by the holy flow.

The Truth Shall Make You Odd

My friend Frank Honeycutt has just published a book entitled *The Truth Shall Make You Odd*. The title comes from Flannery O'Connor's wry editing of John 8:32, "You shall know the truth and the truth shall make you odd." Frank's book is about how pastors are sometimes called to speak uncomfortable things if they are to serve with integrity. But the book and the quotation raise a broader question: Just how odd are we willing to be?

That's our worst fantasy isn't it, to be declared odd by those who matter to us? If the truth be told, our fondest desire is to cozily swim in the cultural mainstream, carried smoothly along like a canoe on a gentle river. We are afraid that being too up-front in declaring our Christian identity will get us lumped in with those who are ignorant and proud, who believe that being passionate excuses lack of compassion, who think that quoting a biblical text is a substitute for understanding basic science, history, law, and courtesy. You need not look very hard to find people doing strange, rude, or vicious things – and justifying them all as faithfulness to God. No indeed, we do not want to be like those folks; we do not want to be odd.

But that is not the kind of odd which Frank, Flannery – or Jesus – have in mind. There is a difference between being a "fool for Christ" and just being a fool. Having fire in the belly does not mean you have to give everyone around you heartburn by being blindly self-righteous. Prophetic and obnoxious are not the same thing.

In a society where religion often wears a snarling face we have some legitimate concern about being identified with those who slander Jesus by claiming His name and despising His vision. But if you are reading these words I suspect you, like me, are more likely to dishonor Christ by silence and inaction than by flawed witness.

Anyway you slice it Jesus was odd. He lived with minimal material possessions. He loved those who hated him. He preferred to hang out with the sketchy folks rather than the pillars of the community. He valued faithfulness to God over loyalty to family, religion, or nation. He suggested that service and sacrifice are the keys to fulfillment in life.

Look at that list again; does it look like the priorities which drive the world in which you live each day? Think about one way you can be a little odd today, a little out of sync with those around you. Flannery O'Connor was right, if we know (and try to live) the truth it will make us odd – and if we aren't a little odd, we might wonder why...

Sweet and Sour

If I kept a daily diary, today's entry would be something

127

like this: "Tech's classes began, with all the possibilities of a new semester...Went to the doctor – he sent me to an orthopedist for my shoulder and put me on blood pressure meds." There is something exciting about the new academic year: fresh faces on campus, new ideas to try, a chance to get it right this time (whatever that means exactly). But this aging Boomer got one more reminder that bodies do not operate on automatic pilot forever. Like my '89 Volvo, my mortal coil increasingly has leaks, creaks, issues with the frame, and sketchy operating systems. This was a day both pregnant with possibilities and shadowed with hints of mortality.

But in fact, if we are really awake, each day is like that. Sometimes we are more aware of what is being birthed: a new love, daybreak over our favorite vista, exciting job challenges which engage our gifts. In other moments, our spirits feel the weight of what is passing away: the death of a marriage, friends growing apart, loss of physical vitality to do the things we love. The mixture changes, but life is always a sweet and sour dish.

The Psalmist writes, "So teach us to count our days that we may gain a wise heart." (90:12). At first glance, these words may seem rather morbid. Isn't life inherently grim enough without, in good times, pondering the sands in the hourglass? Yet the writer's intention is not to cast a gratuitous pall over our joys; it is an invitation to realize that life is finite, our days limited, and, therefore, existence incredibly precious. In frankly acknowledging the darkness of life we gain new appreciation for the things and people who are light on our journey. Recognizing that we do not have the ability to do all things forces us to reflect on whether our daily choices are feeding our souls and healing our world.

If this is a dark day for you, take time to offer thanks for one ray of light which crosses your way. And if your cup is filled to the brim with joy, give thanks for that too – and give a thought to how you might use that abundance to refresh another's parched throat.

Punching Holes in the Darkness

Not long ago I came across a story about Robert Lewis Stevenson, perhaps best known as the author of *Treasure Island*. As a child in 19th century Edinburgh, before the advent of electric street lights, Stevenson observed the lamplighter making his rounds in the city. "There's a man punching holes in the darkness," he exclaimed. If that anonymous lamplighter heard Stevenson, I am sure he smiled and went on his way with an extra spring in his step. "What do you do for a living?" "I punch holes in the darkness," he might have responded, with a little pride, to the next person who asked him that routine question.

I am sitting in my office on Easter Monday. Holy Week is over; many of the Easter lilies have already migrated from beneath the altar to someone's home. The great paschal drama has reached its climax for another year. Like the disciples, once it began to sink in that Christ was truly arisen, we ask ourselves, "Okay, so where do we go from here; what's next, what difference does a risen Jesus make?"

Where I find myself going is to a place of deep thanksgiving for all the people I've been privileged to meet who understood their Christian calling to be punching holes in the darkness. Of course, there are famous people who have brought light to the darkness of oppression, poverty, and injustice – the M. L. Kings and Mother Theresas of the world. We justly celebrate their lives. But I am thinking more about the gentle maid at the seminary who cleaned up pigeon poop on the library steps every single morning and never complained because, "they're God's creatures too." I am thinking about the many nurses I've watched over the years giving patient, compassionate service to unreasonable people in the midst of disgusting circumstances. I am thinking about my Mom, seldom in the spotlight, but always slightly brightening wherever she was. I am thinking about an art historian making funny hats with the children at vacation bible school.

"What do you do for a life (not living)?" Ponder that this week. There are a lot worse answers you could give as a child of the Easter hope than, "I punch holes in the darkness."

Hector

Most of Luther Memorial's members did not notice Hector, but he noticed you.

Early in Holy Week, Hector called the church asking about our worship opportunities. I am not really sure why he picked Luther Memorial. Hector is from Puerto Rico, visiting family in Blacksburg for a few weeks. We are not the closest congregation to his family's apartment. He is not Lutheran by background. And because his English is adequate, but not great, much of the liturgy had to have been a bit confusing to him. Yet he was here for every worship option we offered during Holy Week, from the intimate to the grand. He saw us with a handful of people rattling around the nave during the Easter Vigil. He experienced Luther Memorial's brassy-pull-out-all-the-stops Easter Morning. Like a restaurant critic, he sampled the whole menu. His verdict,

"This is a congregation with much love. I feel love here."

My sense is that Hector is the sort of person who evokes gentleness from those he meets. So maybe part of what he found was what he came ready to give. He found blessing because he came with a heart open to receive whatever might be offered in the liturgy's prayers, scriptures, or hymns. But he was right--there is a lot of love in this congregation, and as one of your pastors I had to smile when I heard his judgment. Finally, that is what you want the stranger to say when he comes into your community, "I found a welcome; I felt at home."

Most of us did not notice Hector, but he noticed us. That is a deeply sobering realization. You never know when the critical moment has arrived, the moment when love flows out of us as effortlessly as breathing in bed – or just isn't there. You can't fake caring for very long. All you can do is practice being a person of compassion in all that you do, so that when someone is noticing they will say, "This is a congregation [or person] with much love. I feel love here."

Ordinary Time

Update on a Familiar Fable

Grasshopper was passionate. When something excited him he went all in; he held nothing back. You had to admire the full bore enthusiasm with which he lived life. The only problem was that he went all in on something new just about every week. True to his name, he hopped from one cause to another: from saving the whales, to fighting the latest cabinet nominee, to whatever outrage popped up on his Facebook page.

"Slow down," said ant, "I get exhausted just watching you flit around. There's nothing worth getting that agitated about! You make yourself – and everyone around you – crazy,…and you know what: No matter what you do or don't do, the sun is still coming up tomorrow. Be smart, save your energy for what really matters."

"I'll rest when I die," retorted grasshopper over his shoulder, heading off to another meeting. And after years of living that creed, that's exactly what he did. He died – vaguely disillusioned that the world was stubbornly unchanged – admired by some, but alienated from many by his habit of riding roughshod over anyone not as passionate as he.

Ant was the picture of prudence. He seldom misspoke because he saw both sides of any dispute. He never gave his money to lost causes because he studiously avoided any group outside the mainstream. Nobody disliked ant. He never took a controversial position; you might as well dislike water. Ant husbanded his emotional and political capital for that day when it would be needed. Ant was a soldier shrewdly saving his shot for the big battle. But the big battle never came; he never found anything he cared enough about to risk his reputation, his friends, or his resources. He too died. Acquaintances remembered him fondly – but only briefly because he had touched few people at any depth.

The moral of this little fable is not subtle. As persons of faith living in the world we face two temptations. One is to dissipate our energies in random busy-ness, often resenting others for not being equally engaged in trying to make a difference in all the ways we champion. The other is to live so fearfully that we never give ourselves to anything which matters. Everything is not worth our passion, but some things are – some causes and people are worth the risk of putting every chip we have on the table and going all in.

In II Timothy, the apostle writes to his child in the faith, "For this reason I remind you to rekindle the gift of God that is within you through the laying on of my hands; for God did not give us a spirit of cowardice, but rather a spirit of power and of love and of self-discipline." As we try to respond faithfully to our world, may we have the discernment to know where Christ most needs our gifts and the courage to go there, whatever the cost.

Two-Dollar Bill

A little girl and her two-dollar bill; that's what's giving me hope today amid the usual sewer gas smell emanating from my news feed. For many years my wife's kindergarten class has done a project called "Pennies From Heaven." The kids bring in their loose change and fill a big jar. The class walks to the bank to have the coins counted. Then comes the highlight of the unit – a trip to the mall where they Christmas shop for a needy child from the "Angel Tree."

Last week Jodie (not her real name) brought in a two-dollar bill. When asked where she got it she said that she had lost her first tooth and this was the money she received from the tooth fairy – and she wanted it to go into the Pennies from Heaven jar. I remember spending my first tooth fairy money on a comic book and caps for my Roy Rogers pistol.

Kudos to the parents who must have modeled caring for others. Kudos to her teachers for building on that lesson. But most of all, kudos to that pint-sized saint, who, in the face of an insistent cultural message of "I've got mine, to heck with you," found room in her heart to care for someone whose true need was greater than her own.

I know we are born with certain instincts for self-preservation. But we are not born with hard hearts which are unmoved when we see children hungry, ill-clad, abused, and without adequate health care. Such callousness has to be learned and cultivated. It has to be buttressed by ideology which devalues community. Jodie reminds me that if we can learn selfishness we can unlearn it, one act of compassion at a time. We are not slaves to our instincts; we can be architects and builders of the kind of humane society in which we want to live.

So, in this week of All Saints Day, when we celebrate all the anonymous faithful who have borne witness to the gospel and modeled its grace in their lives, here's to Jodie! May she find half the joy in giving that two-dollar bill that I have received in hearing about her.

Transformed or Conformed

If you have not found Turkish author Elif Shafak, I highly commend her to you. She has a way of marbling an engaging story with invitations to theological reflection. Her *Forty Rules of Love: A Novel of Rumi* is a wonderful introduction to that great Sufi poet. I am in the middle of her *The Architect's*

Apprentice and I found this exchange between an inquisitor and a Sufi teacher on trial for heresy very thought provoking.

"Is it true that you said you have no fear of God?"

"Why should I fear my Beloved? Do you fear your loved ones?"

"So you accept that you have claimed to resemble God."

"You think God is similar to you. Angry, rigid, eager for revenge…Whereas I say: instead of believing that the worst in humans can be found in God, believe that the best of God can be found in humans."

Notice two things about this passage. First, there is great resonance between the gracious sentiment of this Sufi teacher and the teachings of Jesus and the Old Testament tradition, which speaks of us created in the image of God. These days it seems that we are constantly emphasizing how we are different from our Muslim brothers and sisters. So it is particularly important for us to be attuned to those places where we can find common ground. Every religious tradition is multi-faceted; it is easy to find opportunities to quibble, to focus on nuances in interpretation where we might disagree. But part of living in the spirit of Jesus is seeking to build bridges rather than fortresses.

Second, Shafak reminds us that though we are supposed to be created in the image of God, all too often we create God in our image. Out of our fears, angers, prejudices, and selfishness we easily create a god who is equally petty and punitive, in order to validate our weakness. That is perfectly understandable; it just does not happen to be what being a disciple of Jesus is all about. Our calling is to go beyond being a cipher for our culture and its shortcomings; we are to be distinctive agents of change, which serve a loving God's vision of justice and compassion.

The challenge of being formed by Christ is not a new one. From the beginning Christians have struggled with allowing God to remake them, rather than trying to remake God. Paul's counsel to the Romans is as timely now as it was in the First Century: "Do not be conformed to this world, but be transformed by the renewing of your mind, so that you may discern what is the will of God – what is good and acceptable and perfect."

Me-opia

I was recently at a reception and heard about an experience some friends had last week in San Francisco. In the midst of a long awaited trip to the city they were standing around when other tourists were told their tasting trip to the wine country had been canceled due to raging wildfires. "What do you mean canceled," an irate woman snarled, "I paid good money for that tour and I expect to get it."

This woman was suffering from a very common affliction in our culture, "Me-opia," defined as "the inability to see anything except in terms of how it affects me." Thousands of people were losing their homes and livelihood but the real issue was that she was going to miss out on Napa merlot. Hers is a particularly obvious and egregious case of the disability, but it is hardly atypical. Children are food insecure and suffering from lack of basic health care, but my tax bill might go up if we fix the problem. The planet is in danger, but it might cost me something to cultivate a more sustainable lifestyle. The pipeline may or may not be needed, but the real issue is my property values. Schools in the coal fields or the inner cities are crap, but my schools are fine, so what's the problem?

The devilish thing about me-opia is that it is so hard to "see." It is precisely our perception of the world which is impaired. Our filter is clouded by the very natural tendency to see the world through our own interests. It takes a deliberate choice to ask, "So how might this look from another's perspective; is there a greater good than what works for me?"

Paul writes in Philippians, "Do nothing from selfish ambition or conceit, but in humility regard others as better than yourselves. Let each of you look not to your own interests, but to the interests of others." That is counter-cultural counsel. It is also a pretty good start in dealing with our me-opia.

Lincoln in the Bardo

One of the most unusual books I have read lately is George Saunders' *Lincoln in the Bardo*. Saunders places Abraham Lincoln in a purgatorial world (bardo is a Tibetan state of existence between death and reincarnation) with assorted spirits, wrestling for the soul of Lincoln's beloved son, Willie. It sounds bizarre, but trust me, this no lame Abraham Lincoln, Vampire Hunter. Saunders offers a provocative exploration of what makes for heaven, hell, and a life well-lived.

With his fictional voices Saunders intersperses excerpts from biographies, news accounts, and histories of the period. After meeting Lincoln, Francis F. Brown wrote,

"Oh, the pathos of it – haggard, drawn into fixed lines of unutterable sadness, with a look of loneliness, as of a soul whose depth of sorrow and bitterness no human sympathy could ever reach. The impression I carried away was that I had seen, not so much the President of the United States, as the saddest man in the world."

I read those words shortly after having a conversation

in which someone told me she has stopped listening to the news because it is too painful and depressing. I understand the impulse. Some days it feels like being well-informed is like bathing in a cesspool; you wonder exactly why you should do it. There is certainly something to be said for periodic fasting from the instant news cycle and the breathless urgency of social media feeds. Discernment usually takes some detachment. But if our decision to close our eyes is driven simply by the desire to feel better, to spare ourselves the pain of the world, we might want to think a little deeper.

By all accounts Lincoln intensely felt the consequences of his decisions and the burden of office. He felt the pain of all the mothers whose sons he sent to die. He felt the anxiety of wondering if he was being steadfast or merely stubborn. He felt the slander of opponents who imputed malicious motives to his best efforts.

There is a cost to making the world a better place. Jesus makes that very clear to His disciples, and sometimes that cost is our blissfulness. Part of losing your life for the sake of the gospel is being willing to feel the pain of those less insulated from injustice than most of those reading these words. There are many kinds of sacrifice. Soldiers and police give up their lives and we honor their courage and fortitude. All the more reason for us to stay firmly engaged when we would love to check out emotionally, all the more reason why we should not count too high the cost of awareness and action in our spheres of influence.

....And then there is that promise: "... those who lose their life for my sake and the gospel will find it."

Hope for Change

"Our planet has seen a relentless rise and fall of species and dominant life forms. We ourselves are constantly changing, and there is no reason to assume that homo sapiens is the final form of the human. If we do not destroy ourselves we will probably evolve into something new." That is a rough approximation of what I heard as I pushed through leg presses at the gym, listening to one of those podcasts on science which bring home the tiny time people have been on earth. I don't know why the ongoing transformation of our species had never occurred to me, but I realized my unspoken assumption had been "Yes, life evolved from single cells to humanity, but now we are good.; The process is finished." Yet creation continues.

And not just on a cosmic scale. Governmental institutions change. Neighborhoods change. Worship changes. Our bodies change. Demographics change. The turmoil in our society centers on how much and how fast we want change to happen. The angriest people are those who want to freeze time and go back to good ole days that never were (or were only good for certain people) and those who are so frustrated by the pace of change that they are prepared to blow up the good in pursuit of the perfect. Both reactionaries and revolutionaries have a hard time with the pace of change in the real world. It is equally hard to stop the rain from coming down and to compel it to do so.

Change can be frightening, but the possibility of change is one of the great hopes which the Christian faith lifts up. God is constantly recreating the natural world – and that includes us. We need not stay stuck in old patterns of living because the spirit of Christ is alive in our world and in us. This week we celebrate the coming of the Holy Spirit at Pentecost, an unexpected outpouring of power and possibilities – a down payment on God's promise to make all things new.

We do not get a choice as to whether our world will change; it most definitely will. We can, however, choose whether we will be part of God's action in the world or resist it. Some changes are not for the better, but God is never absent in the midst of transition. That is the witness of the saints who have endured wars, technological upheavals, and intellectual revolutions before us. Wherever our species ends up, we can be sure it is ever in God's care.

Longing for Work

And to Adam [God] said, "Because you have listened to the voice of your wife, and have eaten of the tree of which I commanded you, 'You shall not eat of it,' cursed is the ground because of you; in toil you shall eat of it all the days of your life…" (Genesis 1:17)

Work is a curse. One stream of biblical interpretation takes the above verse to mean that work is the price we pay for sin, for disobedience to God. Life was mellow in Eden; all was provided. There was no need to work. Work is punishment for refusing to trust God.

There's another voice in Genesis, however, which sees work as a wonderful sign of God's trusting humanity with the task of caring for creation. ("The Lord God took the man and put him in the Garden of Eden to till and keep it." – 2:15) God entrusts us with a vocation (literally a "calling") to be what one theologian calls a "created co-creator." Work is not a curse; it is a privilege which allow us to be part of the ongoing drama of creation.

I got to thinking about these two different views of work

as a result of a series of pastoral conversations I had recently. One person I talked with is being crushed by her job. Each day brings stress which has little payoff. Like Sisyphus of myth she feels that she endlessly pushes a pointless rock up a hill – simply do it all again tomorrow. No joy, no satisfaction, no sense of purpose. For her work has indeed become a curse.

From that conversation I went straight to several others, conversations with people who would give anything for the aggravations of daily toil. Their bodies have betrayed them and weakened limbs can no longer take them to any work site. The hours plod. Their spirits plunge because they can no more take up the most basic tasks. They too feel crushed – not by their work, but by the lack of it.

Driving home from those tear-stained talks my mind churned over the juxtaposition of the cries I had heard. How very hard it is to remember that we are precious children of God, totally apart from our work. On one hand we may feel compelled to endure the inhumane in a futile effort to prove ourselves worthy, and on the other, we often doubt our basic value when deprived of the ability to do the work we long to do.

I was also reminded of what a gift it is to do meaningful work. I love my job and know I am blessed to do it in the context of a particularly wonderful congregation – but there are days when you could have it cheap. As I write this I resolve to give thanks for the next workday aggravation because it means I have been entrusted with a task worth doing.

Meaningful work need not be paid. Part of our challenge is to discover in each moment that holy task which God is calling us to do with whatever energy and skill we possess.

That may be planning a massive project from a board room or simply offering the kind word and smile from a sick bed which makes someone's day.

Work is neither our sole source of value nor a curse. It is simply an opportunity, one more sphere of action where we can allow the Spirit of Christ to flow through us to a broken world to bring a little healing.

Hard Year

I did not realize how bad it had gotten until he said that. Most Sunday evenings I call my Dad in Louisiana just to check in and see how he is doing. Our conversations are seldom earthshaking; mostly we bring each other up-to-date on the mundane stuff of our lives. Last week my Dad said, "With all this election mess I can't think of a year I will be gladder to see over." I offered some perfunctory commiseration on our poisonous progression to the polls, and we moved on to other topics. Only later did I reflect on his statement.

This from a 93-year-old man who has seen a lot of hard years. In his youth he endured the untimely death of a beloved brother. He lived through the Depression and served in the Pacific. He saw the upheaval surrounding the war in Viet Nam and experienced firsthand the bitterness of desegregation in the Deep South. And this is the year he is most ready to have behind him? What does that say about where we have come?

You might say his comment was hyperbole, that he would not literally say that this has been the worst year of his life. But the fact that he would say it at all, that he would put this election season in the same league with such desperate, acrimonious times, should give us pause.

Certainly, we want to take a step back from the apocalyptic rhetoric which enflames more than it persuades. From a purely pragmatic perspective we do not want a scorched earth political landscape going forward. But more than that, disciples of Jesus are invited to reflect on whether we are a distinct voice for the way of our Lord or just recruits in somebody else's cause. When Jesus says, "My kingdom is not of this world" He does not mean that we abandon the world to injustice by political quietism. Yet He does suggest that the full rule of God will come in ways other than power politics, with tools and attitudes which value reconciliation more than victory.

One way or the other, this year will indeed pass. The question is whether we are doing things as Jesus' disciples to make the next one better – or just gearing up for act two of toxic times in our nation.

Love is Attention

What does love look like? When I was growing up it looked like my Dad working very long hours in a dim study to ensure that my brother and I had a safe, secure home and every opportunity to realize our potential. It looked like my Mom teaching me to read with a primer called *Little Lost Bobo*, sacrificing a job she loved and a career in which she could have excelled so that I could thrive (a sacrifice for which I never really thanked her). Once a year it looks like me trying to write a poem for my wife, Gail, on our anniversary. Every day it looks like her choosing to appreciate my smallest virtue and forgive my manifold failings.

Think for a minute and I suspect you can come up with

your own mental picture of what love has looked like in your life. This week I ran across a phrase which sums it up, "Love is attention." It was a throwaway line in an NPR interview, but it lingered in my thoughts all day because it is the golden thread which runs through virtually every expression of love I can think of.

In our "click and go" world there is no more precious currency than our undivided attention. Some have money to spare; a big check may or may not mean love. But ignore your phone while you are talking to someone, take time to write a thoughtful note of condolence or thanks, listen intently while another pours out her sorrows – then, my friend, you have given a priceless gift which is rarer than rap at the Grand Ole Opry.

When we give our attention we give our verdict, "You are very important!" We give an invitation, "Let me know you better; tell me what is important to you and how we can enrich one another." We give warmth to one who may be chilled to the bone by the world's apathy and antagonism. By the same token when we are habitually late for meetings with someone, when we fidget with our text screen during conversation, when we never willingly linger to "just talk," we make it equally clear what we think of a person.

On our best days we may aspire to being one of the movers and shakers who accomplish great things for the good of humanity. Such is a worthy goal, but the truth is that most of our grand projects, which seem so important in the moment, really aren't. In terms of changing the direction of the world, our agendas usually have about as much impact as a six-inch rudder on an aircraft carrier. In contrast, a moment of attention at a critical moment may turn someone's life around.

Think about the people who have made the greatest impact on your life. I am willing to bet it was someone who gave you the gift of their full attention. Maybe you can be that person for someone today.

Mucinex

It was not the best breakfast buffet you've ever seen, not even in the top hundred. Stale pastries, bruised apples, and brown bananas would have been a step up from what was laid out at the conference I attended last week. The coffee was good, but the rest left a lot to be desired. Indeed, it was not immediately obvious exactly what was being offered. At one end of the table were juice glasses filled with an unknown gelatinous substance that came in a variety of colors (including that industrial green they painted my elementary school bathroom). Best bet: fruit smoothies – though folks seemed reluctant to take that bet.

The other option was a brownish glob with a white film on top, served in a parfait glass. In the tone little boys use as they poke a dead insect with a stick, someone asked, to nobody in particular, "What's that?" Carl piped up, "I think it's Mucinex." We all did a small double-take because Carl is not the sort who makes snarky comments (in contrast to yours truly). Then, like sun slowly peaking through the clouds, it hit us. "Do you mean Muesli?" Ed ventured. The line exploded in laughter – with Carl laughing the loudest of all.

Carl is one of the smartest pastors in our synod and yet he was totally unconcerned by his faux pas. I realized that is one reason I like him so much. He takes his work very seriously and does it with exceptional skill, but he holds his ego with a light hand. He admits his limitations and acknowledges his mistakes, without being overly concerned about either. I envy him. I am more likely to be mortified by failings and become either defensive or brooding.

The ability to laugh at yourself is to be prized, but my point is a little more than that. Carl knows Martin Luther's writings far better than most, and I suspect one reason for his healthy attitude is that he has internalized the core of the Lutheran confession that we cannot – and need not – justify ourselves. Carl's self-worth is not rooted in his accomplishments or lack of screw ups. I think he actually believes that he is valuable because God has called him beloved, apart from his manifold gifts and accomplishments. Because God has pronounced him precious, he worries less than most about proving it. He just goes about living as faithfully as he can.

Theology can be terribly abstract. "Justification by grace received through faith" easily becomes a slogan. Sometimes it shows up in something as mundane as confusing Mucinex and Muesli and being able to laugh instead of cringe. Whatever challenges you face this day, may you rest in the assurance that you are loved beyond measure, that no mistake or failing can take that away.

Many Modes of Violence

Periodically I have a "thou art the man moment." The allusion it comes from is the confrontation of King David and the prophet Nathan. David, out of hubris and lust, murders one of his loyal commanders and commandeers his wife. Nathan comes to David and tells him the story of a rich man who had a big flock but, for a feast, killed the one lamb of his poor neighbor. David is enraged and vows judgment on this wicked man. Nathan replies, "Thou art the man."

My latest moment came last week as I was reading a passage by Joan Chittister on the subject of non-violence. She writes, "…nonviolent resistance is committed to making friends out of enemies…The goal of nonviolent resistance is to concentrate on issues rather than belittling, demeaning, or destroying people who hold positions different from our own."

As I read those words my heart was strangely warmed, not with the joy which John Wesley describes at hearing Luther's *Preface to the Epistle to Romans* read in Aldersgate, but with shame at how often I have failed to make the distinction between perspectives I find troublingly dangerous and the people who hold them. We should not be afraid to bear witness to the often unpopular way of Christ. But there is never any excuse for making those to whom we speak feel dismissed and disdained. Even if others are mistaken they will never consider a new way if they believe we have no interest in understanding and respecting them.

There are a lot ways to be violent and only some of them involve guns, knives, and fists. When we are more interested in being right than in understanding, we yield to violence. When we are more interested in coercion than persuasion, we yield to violence. When we oversimplify and stereotype another person because nuance is too difficult, we do violence to a child of God.

It did not take me long to think of moments when I have done violence to another in talking with my children, in casual conversation, in Facebook postings, in writing a sermon. Words are powerful tools and in these days when there is so much violence around us, when guns are blazing in Paris, Syria, and San Bernardino, and verbal blasts are exploding on the campaign trail, we do well to consider how we can be agents of non-violence. We do not have to agree with one another, but we can at least commit to respecting the dignity of all with whom we come in contact.

Sharing the Load

My friend, Ginnie Aebisher, recently posted this on her Facebook page: "Leadership is a set of functions that need to be performed! It is not housed in one single person. Organizations/Systems are forever looking for that special person who can and will do it all! But leaders can't do anything without those who support them and take up the cause to walk with them."

The words have the ring of modern systems theory, but the insight is as old as Moses getting run down by trying to adjudicate every dispute among his recalcitrant band of wilderness wanderers or the early church commissioning deacons in Acts. It is not a hard concept: Nobody can do it all. Nobody has all the gifts necessary to do the task. There is no leader without great followers. So why do we – and here I am really thinking I – have such a hard time getting it?

A mixture of motives gets us in over our heads; some are admirable, and some less so. We want to use our gifts well. We want to serve noble causes with great passion. So we try to do more than our skills and energy allow. But there is also the need to be in control, the lack of trust in others, and the aspiration to be the irreplaceable messiah who makes it all happen. I cannot speak for you, but I know the drive to do too much leaves me frayed, scattered, and unreasonably resentful because folks have not done things I never asked them to do.

So my spiritual discipline for this day is to remember that I am not the messiah; in the Church that slot has already been filled by someone much more suited to it. I am also making it a point to give thanks for the many people who step up long before I ask them to, the people whose love supports me each day in ways great and small.

If you are feeling a little stretched, let me suggest that you allow yourself to ask for and receive the gifts of others. That is smart, honest, and ultimately the path to more effectiveness in the tasks we take up and a healthier life/work balance.

A.M.D.G.

From Pentecost through Christmas in 1974, priest and writer Henri Nouwen spent seven months as a "temporary monk" at the Abby of the Genesee, in upstate New York. During that time he kept a journal which later became, *The Genesee Diary: Report from a Trappist Monastery.* I have been using that book in my daily devotions. Part of the entry for June 9 reads, "I remember vividly how the Jesuits in high school made me write above almost every page A.M.D.G. (Ad Majorem Dei Gloriam – to the Greater Glory of God), but I am overwhelmed by the realization of how little of that has become true during the twenty-four years since high school."

That one sentence got me thinking about several things. Two of the most fundamental questions we can ask ourselves are, "Why am I here?" and "Why am I doing this?" Simply putting four letters at the top the page did not ensure that all of the Nouwen's work would indeed be "to the greater glory of God," but I have to believe it raised his consciousness that life is a gift meant to be spent in more than mere existence. Most of the time we imagine life as a series of tasks which we tick off, one after another. A good day, we think, is when we fall into bed exhausted but with no leftovers from the "to do" list.

Think how your day might be different if you thought of each encounter, each mundane action, as an opportunity to bear witness, in some small way, to what God has done and is continuing to do in the world. My guess is that that two things might happen: You would find more value in certain tasks which now seem tedious, and you would stop doing other things because they are clearly not worth doing. Small activities can be filled with great significance if done in a thoughtful way, but sometimes we discover we are investing too much precious time and energy in the wrong things. "How can this bring glory to God" is a question which can help us find the holy in the ordinary – and save us from a lot of grief if there is no good answer.

Nouwen's words also got me thinking about the power of rituals and signs. Luther suggested that when we wash our face in the morning we should remember our baptism. The cold splash becomes, says Luther, a reminder of whose we are, the promises we have been given, and the call to ministry which comes in baptism. Maybe writing AMDG is not for you. Perhaps you, like me, are too groggy first thing in the morning to make the association between shower and sacrament. But consider some little sign which might remind you of what is important: a note on the mirror, a string on your wrist, a small rock in your pocket, anything which jolts you out of sleepwalking through life.

One final thing: Nouwen was stricken by a guilty conviction that his twenty four years since high school had not been to the greater glory of God. In fact, when he penned those words he had already written some of the 20th Century's most profound and popular books on spirituality – and he would write many more. Any objective assessment would say that he, if anyone, had lived the intention of AMDG. His struggle reminds us that we need to be gentle with ourselves. Yes, we do the best we can. We strive to remember whose we are and why we have been given life. But at the end of the day we have to be willing to let go of our need to be perfect and allow ourselves to rest in the love which is the heart of the gospel.

Find Your Ministry

I am a big fan of our national parks. When I think of the places which have fed my soul over the years, names such as Smokies, Yellowstone, Tetons, Rocky Mountain, Olympic Peninsula, Grand Canyon, and Acadia immediately spring to mind. Whether your idea of roughing it is backpacking in the wilderness or an RV without a TV dish, you can find something in our national parks to celebrate. That is the assumption behind an advertising campaign which marks the centennial of the National Park Service. The tagline invites you to "Find Your Park." As you plan your summer vacation, I hope you will consider doing just that; our park system is a multifaceted gem which is worth exploring.

That tagline got me thinking about something similar. So herewith I launch my own micro-campaign: "Find Your Ministry." Summer is usually a time of respite from some of the duties which consume us the rest of the year; so use at least a little of the time to reflect on where you would like to invest your time and energy. Ministry is not one size fits all. Each of us has gifts which we would love to invest if we could find that place which both meets a need and energizes our heart. The genius of the National Park Service campaign is that it invites folks to discover that whether a person's tastes run to deserts, glaciers, sea shores, historical sites, or urban landmarks there is something in the system to savor.

I wonder if one of the reasons Christians are not always deeply engaged in ministry is that we are asking the wrong question, never getting beyond, "What has to be done?" Yes, there are certain tasks which must be done in a church, and I am thankful for those who do them. But I would love for more folks to ask, "What is my ministry; what is it – out of all the possible ways I could serve God – that I am blessed with the time, energy, and ability to do?" I am pretty sure that our enthusiasm for ministry would grow if we took a little time to listen to how God is calling us in the things which make our eyes light up and our hearts swell.

This day, "Find Your Ministry." The world will be better for your efforts, and you will discover the deep joy which arises when gifts and calling match like a tongue and groove.

Tar Paper Roofs

I was recently at the beach, and it happened again. Sitting there, staring out at the Atlantic, with the gentle breeze kissing my cheek and the swoosh of the lapping waves lulling me into a torpor, my thoughts turned to – tar paper roofs. There must be some strange kink in my brain's wiring which makes this happen; I never go to the beach without thinking about those roofs.

At least I know where the image comes from. For many years I had a campus ministry conference each summer in

Chicago. Often that conference was at the Lakeshore campus of Loyola University. If I was very lucky I got a room near the top of a high rise dorm with a breathtaking view of Lake Michigan. If I was not so lucky I got the tar paper roofs. The back side of that dorm faced out, not on blue water and sailboats, but on a sea of black roofs baking in the sun. As far as the eye could see was an ocean of blackness. I sometimes wondered what it would be like to spend your whole life sweltering beneath those roofs, perhaps with an El track clanking outside your window day and night.

Time away is a wonderful gift in our busy world, space to take a deep breath and let the cares of life drop away. Respite in the green places of creation I find doubly refreshing for the soul. I rejoice in those times and places. I need them for mental and physical health. I commend them to you as sources of healing.

But maybe as we savor this gift we might remember that it is a gift – that not everyone has the option to check out for a week or more. Maybe we can spare a thought for those who labor just as hard as we do, but in jobs which do not afford the time or excess income to escape the tar paper jungle. And in remembering them we might begin to understand some of the anger and despair they feel. Those tar paper roofs are more than an urban sight; you see them in rural trailer parks and on shotgun houses, in the coal fields of Appalachia and the Native American reservations of South Dakota and Arizona. They represent a lack of choices and the sense of being stuck on a treadmill with no relief in sight, which feed frustration with a rigged, callous system.

I do not mean to bring a thunderstorm to your beach week, but when you get back you might ponder Jesus' words, "From everyone to whom much has been given, much will be required; and from one to whom much has been entrusted, even more will be demanded." (Luke 12:48)

Cancerous Question

It was an exchange like hundreds I've heard on news programs before, but for some reason this time it rang in my ears like a siren at 2 am:

Reporter: This bill will hurt a lot of people.
Congressman: We feel like we can win on this.
Reporter: But it will especially hurt a lot in your district.
Congressman: We are sure we can win on this.

And there, in a nutshell, is the problem. I don't know whether the proposed law would be good, bad, or indifferent for Congressman Gladhand's district. I just know he is asking the wrong question if we want a healthy society. Plato said our quest should be to know and promote the good, the true, and the beautiful. Jesus, echoing his Torah tradition, called us to love God and neighbor. But the question we increasingly ask has nothing to do with discerning whether something is good, true, beautiful, or in keeping with the mandate to love. We ask, "Can I win?"

"Can I win?" That is the question a cornerback asks just before delivering a cheap shot outside the official's vision. It's the question Wells Fargo executives asked in calculating whether they could get away with opening fraudulent accounts and milking their clients. It's the question that gives us political campaigns which dog whistle to our fears and prejudices instead of inviting us into serious discussion of urgent issues. Manipulating ignorance is a lot easier than seeking what is good, true, beautiful, just, and compassionate. We value winning, not wisdom – and thus we get the

155

acrimonious society we deserve.

"Can I win?" is a cancerous question consuming our public discourse; it destroys healthy exchange and flattens out the goal of discernment to nothing more than getting your way. The ascent of "Can I win?" as our guiding principle is the reason we often think statesmen (legislators who are concerned with the common good instead or pork barrel payouts) are like unicorns – noble, beautiful, and only mythical.

I am not naïve. Politics is the art of the possible; you have to win an election in order to implement policy. Sometime you have to ask, "Can I win?" (Though you could act out of principle instead of popularity, whatever the answer.) It's a fair question, but it can't be the only question our leaders – and we – are asking. "Can I win with this?" is a question utterly devoid of a moral center, so we shouldn't be surprised when our public life is increasingly coarse, bitter, and without a unifying vision.

People of faith cannot singlehandedly reverse this trend. But we can at least ask other questions along with "Can I win?" How about one posed to Jesus, "Teacher, what must I do to inherit eternal life?" [Luke 19:25]…You might check out where that leads…

Winery Sign

I just about blew cab franc out my nose. Gail and I were enjoying a tasting at a local winery when she gestured to a sign on the wall: "Lord, give me coffee to change the things I can, and wine to accept the things I cannot." For some reason this variation on the Serenity Prayer (generally attributed to theologian Reinhold Niebuhr and popularized by Alcoholics Anonymous) struck me as particularly funny that

156

day. Maybe I just needed to laugh, but I think it was because most of us alternately have a hard time getting energized for hard tasks and staying mellow in the face of intractable problems with no easy solution. The sign was wry acknowledgment of the human condition where we all need a little help to keep on keeping on.

Still, at the risk of killing a delightful piece of whimsy by over-thinking it, I wonder if this says more about the way we approach life than we would like to admit. Do we not have a tendency to look outside ourselves for happiness? We buy a car to feel sexy, pop a pill to be energized, suck down a cold one (or three) to relax, change our job repeatedly to feel fulfilled. Whatever the problem, we assume that something "out there" can fix it, if we just find the right thing. But as Cassius observes in *Julius Caesar*, "The fault, dear Brutus, is not in our stars, But in ourselves..." The discontent we feel is often rooted in a mismatch between what we are doing and what we value.

Don't get me wrong. Anyone who knows me will tell you I am a big fan of good coffee and fine wine. I just don't want to depend on them for attitude adjustment. If you are lucky enough to have some summer hours when daily demands are not so pressing, let me suggest that you spend some time (maybe with the beverage of your choice) pondering what is most important to you – and whether your average week reflects those priorities. You might need a little less coffee and wine.

Sucking Sand

The other day I asked a friend how things are going. "To tell you truth," he said, "I'm sucking sand." I suspect the phrase refers to either a depleted oil well or a pump trying to pull water from a dried up irrigation pond. In any case the image is wonderfully descriptive. All of us get to a point when we feel we have little to offer. It's not necessarily that the demands of the job are so great or that our family schedule is any more hectic than usual. No, the issue is that we are pulling from a pool of energy and enthusiasm which is not being renewed. So what do you do when you are sucking sand? A few things that may help refill the pond:

Put a walk on your schedule. You cannot read the gospels without noticing that Jesus constantly takes time to draw aside from the demands of his ministry. He does not always succeed in getting away, but it is clearly a priority. So treat a walk – or time at the gym, or whatever allows you time to disengage – as an important part of the day.

Make time for people who love you. Sometimes being around people draws the energy out of you, as you try to meet multiple expectations. But being with those whose only agenda is to enjoy your company is great way to recharge the battery.

Keep learning. We often feel tired when we are really just bored. Life loses its zest when we cease to grow. Read a book which stretches your mind. Take up a hobby which engages your soul. Cultivate curiosity about the world around you.

Find a way to listen for God's voice. There is no one size fits all spirituality, and God has a way of surprising us, coming in unexpected ways. Yet there are places where parched Christians through the centuries have consistently found a refreshing pool: in reading the scriptures, in gathering with others in worship, in sharing the Sacrament, in being immersed in the wonder of creation. Our days are filled with insistent voices which make demands and offer only conditional affirmation. Be sure to allow yourself to hear the voice which spoke at your baptism, "This is my beloved."

It is hardly profound, but nevertheless true: You can't give what you haven't got. No matter how important the work, if you do not take time to fill the pool, you will soon be sucking sand. Find a way to allow the living water of God's love to flow into your reservoir this day.

Filters

My morning Facebook feed brings this quotation from Martin Luther: "Whoever drinks beer, he is quick to sleep; whoever sleeps long does not sin; whoever does not sin enters Heaven. Thus, let us drink beer!"

I have no idea whether the attribution is authentic. Luther said some pretty outrageous things, but the theology is sketchy to say the least. True or not, the sly, tortured logic illustrates our very human capacity to create justification for what we have already decided to do. We like to think our actions and opinions are driven by an objective assessment of the facts, but it is far more likely that we filter the facts to fit our assumptions. Each day we take the pieces of reality which bombard us and try to fit them into some sort of matrix which gives them order and meaning. About the last thing we want is truth which stubbornly refuses to fit into our neat world view.

Sometimes we just misinterpret. Consider the little children whose teacher dropped an earthworm into a glass of vodka. It quickly shriveled up before their eyes. "Now," she said, "what do we learn from this?" One quickly replied, "If you drink a lot you'll never have worms." Probably not the lesson she intended, but data has no meaning until it is interpreted and seen in a context.

Filtering and misinterpretation have serious consequences for our life together. In our politics we assume stupidity and ignoble motives in those with whom we disagree. In our relationships we are hyper-attuned to the smallest slight and blind to what we might learn from another.

When Jesus asks blind Bartimaeus what he would like Jesus to do for him, Bartimaeus replies, "My teacher, let me see again." Maybe that is what we need to be praying for this day and every day – clear sight. Few things are harder than getting beyond our own fears, assumptions, and biases, yet until we do so, all our judgments are flawed. We are like one who wears yellow sunglasses 24/7 – and then assumes the whole world has an amber cast.

We will never totally get beyond our biases. Still, a good starting point is to acknowledge that we have blindspots and then consciously make an effort to see the world through the eyes of those with whom we have the most trouble. As uncomfortable as that may be, the payoff is likely to be both greater compassion and a more accurate view of the world.

Daniel Berrigan

Daniel Berrigan died recently. If you are a certain age that name is likely to inspire intense emotion. Daniel and his brother Philip were highly visible faces of the anti-war movement of the '60s. For some, these men, a Jesuit and a former priest, were the embodiment of what religion looks like when it engages the world with faithfulness and courage. Others saw the Berrigans as symbols of religion taken captive by political agendas. Daniel Berrigan was a hero to many (I think he and Farrah Fawcett were the top two dorm posters on my hall). But to many, he was like sex, drugs, and rock and roll – a force destroying America. Few were neutral about Daniel Berrigan.

One obituary of Berrigan quoted him as saying, "Know where you stand and stand there." That is either simplistic or sublimely profound. I lean toward profound because it calls us to two things which we need but so often lack – discernment and courage. Discernment is hard work, which is why we resist doing it. Discernment demands that we consider many paths, weigh many options, and make a decision. Discernment involves being willing to be in that uncomfortable place where we see complexity rather than simplistic answers. Discernment demands patience when the future is still shrouded and the humility to consider that we may need to change our minds. Discernment is the antithesis of zealotry and political partisanship. Discernment is difficult but its fruit is the conviction that we have arrived at a path we can walk with confidence because we have asked harder questions than any critic can pose.

Knowing the right path is one thing. Walking it is another. Nothing is easier in our "trending culture" than to see where the crowd is going and fall in line. The herd is a comfortable place to be, but it is in living on the edges that we see the new, the challenging, and the transformative. It takes courage to be on the edge, doing what is right simply because it is right.

You may or may not think Daniel Berrigan's stand on war or his interpretation of the Christian faith was correct. What is undeniable is that he knew where he stood and stood there against great odds. He showed both discernment and courage. Can you and I say the same?

St. Cassian of Imola

Fun Fact: St. Cassian of Imola is the patron saint of afflicted teachers. According to legend, this 4th Century teacher was condemned for refusing to sacrifice to the Roman gods. The authorities turned him over to his students who stabbed him to death with their pointed metal sylii, the instruments used to mark wax or wood tablets. I live with a teacher and I can imagine a few prayers being offered up by her and her colleagues to St. Cassian in these first days of school. There are days you can use all the help you can get.

I wonder what St. Cassian thought as he was tortured by those to whom he had given so much energy. Surely there was a sense of sadness and betrayal. He had offered them his best and the result was martyrdom at their hands.

We need not worry about being skewered by a colleague's pen or impaled on our child's tablet stylus. But we certainly know that sense of being misunderstood and receiving anger when we sought only to offer our best counsel. St. Cassian bore witness to the truth as he understood it and that honesty was not appreciated. Jesus said that the truth will set us free; he did not say it will make us popular.

One of the hardest challenges of discipleship is speaking the truth without sounding self-righteous. It is hard to disagree with prevailing norms without being merely disagreeable. Yet that is part of our calling, to speak with both courage and gentleness, with both confidence and humility. Here, as in so many places, we cannot find a better example than our Lord. Before speaking He regularly took time to go apart and pray. Faced with the perceived need to speak an unpopular word, we do well to take time to gather our thoughts and soften our wrath.

That does not guarantee that we will escape being stabbed

to the heart by an angry retort, but we will have at least borne witness to the reconciling attitude of our Lord.

Required Religion

"What we need in our country is value-based education, education that will build character…We can't do that without religion, so religious studies must become a part of school curriculum. The second thing that is required is a complete overhaul of the current setup – every single textbook should be rewritten to reflect national pride."

There is nothing particularly striking about the paragraph above; it expresses the sentiments of many in our country: Squishy, value-neutral education is undermining the nation and the solution is to force feed religion and national pride to our children. You hear this every time there is a debate on a controversial book, home schooling, or what ought to go in an American history textbook. Except….this was not an Alabama state senator trying to return America to its supposed Christian roots. These are the words of India's Prime Minister Narendra Modi urging education reform which would put the Hindu scriptures at the heart of the country's educational system.* Suddenly they sound very different don't they? "Hey, I didn't mean those religious studies…."

It is one thing to be in the majority, when you are in position to impose your will on others, but it is quite another when you are the one being imposed upon. When we start defending the practice of imposing faith on others, the implicit assumption is that we will get to choose what version of faith gets imposed. I'm pretty sure the folks who want to require Bible study in the public schools would not want me to teach the unit on Genesis 1. Hint: I think Creationism is lousy science and worse theology. Likewise, I wonder how they would respond to Mr. Modi when he says, "I am perfectly happy to teach religion in the schools – let's start with the Bhagavad Gita"(which is what he has proposed).

I am certainly not trying to demonize Mr. Modi. Quite the contrary, my point is that he holds a position you can find all around the world – among Christians, Muslims, Hindus, Marxists, and assorted ideologues – a position which causes untold pain and suffering. We think we can solve the problems of the world by imposing whatever idea can command majority support and by squelching honest critique. What we usually get is sectarian violence.

Perhaps you are wondering what this has to do with Jesus. All of the above would be worth saying in a discussion of Madisonian democracy (one of America's great contributions to the world, with its eloquent defense of minority rights), but why in a Bread for the Journey?

Jesus never felt the need to coerce others into belief nor did He prostitute religious faith to ethnic identity and national pride. He bore witness, lived faithfully, and loved without limit. He assumed that if you do that you do not need to hammer people with governmental coercion – or the equally brutal will of the cultural majority. Those who want to force religion into education are not crazy; there is hedonism and a cynical "me-firstism" in our social fabric where values such as justice and mercy should be. There is indeed a rot in our value system.

They are just wrong in the solution they propose. The sad thing is that their actions betray that they do not trust the faith they espouse or the God they confess. Bullies are insecure – count on it. They doubt that their ideas can withstand honest scrutiny. Jesus commissioned His disciples, "As the Father has sent me, so I send you." Do we dare to simply bear witness to His teaching and example – eschewing coercion – and trust that the Spirit's movement in another's life is all the power we need to see genuine transformation in lives and society?

*(*The Christian Century*, 4/15/15, p. 14)

Name and Frame

My congressman sent out a questionnaire that included this question, "Do you support or oppose the Environmental Protection Agency enacting new regulations that make it harder to use coal as an energy source, killing local jobs, and driving up electricity rates?"

You will not be surprised to find out that the overwhelming majority opposed the EPA's action – and that, of course, was Congressman Griffith's intention. This was not a true survey; this was a ludicrous, ideologically driven phrasing of a question to get the answer he wanted. My focus, however, is not primarily the politics of coal, but the power of words.

Suppose the question had been phrased, "Do you support or oppose policies which help make air clean, water free of pollutants, and Southwest Virginia and the rest of the world a fit place to live for generations to come? Do you believe that we should pursue short-term expediency at the cost of our children's health and future?" The numbers might have been a little different. It's all in how you ask the question.

The ability to name and frame is among the most important powers we have. It matters whether we call the poor among us "unfortunate neighbors" or "deadbeats." How we respond to immigrants is driven by whether we see them as the source of "cultural enrichment" or a "threat to our way of life." Our attitude toward the plight of those without access to good healthcare pivots on whether we see it as "their problem" or "our problem." Words matter. Our words construct the filter through which we see the world.

There will always be those who deliberately frame questions so as to evoke fear and to appeal to the basest, most short-sighted selfishness. Christians are called to frame our questions and responses so as to seek the common good. Not once did Jesus make a decision based on what was in His personal best interests. He sought what was best for the least and lost. When we follow Him, we do the same.

Power of Gratitude

The devotional book I am reading recently included this observation by 13th Century mystic Meister Eckhart, "If the only prayer you say in your life is 'Thank You,' that would suffice."

My thoughts immediately ran to a circle of which I was a part a few weeks ago. "Sisters in Sobriety," the Alcoholics Anonymous group for women that gathers weekly at Luther Memorial, graciously invited me to join them for an "open meeting" (in contrast to closed meetings, which are limited to those dealing with alcoholism). The women who took their places in the corner of the fellowship hall were a cross-section of our community. Some obviously bore the marks of poverty or a long battle with addiction. Others could just as easily have been heading out to their children's soccer match as attending an AA meeting. You would pass them on the street and never guess the internal life and death struggle in which they are engaged. Whatever their differences the sense of community was palpable.

The focus of this particular meeting was "gratitude." For an hour I sat in increasingly moved silence as one after another bore witness to the power of simply giving thanks. Several told essentially the same story. "The turning point came when my sponsor demanded that each day I write down three things for which I am grateful. I hated her for making me do that. I thought, 'This is so lame.' But one day I realized that I really did have something to be thankful for. Then I did not feel quite as much need to drink."

The meeting was an outpouring of thanksgiving: thanks for a day of hiking, thanks for the women in the circle, thanks for a new job, thanks for seeing that they did not have to be perfect, thanks for patient friends and family. Above all, they gave thanks for just one more day of sobriety, one more day of experiencing life, with all its joys and sorrows, without the haze of alcohol.

All too often we do not savor the preciousness of the ordinary. We take for granted the ability to see the sun rise, to hear a baby's laugh, to walk without pain. We assume as our due friends who care for us, abundant food, and a secure home. We are much more likely to focus on what is wrong than the thousands of blessings which fill our laps, to become outraged when something which was ours as pure gift is taken away. Whatever the hard lessons losing much to alcohol had taught them, the women in that circle had learned to give praise for the simple things – and it was transforming them bit by bit.

Gratitude is not a sappy denial of the pain we experience; it is simply noticing that in the midst of that pain there is also much which is fundamentally right, precious, and joygiving. It is the commitment to echo the Creator's judgment

167

on our world, with all its sadness and setbacks: "It is good." Gratitude flushes the pus out of our festering sense of self-pity and allows us to heal from whatever has wounded us. It is the stream which cools our pointless rage at the world and opens us to receiving blessing in all circumstances.

Take a page out of the Sister's playbook: On rising and retiring this week, take time to explicitly say "thank you" for three specific things. You may be surprised at what a difference it makes.

[Note: Before writing this Bread I explicitly asked the convener of the Sisters in Sobriety group if I could share my thoughts on their meeting. She assured me that as long as no personal details were shared, it would be fine. I would never want to compromise the good work they are doing. If you are aware of someone who could benefit from this group, they meet each Monday and Thursday at Luther Memorial, 6:30 p.m., and except for rare exceptions, such as the invitation extended to me, meetings are closed for the sake of confidentiality.]

Single-Minded or Narrow-Minded

In preparing for our Sunday morning adult educational opportunity, the Luther Forum, I ran across an observation by Henri Nouwen. After an extended time of prayer he wrote, "I felt the great difference between single-mindedness and narrow-mindedness. For the first time I sensed a real single-mindedness; my mind seemed to expand and to be able to receive endlessly more than when I feel divided and confused."

"I felt the great difference between single-mindedness and narrow-mindedness." I suspect many find Nouwen's words paradoxical. We tend to think that these two attributes go together. Certainly, that is what we often seem to observe among those who receive press attention as church leaders. Passion for Jesus is too often associated with an accompanying unwillingness to grant anything good outside the community of faith. Those who claim to be single-minded in devotion to Jesus are often equally passionate in their antipathy for Muslims, immigrants, and science.

Nouwen reminds us that passion and bigotry are not the same thing. Devotion to the way of Jesus is going to be make us more, not less, likely to see in a more expansive, accepting way.

Great scientists often observe that the more they know about the mysteries of the physical universe, the greater their awareness of what they do not know. Their passion for the most comprehensive theory prompts them to greater humility in making dogmatic statements. Something comparable happens when we devote ourselves to understanding the depth of the revelation we find in Christ.

To seriously ponder what it means that God came among us in love is to see that the barriers we put up between our little national, ethnic, and religious tribes are both absurd and a denial of what Jesus lived and taught. When we are single-minded in following Jesus, we discover that many of things which divide us are much less important. The more we make seeing the world through the eyes of God our goal, the more beauty and truth we see in places which had been beyond our gaze.

Historians have often observed that great cracks in the wall of racial segregation in America appeared as a result of soldiers fighting side by side in wars. When your only goals are survival and the military mission, you simply have no time or energy for bigotry. Racial divides were relativized and rendered unimportant by an overwhelming common cause.

Paul says, "God was in Christ reconciling the world to Himself, not counting their trespasses against them, and entrusting the message of reconciliation to us." There is our mission – we are part of God's reconciliation – everything else in discipleship is secondary. The more single-minded we are in our devotion to that call, the less justification we find for our narrow-mindedness. This week make living and emulating Jesus your single priority – and discover how things which you thought were so very important and divisive fade into irrelevance.

Walk Facing Traffic

I know it's not a big deal, but it's a peeve. In a desperate attempt to fight the battle of the bulge I walk around my neighborhood every morning. Maybe I missed the memo which changed the protocol, but when I was a wee lad in first grade I learned to walk on the left side of the road, facing traffic. So that is what I do. By actual count, nine of the ten people I met this morning were on the right, which is to say putting them and me on a collision course. Joggers, other walkers, people with dogs on long leashes – I did a dance with them to decide who stepped out into the street.

What is wrong with these people? Why would you NOT want to be facing traffic, particularly when music pumping through your ear buds makes you functionally deaf? What makes people so into themselves that they ignore the rules? What makes me…care…?

When I stop to think about it, I realize my aggravation is rooted in a few assumptions: that my way of walking is empirically better, that these folks were taught the "rule," and that they are deliberately choosing to flaunt it. Put it that baldly and my peevishness looks pretty silly.

I lift up this micro-crisis of social interaction because it is an example of something much bigger. Most of the anger we feel toward others and which festers within our hearts is rooted in just these assumptions: we are right, others really know that, and they are either stupid or choosing to be difficult. Take your pick – religious intolerance, lack of political civility, tension with spouse or kids – all are rooted and fed by unspoken presumptions.

We save ourselves a lot of heartburn by realizing that most preferences are just that, preference, not eternal truth. Life is a lot better if we live it as graciously as we can, assuming, not that others are stupid or intentionally mulish, but that they happen to see the world a little differently than we do. Luther put it this way; we are to put the best construction on the actions of our neighbor, trying to give his or her behavior the most charitable interpretation....

...but I still don't see why you wouldn't want to see something coming which can splatter you like a bug...

Barolo Day

I opened the aged Barolo last week – and it was wonderful. If you know a bit about wine you know the Barolo region produces some of the great wines of Italy – usually with a price to match. But this Bread is not about how good the wine was but why it took me so long to open it.

When I pulled it out of the rack, the bottle was so dusty I could hardly read the label; that tells you how long I'd saved it. This was a special wine, and it deserved a cosmic convergence of the stars: the perfect main dish, the perfect group of friends to share it, the perfect occasion. This was not for mindless quaffing; this was for savoring. The only problem was that the perfect alignment never came. I could always find an excuse for leaving the Barolo on the shelf. So there it lay, like a fine painting hanging in the linen closet.

In a rare moment of lucidity I realized that if I was never going to drink this precious Barolo, I might as well have a rack of Boone's Farm Strawberry Hill. So with Gail, a valued friend, and some pretty good Lasagna we popped the cork and had a great evening.

There is certainly a place for extravagant gestures, for killing the fatted calf on a special occasion. An anniversary or graduation ought to be suitably marked. And most of us can't afford Barolo every night. Still, I wonder if we often fail to celebrate as much as we could. Instead of waiting for the perfect occasion, we can savor the ordinary, but still wonderful, moments of life.

I once read that Americans suffer a great deal of depression after their summer vacations. Researchers speculated that the reason is that people work solid for 50 weeks and depend on two weeks away to give them enough joy to last the year – and are inevitably disappointed because no vacation can measure up to such expectations. Better, researchers said, to intersperse fun over the course of the whole year.

Are you vertical today? Do you have a friend? Is there food in the pantry? Is the bursitis in your knee not quite so achy? Is the tree outside your office window blooming? Has someone shown you a small kindness? Sounds like ample reason to pop the cork on the Barolo to me! Don't wait for the perfect moment to rejoice; declare it.

Who Do You Love Least?

Sometimes it is the juxtaposition which gets you thinking. Three things are on my mind today. Last evening I saw Selma, the movie which deals with the pivotal marches and brutal police repression which galvanized the civil rights movement. I am thinking back to how I reacted to the news footage of those events on the Huntley-Brinkley Report. I wonder how Jim Crow could ever have been a position anyone defended. We've come a long way, I think. But...

As I write this there is yet another Alabama governor vowing defiance and yet another chief justice of the Alabama Supreme Court refusing to honor the law of land because they believe civil rights are gifts which may be granted or denied based on a majority vote. Fifty years later and Bull Connor is alive and well. Now the issue is not race, but sexual identity and the freedom to marry. I feel this toxic mix of disgust and despair welling up in my gut – disgust that cynical politicians never tire of pandering to prejudice, despair that it continues to be a winning political strategy in the South which I love...

And then comes the third thing, one of those "quotation for the day" emails which many of us get. From Catholic reformer Dorothy Day: "I really only love God as much as I love the person I love the least."

Just when I was settling into a nice comfortable seat of self-righteousness. Just when I was all set to cast thunderbolts toward those benighted souls who shamelessly defend injustice. Just when I was neatly dividing the world between those I care about and those I can easily dismiss, Dorothy Day reminds me of Jesus' pesky call to love even those I find most unloveable. It is easy to care about the oppressed – and make no mistake, we can and we must give special care to those who are most vulnerable – what's hard is loving those so bound up in their fears that they are blind to the hurt they cause. It's hard to remember they are like cats thrown into a sack, more scared than deliberately malevolent. When the nastiness is so overt it takes great effort and a healthy measure of grace to remember that those folks are deserving of both censure and compassion.

Who is the person for whom you are feeling the least love right now? Is it possible to see God in his or her face? To the degree that we allow ourselves to love the unlovely we free ourselves from pointless rage and create a small place for understanding to grow.

Acknowledging Our Debts

When you read Paul's letter to the Romans there is absolutely no doubt concerning the centrality of Jesus Christ in his personal and intellectual life. Romans is the closest thing to a detailed systematic theology of Christianity which you will find in the New Testament. It is a letter which asserts with total confidence that in Jesus we see the definitive picture of God and in Christ's death and resurrection we glimpse Holy Love at its fullest.

So it is striking to see how Paul talks about the Jewish faith out of which both he and the Lord have come and how much love he has for those he regards as, at best, lacking in some critical insights. In Romans 9:3-5 he writes, "For I could wish that I myself were accursed and cut off from Christ for the sake of my own people, my kindred according to the flesh. They are Israelites, and to them belong the adoption, the glory, the covenants, the giving of the law, the worship, and the promises; to them belong the patriarchs, and from them, according to the flesh, comes the Messiah, who is over all, God blessed forever. Amen."

What I notice in that passage is how Paul bends over backwards to acknowledge the profound religious debt he has those who have often been his adversaries in spreading the gospel. They may be "wrong" in their failure to appreciate the full import of Jesus, but they are still heirs of promise.

All of this came to mind for me this week as I thought of two ways of relating to other faiths. On one hand we have had the example of ISIS, the radical Islamist sect in Iraq which is so bigoted and religiously root-bound that it even blows up the shrines of other Muslims who see their common faith a little differently. If that were my only frame of reference I might well be tempted to regard the followers of Islam with a mixture of fear, pity, and anger.

But I am fresh off a continuing education trip to Turkey where I repeatedly encountered devout Muslims who were at pains to acknowledge the witness of Jesus with appreciation. More often than not the mention of His name would be followed by a reverential "peace be upon Him." I have no illusions that my new Muslim friends would agree precisely upon the significance of Jesus, but I am pretty sure we could find a lot of common ground as we confront the suffering of the world.

Globalization, obscenely powerful weapons, and ecological crisis make interfaith dialogue more than a good idea, they make it a necessity. Paul gives us a hint about how we might proceed: Make a list of everything you can possibly affirm in the other before you tee off on his faults. Think how different religious disagreements would be if we started with a commitment to find common ground before we began fighting....

….And you know, affirming all we can in the other is a pretty good exercise in our families, our church, and our political life together. Admitting that another person may have wisdom is not the same as caving on your convictions. It is just valuing the deepest truth more than the illusion of having all the answers.

Everyone Thinks They Are Welcome

Last week Luther Memorial's Visiting Theologian, Kristin Largen, shared many stimulating thoughts on inter-faith dialogue, but the quip I most remember was not specifically focused on that particular topic. It was almost a throw-away line, "One hundred percent of congregations say that they are welcoming, but most of the time that means they are welcoming to people just like them." When you stop to think about it, of course that is true. Few people get up in the morning and say, "Today I am going to be unfriendly; I really want to communicate how little I care about other people." We all intend to be welcoming and friendly, yet that comes a lot more naturally when the other person looks, thinks, and acts like us.

Psychologists often observe that the message sent is not necessarily the message received. What we say is not always what others hear. Others may well perceive something different than we intend. It's easy for us to think we are reaching out to others when that is not how it feels to the strangers in our midst. We think we are respecting their space; they feel ignored. We think we are flashing a winsome smile; they feel like we are smirking in judgment. We think we are opening our community to them; they feel the implicit condition for inclusion is their conforming to our way of doing things.

As an introvert I understand how hard it can be to cross the line and put yourself out there. You are not sure exactly what to say. Maybe there will be an awkward pause. Some of us naturally have the gift of gab; those folks could engage a brick in stimulating conversation and make a skunk feel like an honored guest. I envy people for whom welcoming is an instinct and not a skill gained with hard practice. We do not all have that gift, but we can cultivate concern for those on the edges. Hospitality is less about techniques than about caring.

In the gospels Jesus heals a woman with an issue of blood. We don't know what exactly her problem is. All we know is that she is embarrassed and feels shame because of her ailment. She sneaks up behind Jesus, touches His garment, and immediately experiences healing. We call this a miracle story, but I have always thought the miracle is that in the midst of a crushing crowd, Jesus noticed that soft, fearful touch. In fact, it is not so much a miracle as an example of how Jesus was attuned to those on the margins, the folks who were not sure they belonged.

That awareness of a hardly expressed need is the first step to being genuinely welcoming. This week, at worship – or wherever you spend most of your days – look around. Is there someone on the margins who might be hoping for an unambiguous expression of interest and welcome?

Unburned Sin

I had to laugh; it's every pastor's nightmare. My close friend, Chris, recently wrote about a worship service he planned. The focus was forgiveness. So he had everyone take a small slip of paper and write something on it which they needed to confess, something which embarrassed them or made them ashamed. The plan was to gather all the slips of sin together, light a fire, and let God's forgiveness symbolically consume them. Beautiful idea. Powerful image. Except some folks, in an effort to make sure nobody knew their shameful secrets, had so tightly folded their sin-full slips that the paper refused to burn.

Now that really messes up your moment. What's the symbolism of those unburned slips peeking through the ashes? God's love can cover most things, but there are a few stubborn sins that even Christ's grace can't handle? For some reason I imagined Chris presiding in a Saturday Night Live skit, trying to salvage the symbolism and becoming increasingly desperate to get those hold-outs to burn – drenching them in lighter fluid or maybe hitting them with a flame thrower. As I said, I had to laugh. There's many a twist between a preacher's beautiful plan and its often flawed execution.

As I thought further about that incident I realized that it says something powerful about our inability to let go of the past. Each Sunday we make our confession; we at least nominally put all those slips of sin into the bowl to be burned. Maybe we don't always think much about the act; maybe more often than not we are going through the motions, but we at least speak the words of confession. Yet I suspect for most of us there is at least one thing which we cannot let go of, something which haunts our hearts and fills us with regret over what might have been, should have been. We are literally so tightly wound up by the past, that we don't allow ourselves to "go in peace," despite what the minister says.

As the appointed gospel lessons over the past few weeks have illustrated, sometimes we are blind to our sin and oblivious to the suffering around us. Sometimes a little guilt is the appropriate feeling when we have been callous or apathetic. But I also know a lot of folks who have a hard time accepting that they do not need to keep beating themselves up for what is in the past. Maybe it was a fateful night that involved too much drink and a predatory date. Maybe it was hurtful words which sent a beloved child out into the night. Perhaps it was the failure to stand by a friend when the stakes were high. Most of us have something which is our "unforgiveable sin" the thing which, though God may forgive it, we keep twisted tightly in our heart.

So let me invite you: If you have one of those little sin slips sitting in the ashes, gently unfold it and allow the healing fire of God's love to consume it once and for all. We do not simply ignore the past; when we can, we make restitution for the hurt we have caused. Certainly, we should take sin seriously. But finally the gift of knowing Christ is that we can take God's offer of forgiveness even more seriously.

Tradition and Innovation

C. S Lewis was no great fan of innovation in worship. In *Letters to Malcolm: Chiefly on Prayer* he quotes with approval one disgruntled parishioner, "I wish they'd remember that the charge to Peter was, 'Feed my sheep,' not, 'Try some experiments on my rats,' or even, 'Teach my performing dogs new tricks.'"

Lewis lifts up one side of the tension we face in cultivating a rich spiritual life. Sometimes we think merely new is innovative. But novelty is not, in and of itself, an improvement. Whether we are talking about laundry detergent or liturgy, software or biblical translation, sometimes the new is inferior to what we already have. Indeed, we might even presume that something which has fed generations before us is likely to have more depth than a slang-filled stab at "relevance."

Still, there is a corresponding danger that we will become so familiar with our favorite liturgy, prayer, or text that we cease to really hear it, cease to engage God through it. Periodically, just on principle, we need to force ourselves to sing a song which is not our favorite, pick up a translation which may be a little grating to our ears, entertain a worship style which forces us to recognize that there is no single divinely sanctioned path to the presence of the Holy One.

A few weeks ago I heard another pastor comment on the call of Isaiah in a mystical vision (chapter 6). Part of the text says, "...I saw the Lord sitting upon a throne, high and lifted up, and His train filled the temple." My friend noted, "Just the edge, the hem of the robe filled up the whole massive temple; maybe we need to be a little more humble in what we claim to know about the mind of God." Good counsel. God is way bigger than our preferences; wisdom lies in being open to a plethora of holy possibilities.

Vacation and Sabbath

What do a visit to the Gettysburg battlefield, a guided tour of the Philadelphia Museum of Art, reunion with old friends, wine tasting in the Finger Lakes, riding roller coasters, hiking in the Poconos, long drives with your spouse, and seeing a production of Antony and Cleopatra have in common? They are all things I did on my recent time away.

Before you hit delete, let me assure you this Bread is not merely, "How I Spent My Summer Vacation." Nothing is more tedious that a detailed description of someone else's fun. I share this list, not to tell you what I did, but why. All these pursuits fed my soul in one way or another.

This is the season when many of us are blessed with the luxury of taking a break from the tasks which occupy our energy most of the year. (In passing, remember it is a luxury, many do not have the gift of respite, due to a lack of money, time, or schedule flexibility. We do well to begin time away with a bit of thanks.) Let me offer a suggestion as you head out: Make it more than just vacation, make it a time of sabbath.

Vacation is more than not doing what you usually do; it is ceasing to work. There is certainly value in ceasing our usual routine. Sometimes our most pressing need is to stop pushing ourselves. But a vacation which is no more than ceasing to work is a bit like a diet which is only not eating bad stuff; a good diet is also choosing that which builds up our bodies.

Sabbath is different from vacation. Sabbath is more than ceasing, it is actively embracing that which heals, energizes, inspires, and renews. Sabbath has an intentionality which carves out time and energy for the pursuit of what feeds us. I do not mean to suggest that our time away should be as driven as our time at work. Rather, my suggestion is that you think about what really gives you joy, what eases that crush in your chest, what puts spring back in your step – and be sure you use precious time away wisely.

Most of us do not give much thought to what really gives us energy. Before you head out, think about what will re-center and renew you. Your list will be different from mine; Shakespeare is not necessarily better for this purpose than a few days at the beach with an escapist novel. I do invite you, however, to think about what you need so that you do not waste the gift of time. Don't just take a vacation; receive a sabbath for the sake of your soul's health.

Spiritual Numbness

I've been told that the servers at fine restaurants reach the point that all they want for dinner is a burger and fries. Surrounded by fine food day after day, they cease to experience that rush which patrons get when a perfectly presented plate is placed on the table. That symphony of scents, which is such a treat for the diner, thrills them no more than a can of beanie weenies. It's hard for me to imagine, but I am told it's true.

On second thought, it's not so hard to imagine. One of the occupational hazards of being a pastor is that you can find it hard to receive the blessings you serve to others. You read a passage of scripture and immediately begin to ponder how you would preach it. Instead of hearing the text as a life giving word from God, you automatically dissect it, hoping to identify context, author, and style – and, please dear God, a pithy hook on which to hang a sermon. Rather than precious gifts by which God speaks to the deepest places of your heart, the liturgy and the scriptures become "tools of the trade."

Does that ever happen to you? Do you ever find yourself, like a jaded waiter, holding a precious feast in your hands, unable to savor it? The preacher proclaims, "God loves you just as you are; you can let go of all the guilt and self-hate you are carrying." And you are thinking, "Yeah, yeah, God loves me...now when is it we need to be at the soccer field." The pastor presents bread and wine with the solemn affirmation, "for you." But that promise, that the creator of the cosmos actually knows and cares for you, fails to move you to awe or lighten a leaden spirit. It is not so much that familiarity breeds contempt as that it breeds spiritual numbness.

One way to appreciate fine food is to eat the dish while

trying to notice exactly what makes it special. You ask yourself, "Is that oregano I taste? What are the shallots bringing to the sauce?" Try that this week in worship. Pay attention to the ingredients while you eat. Twirl the words of the hymns on your spiritual palate. Attend to the sweetness of the gospel and linger with a bite-sized phrase. There is a reason that the Bible often compares life in harmony with God to a fine feast. Pay attention. God's Word will delight and nourish.

Speaking With Care

In his *Return of the Prodigal Son*, Henri Nouwen discusses the symbolism of shoes. In many parts of the world shoes distinguish the rich and free from the poor and disenfranchised. He writes, "For many poor people, getting shoes is a benchmark passage. An old Afro-American spiritual expresses this beautifully: 'All of God's chillun got shoes. When I get to heab'n I'm going to put on my shoes; I'm going to walk all ovah God's heab'n.'"

Perhaps it was the recent controversy at the University of Missouri over the racial climate which made me notice, but I looked at those lyrics and reflected on how some might react to Nouwen's rendering: "This is just what you would expect from a white European. Blacks are portrayed as illiterate and unable to speak proper English. This is the Uncle Remus image of the American Black which perpetually condescends and infantacizes a people."

Nouwen could have written, "All of God's children have shoes. When I get to heaven, I'm going to put on my shoes; I'm going to walk all over God's heaven." But then the critique might read, "In the midst of bondage no slave ever sang the words like that. To render the lyrics this way is to sanitize a dark time and render invisible a heroic people who crafted a distinctive voice in the face of oppression."

Let me be 100% clear: The civil rights struggle in our country is ongoing and in some ways more challenging than in earlier times because deeply ingrained attitudes are a lot less visible and much harder to confront than Jim Crow laws. De jure racism was the low-hanging fruit – and brazen racial gerrymandering and voter suppression laws make it clear that even that battle is not over. We still have a long journey to racial justice and harmony and we need to be on the road.

I mention a song lyric to illustrate that even when we want to move ahead we may not be sure of the language to do so. We want to be respectful but we are not always sure what that means. I have heard both black and white persons offer each of the above critiques or ones very much like them. Each, in its own way, lifts up an important facet of the challenge we face.

We are going to be on this journey for a long time. May I suggest two principles? First, let's listen to one another. Let's listen especially to those who daily live the legacy of racism. This is not about political correctness. It's not about what folks "ought" to feel or see. This is about the empirical reality that I can only understand you if I let you tell me what you experience day after day.

Second, let's assume, unless there is overwhelming evidence to the contrary, that folks are trying to understand and be respectful. We make mistakes. We unintentionally offend. Can we make the default assumption that another is unaware rather than malevolent?

In his exposition of the Ten Commandments in the Small Catechism, Luther says that part of not bearing false witness against our neighbors is that we "come to their defense, speak well of them, and interpret everything they do in the best possible light." Whether the context is the struggle for racial justice, disagreements on the youth soccer field, or the upcoming political mud wrestling matches we call presidential primaries and elections, Luther's words are worth memorizing and displaying as your computer's screen saver.

Sometimes a Cigar...

"Sometimes a cigar is just a cigar." Though some attribute the quotation to Sigmund Freud himself, most believe it to be a witty critique of Freudian over-analysis of dreams and symbols. We can see great significance where there really is none. I thought of that observation last week as the drama of a Clerk of Court, jailed for refusing to issue marriage licenses to gay couples, played out in Eastern Kentucky,. Some have tried to frame this as religious persecution, but sometimes ignorance and bigotry is just ignorance and bigotry – nothing more or less.

To risk belaboring the obvious, there is nothing new here. This is the same defense that prejudice has been offering for at least sixty years: "My faith tells me that blacks are inferior (Ham cursed in the Noah narrative)." "The Bible says that the races should not mix." "God does not want blacks and whites to marry." "Scripture says that the woman's place is in the home – and therefore it is fine to pay them less in the workforce..." The intellectual pedigree of these arguments is not Jesus, the Apostle Paul, or Martin Luther King Junior; it is George Wallace, Strom Thurmond, and Jesse Helms.

As I said, I risk belaboring the obvious, but I think there is a bigger issue to which persons of faith do well to be sensitive. Some believers act as though calling an action or belief "Christian" or "religious" somehow places it beyond critique. Music can be trite, repetitive, and unimaginative, but that is okay because it is "Christian Rock." The characters can be stiff as dry wall and the plot totally predictable, but we are supposed to give it a pass because it is "Christian literature." Calling creationism "biblical" is supposed to magically make appalling bad science somehow credible. By the same token some suggest any attitude or belief should receive credence just because its adherent claims it is rooted in his or her "religion."

This sort of uncritical thinking does religious faith no favors; indeed, it gives evidence to those who say that religion is just a way to give divine sanction to ignorance. Calling something Christian should not free it from scrutiny; it subjects it to the greatest scrutiny of all: Does it really reflect the life and ministry of Jesus? Of course Ms. Davis, the clerk in Kentucky, should have the freedom to believe homosexuality is wrong (which is different from ignoring the law she had pledged to uphold), but she does not have the right to assert ignorance as fact. She does not have the right to claim the sanction of Jesus when she so clearly has little of His spirit. She does not get a free pass because she is sincere, anymore than my neighbors should have gotten one in 1964 because they sincerely believed Blacks were too dumb to vote.

The sad thing is that unless other Christians, ones who have caught the gracious vision of Jesus Christ, call her and her ilk on it, the world easily sees Christians as intellectually lazy and morally hidebound. At some point you just have to say it: The rotting fish head of prejudice stinks no less if you call it a "religious" fish head.

In criticizing Ms. Davis I know I risk becoming that

which I critique, self-righteous. I only mean to say that I believe she is wrong and that measured by the standard of Jesus, her actions are more a betrayal than an affirmation of His Way. I invite you to make your own determination of whether she reflects the spirit of Jesus. Just don't say the question is out of bounds just because her actions are rooted in her religious beliefs…

Catherine Booth on the Future

Catherine Booth, co-founder of The Salvation Army, observed, "If we are to better the future we must disturb the present." These are words simultaneously simple, eloquent, obvious, and profound. They point to a paradox of life: everybody wants to go to heaven, but nobody wants to die. All of us long for a better future, but we generally resist anything demanding change.

Last week I was counseling with a young woman who has found it hard to get her life on track. She knows she cannot continue in a dead-end job, living hand to mouth, but finds it hard to move in another direction. "I'm just afraid of shaking things up; I guess I've gotten comfortable in a strange way, even though I know this is not what I want." She could just as easily have been a woman in an abusive relationship, a man in a bad marriage, or anyone who gets up in the morning dreading another mind-numbing day on the job. Until the cost of staying put is more than the fear which change ignites, we prefer lethargic misery to the anxiety of the new.

A similar dynamic operates in groups and organizations, including the church. Luther Memorial congregation is in the midst of strategic planning, and one way to think about the overarching question we are asking is, "What are we willing to disturb in the present in order to be where God needs us to be in the future?" That is a particularly hard question to face when there is much about our present which we value. It is one thing to boldly set out for a new land when the place you live offers few prospects; it is quite another to turn your back on a comfortable home with only the possibility that the distant country will offer new delights. Still, there is an iron logic which we cannot escape, "If we are to better the future, we must disrupt the present." There is no beautiful garden without the temporary ugliness of plowing and seeding, no exhilaration of reaching the far shore without the terrifying disorientation of time on the open sea.

Fear of change seems so powerful these days. Politicians pander to our anxious awareness that the past (often viewed through a rosy, nostalgic haze) is gone and will never come again; they invite us to dig in our heels against new realities – and possibilities. That young woman I mentioned is hardly alone; she is legion in our society, despairing that her future can be better than her limited present.

There are scary challenges before us, but Scripture bears witness that our God is a God of journeys, one who calls us to boldness and dares us to trust that we will be sustained as we are faithful. God desires that we live with joy – as individuals, as a society, and as a community called together in Jesus' name. Are you feeling the need for a change? Dare to disrupt your present in the hope of realizing God's future for you and our world.

House in Indy

Gail and I spent our Thanksgiving in Indianapolis, visiting our son. Scott has just purchased a new house, and he was eager to show it off. Scott's house was originally built almost a hundred years ago and is located in a neighborhood which was once very nice, became blighted, and is now on the rebound. Creative, adventuresome folks are buying houses on the edge of demolition and fixing them up. Like many of the houses in his neighborhood, Scott's was taken down to the studs before the rehabilitation began.

The walls are now pristine, and the appliances are new. The colors are slightly edgy; the general vibe is more steel and glass than suburban beige. But the dark hardwood floors, windows, and door frames are the originals. You can see the marks, dents, and distress which come from decades of a house being inhabited. The creaks when you walk around remind you that this house could tell some stories.

And that is why I love it. Neither "cookie cutter modern" nor "stuck in the past faded glory," this is a house which brings together the best of two worlds. It has a sense of history, but is fitted for the present.

Reflecting on that fact got me thinking about some words from Jesus. "…Therefore every scribe who has been trained for the kingdom of heaven is like the master of a household who brings out of his treasure what is new and what is old." [Matthew 13:52]

The challenge of faithful discipleship often consists in knowing what to carry over from a rich tradition and what new ideas, methods, or perspectives to embrace for the sake of making a more effective witness to God's kingdom. So, for example, the King James Version of the Bible is unsurpassed in poetic beauty and cadence – but its language can be incomprehensible to one encountering the gospel for the first time. Sometimes we need to use words which are less eloquent but clearer.

The treasure of the church is that we have a rich tradition AND creative people who can take liturgy, organization, or theology down to the studs and create something beautiful and functional for God in a new world. This week think about what God needs you to be doing in the wonderful, ongoing renovation of the house of faith.

Volcanic Eruption

Like many pastors I have about half a bookshelf of devotional books. Over the years I have accumulated a variety of books in the genre, "A year with…" I have everything from *Morning and Evening*, by the great 19th Century Baptist preacher Charles Spurgeon, to *Bread for the Journey*, a collection of readings by my favorite modern spiritual writer, Henri Nouwen. I do not think I have ever followed one of those books for a whole year, but I dip into them when I need a little inspiration. As an aside, I commend to you finding a writer who feeds your soul and getting a book of his or her writings, organized into digestible pieces, to prime the pump when you are feeling spiritually dry.

Lately I have been reading *A Pilgrim's Almanac* by Edward Hayes, a collection of stories, anecdotes, and reflections which spans a variety of religious traditions. This is the offering for June 8: "The Laki Volcano erupted on this day in 1783 in southern Iceland. One of the most violent volcanic eruptions in recent history, it caused the death of ten thousand, and its acid rain after-effects brought about climactic changes worldwide. Every violent eruption of anger follows the same basic principles of the volcano and has the same effects. Check today to see if deep inside your heart there is a bubbling fear that churns into a roaring anger ready to erupt, later to rain down more fear into the environment."

I read that entry and then went to check my Facebook page. It just so happened that several folks on my feed were not in a happy place. That got me thinking about the times when I have been snarky in my response to people, more interested in venting than really making the world a better place.

At times we need to say hard, even confrontational, things but it is worth pondering, just before we let fly, what is going on to make us so angry. Are we afraid? Are we needing some self-care? Have we lost our perspective? Each of us has some responsibility for the climate he or she creates by word and action. This week think of some ways you can be a force for positive climate change.

Royal Waste of Time

Last week I was sitting in the Virginia Tech Horticultural Gardens during the afternoon. It was a perfect day, the kind which prompts poetry. The humidity had finally dropped below needing a snorkel just to breathe. Though the sky was sunny, the canopy of trees over my shady bench made the temperature perfect. A little stream's constant burble was punctuated by assorted avian chirps. And I was having a very hard time enjoying it.

I knew this was good for me. I knew it was good for my ministry. I learned long ago that taking time away from the office to read, ponder, pray, and journal is absolutely essential for my emotional well-being. There is nothing like a serene, beautiful place to allow the minutia of living to fade into the background, nothing like sitting quietly to give random thoughts space to sort themselves until the tender shoot of an insight emerges from the muck of distraction. I know prayer is possible at any time and any place, yet it is more likely to be rich when the phone cannot ring. I knew all this intellectually.

But it sure looks like slacking off. Even though I had a couple of books and a pad at hand to prove that I was "working," a piece of me wondered what the good folks of Luther Memorial would say if they saw me sitting quietly in a garden in the middle of a work day. In the midst of whatever chaos fills our days, God enjoins, "Be still, and know that I am God [Psalm 46]." But how very hard that is for this pastor! I imagine it is even harder for you, who can't even claim "professional development."

Marva Dawn calls worship a "royal waste of time" and another writer has said that prayer is "wasting time with God." Both are being ironic; there is nothing more important than being present to God. But they capture how the practices of faith look to a world which always values doing at the expense of discerning, which thinks we should be perpetually running – even if we are not sure where.

Summer is the time for vacations. I hope you get some time for decompressing. But taking time for spiritual growth is different from that. Being still before God is not the same as playing golf or reading on the beach – though those are great stress releases – it is the way we stop and make space for a friend to touch and enrich us.

My prayer for you, in the middle of your very busy lives: that you may find your own Horticultural Gardens, that place where you can receive what God is eager to give you.

Reflection on Psalm 137

When I saw the look on his face I knew what today's Bread was going to be about. Worship was proceeding smoothly along as we chanted the psalmody in a properly pious way. The appointed Psalm for the day was 137, a searing lament which articulates the pain of Israel in exile. Its words have been borrowed by generations of believers who have felt that, in the midst of present pain, God has suddenly gone absent or apathetic. "How shall we sing the Lord's song in a foreign land?" the psalmist asks. All of us have been in that foreign land of despair at one time or another, and there is a certain consolation in knowing we are not the first to hear only the sound of our sobs when we longed for the voice of God. To read Psalm 137 is to know others have traveled this way and somehow come out on the other side.

But then there are those final two verses… "O Daughter of Babylon, you devastator. Happy shall be he who requites you with what you have done to us. Happy shall he be who takes your little ones and dashes them against the rocks."

As the congregation heard itself chanting those words there was an audible drop in the fervor of our singing, eyes bugged out all around the nave, and I saw a young man punch his dad's side and look up as if to say, "Are we really saying this in church; how does this fit in with love, grace, and forgiveness?" Awkward! There is no way around it; these words are an embarrassment if you believe God in Christ calls us to more than tit-for-tat violence.

In this brief reflection I cannot enter into a detailed exploration of these brutal words. Rather, let me pose a question: When you read the Bible, do you regard it as more of a lecture or as an invitation to a conversation? Sometimes we assume the Bible is simply a one-way communication from

God's lips to our ears. So whatever we read, no matter how incongruous, we take to be God's directive. If that is our assumption, we probably find Psalm 137 barbaric, but might try to force ourselves to believe its vengeful tone is divinely sanctioned, since it is in the Bible.

In fact, Scripture does not speak with a single voice and every voice in it is not necessarily the voice of God. A great gift of the Bible (and the psalms in particular) is that it is brutally honest about the human condition. It allows people, such as the writer of Psalm 137, to speak about their experience, their gut hopes, their longings – without saying that what is natural is necessarily God's intention. In the pages of Scripture we find many different, often dueling, perspectives (think about the various voices in the book of Job, wrestling with the mystery of suffering). The writers of the Bible invite us to join the conversation. We are invited to put ourselves into faith's struggle to make sense of life's deepest mysteries.

Psalm 137 presents us with a particularly jarring example of a voice which invites reflection and response, but it is not unique. God's voice is often mixed with the voice of the messenger. That does not mean we cannot trust Scripture, but it does mean we have to listen carefully and ask hard questions about how a text compares with the life and witness of Jesus. That is our ultimate standard for knowing God's intention for us and our world.

Ina's Legacy

One of my favorite parts of the week is the time I spend with my "reading buddy." Valley Interfaith Child Care Center (VICCC) has a program that pairs a child with an adult for half an hour of reading each week. It is a laid back time when the only agenda is for a child to receive a little extra attention and develop a love of books. Two weeks ago I went to the VICCC library and pulled an assortment of books off the shelf. My little guy and I settled down on the couch and prepared to read. On the title page of the first book I opened, up in the right hand corner, was a single word, "Dunford."

Ina Dunford was my daughter's kindergarten teacher. Over the years our paths crossed many other times as she worked with the Christmas Store, To Our House, VICCC, and other volunteer organizations in our county. She was one of those folks who are habitually found planning and staffing ministries of compassion. And sitting on that sofa I knew I was going to her funeral the next day.

I'm pretty sure that the book I held in my hands came from her kindergarten days. It had the heft and content to be a "class book," one of those books which teachers put out each year in their rooms to enrich the learning of a new generation of students. After she left the classroom I suspect Ina decided that donating the book to VICCC would touch a few more kids.

It was a little eerie, but in a warm way, to see her name in that book. After her death, Ina's legacy of caring continued. It got me thinking about the influence we have on people through little things. Like ripples from a stone cast into a pond, the effects of our daily actions radiate out, so that even beyond death we may have an impact on others. She, of course, had no idea that I would pick up that book and share it with my buddy. But her act of kindness reached far beyond where she could see.

The thing about a legacy is that it is seldom the consequence of a self-conscious effort to leave one. The best legacies are those formed, like stone walls, by hundreds of single acts of faithfulness and care. So, what kinds of stone are you putting in your wall today?

In *Julius Caesar*, Marc Antony says, "The evil that men do lives after them; the good is oft interred with their bones." I am thankful that this was not true of my friend Ina; may it not be true of us. May we scatter seeds of care which keep sprouting long after we have drawn our last breath.

Giving Thanks for Seeds

Periodically someone comes up to me and says, "Pastor, I don't know how you do it. I could never stand up and preach every week (by the way, how do you make sense of that tiny sheet of paper?). You get pulled in so many directions; your schedule's always getting turned upside down; people nipping at your heels for the smallest thing…."

I won't lie. There are days when I might trade my calling for something else, but then I suspect you would say the same thing about your job. Whenever I have "one of those days" I sit back, close my eyes, and flip through my mental rolodex (okay, so that dates me) of all the saints in the congregation whose faithfulness is so much a given that it's like respiration in the body – essential yet easily unnoticed. Week in, week out, money is counted, linens laundered, bulletins folded and stapled, grass mowed, schedules painstakingly made, meals cooked, rides arranged, planning done, coffee brewed, clean ups completed, forms filled out, visits made, prayers offered, caring telephone calls made, backpacks gathered, food distributed, children taught, words of affirmation spoken….

The privilege of being a pastor is that I get to sit at the

nexus of where so much care and compassion is being offered. I am blessed to see how the care of my people makes a difference in people's lives.

Jesus said that the kingdom is like a little seed. It starts out small and grows big. It gets planted and when you turn around twice it has somehow come to maturity. Sometimes the fruits of the Spirit's action are dramatic and obvious. I write this on the day when the Supreme Court has upheld the dignity of gays who desire to marry. I rejoice in this fruit come to maturity. More often the kingdom's fruits are less obvious, but no less meaningful for the one person whose heart is lifted by a moment of care.

In a world where there is murder in Charleston, ISIS on the rampage, misconduct in the pastoral ranks, naked selfishness in regard to the health needs of our neighbors, and a glut of vicious pundits who are often wrong but never in doubt, it is easy to lose sight of the seeds which are growing slowly but inexorably to make Christ known.

I invite you to join me in flipping through that rolodex (or contacts list) and giving thanks for all those you know who give Christ a body in our world.

Facebook Birthday

I understand that Facebook is piloting a new setting. Whenever a friend's birthday comes up on your feed, it will automatically type "happy birthday" or "have a good one" (your choice) on their timeline. That way folks who have a lot of Facebook friends don't have to waste a lot of time typing…

No, I'm kidding. To my knowledge this new setting is not in the works, but I wonder why not. I am not sure why so much typing goes into expressing sentiments with all the personal warmth and thoughtfulness of an election season robo-call. Just out of curiosity I clicked on all 123 greetings posted on a friend's birthday. There were precisely two which could not have been just as appropriately posted on the Facebook pages of Attila the Hun, Godzilla, or Snoopy. Virtually nobody spoke to the unique humanity of this person I know to be very special indeed.

Perhaps I sound like a grump, an old geezer screaming at the kids to get off his Facebook lawn. Don't get me wrong; I like being remembered as much as the next guy. I'm not against giving folks a shout out on their birthdays. Au contraire, we desperately need to create genuine community in a world which treats us as numbers and interchangeable pieces. We should take time to offer genuine appreciation to one another. When so much of daily life conspires to make us feel unimportant, someone naming why we are special to him or her is a great gift.

I worry that the faux intimacy of dashing off a formulaic birthday post fools us into thinking we are creating the real deal. Community happens when we know and are known by other people at more than superficial levels. Affirmation is meaningful and supportive when it reflects some awareness of the complex combination of traits which makes me who I am. Friendship is cheap when it does not cost us at least a little time and thought.

A modest proposal for those who use Facebook: Tomorrow when all those birthday prompts pop up ("Today is Joe Blow's birthday, send him a greeting…."), instead of responding with a Pavlovian, "Happy birthday" to them all, pick out one person who really has meant something to you, one person who might need you to name their specialness, one person whom you've appreciated but never gotten around to telling – and write them an actual note that tells them exactly why you are glad they were born.

Maybe it's just me, but I'd rather get one diamond than a hundred pieces of gravel – wouldn't most folks?

Real Loneliness

Many people have a romantic fantasy of escaping the daily grind and finding a simpler way of living. Last week, while I was exercising, I listened to a podcast story of a man who took that desire about as far as you can. He rode a train to Alaska, hitched to the last town at the end of a dirt road, canoed 125 miles downstream into the wilderness, hiked 25 miles away from the river – and then built a shelter where he spent the next ten years or so. His goal was to live off the land.

He pretty much succeeded in doing that. The only thing he could not find in the wilderness was a woman, so he reversed his trek and ultimately found someone who wanted to share his lifestyle. They lived happily in the wilds until a lawyer convinced the Indian tribe on whose land they were squatting that there were liability issues if they were to be injured. So the two ended up back in Fairbanks.

An interviewer asked how he and his partner dealt with the loneliness of the wilderness. He responded with something that stopped me dead in my tracks. "Loneliness is not being alone. Loneliness is being in a room of people who don't want or need you."

That is as succinct a statement of the modern malady as I have heard. It explains how the bar scene can be both frenetic and depressing. It shows how retirees can have so much free time and so little fulfillment. It illustrates how the cost we pay for our mobile society, which often puts us far from the squelching expectations of family and community of origin, can be a deep longing to know and be known.

In the Genesis creation narrative God observes, "It is not good for the man to be alone." This is much more than a statement on sexuality and marriage; it speaks to the absolute necessity of community. We need to be needed. We need to matter to one another. We are not fully what we are intended to be until we find a way to give ourselves.

Loneliness and depression are complex, often debilitating conditions. It would be presumptuous to suggest there is a one-size-fits-all solution for every loneliness. But I offer one suggestion. If you often find yourself feeling lonely, instead of just looking for places where you can cohabit space with a lot of people, find a place where someone needs you, where you can give your best self.

Peace Through Reproof

I confess that Proverbs is not one of my favorite books of the Bible because
- It does not have a coherent point of view; one proverb often contradicting another.
- It is more a collection of random bromides from all around the Middle East, rather than a bold statement of Israel's rich, distinctive theological vision.
- It is (with a few notable exceptions) to literature what a jingle is to a symphony, easily accessible, but lacking new depth after that first hearing. There is a fine line between pithy and platitude.

Many folks hold Proverbs dear. Bless them; it doesn't usually feed me.

So I was mildly surprised when I found myself lingering over a portion of Proverbs which showed up in the daily lectionary I use for personal devotions, "He who winks the eye causes trouble, but he who boldly reproves makes peace. [10:11]." Maybe what I found interesting is the idea, which seems a bit counter-intuitive, that bold reproof makes for peace.

That's not usually what we think is it? Most people will move heaven and earth to avoid speaking a word of reproof (which Webster defines as "criticism for a fault") precisely because they are afraid it will result in a blow up, hurt feelings, and a testy relationship. We generally prefer to put on a plastered smile, grit our teeth, and eat our frustration, because we think the alternative will be decidedly unpleasant. We certainly do not expect "bold reproof" to make things more peaceful.

Yet if we think about it just a bit we realize that the writer of Proverbs has a point. Pretending that everything is hunky dory, when it isn't, does not make our resentment go away; it just makes it squirt out in unexpected ways and at odd times. Think about how many times you have made a snarky comment about something trivial (for example, someone being 5 minutes late) because you were afraid to broach the real issue. Denial is seldom a healthy strategy, whether we are talking about an ache in your back or that churning in our gut. Better to face the issue straight up and speak a bold, but respectful word.

The point is not to give someone both barrels of anger; that suggests we are more interesting in venting than in making peace. Here, as in so many things, we do well to observe our Lord. He was never shy about confronting people when he thought they were being less than honest (think about his encounter with the Samaritan woman in John 4) or were engaged in destructive behavior (many of his encounters with the Scribes and Pharisees). But he reproved in a way which sought to educate or take the relationship to a better place, if that was possible.

Relationships are hard work. Sometimes we have to take the risk of being misunderstood when we are honest. But a marriage, friendship, or working team built on gentle untruth is like a house framed on poorly packed fill – at some point it's going to crack. So we speak the truth as we see it – with all the gentleness we can offer – and hope that a real, rather than superficial, peace will be the fruit.

Passion on the Thames

There's a controversy brewing on the banks of the Thames. The prestigious Southbank Center of the Arts is host to four resident orchestras and a variety of other musical artists. Beneath the center is a graffiti-covered concrete cavern known as "the undercroft," which skateboarders regard as hallowed ground, the birthplace of their sport. The Center wants to open up more space for much needed rehearsal rooms and outreach to the neighboring community, but that would mean moving the skateboarders down the river.

As I listened to the story on NPR I was struck by how passionate each side is about its art – and that is how both the musicians and the boarders see their pursuits, as art. Perhaps it is obvious that music is art. But so, too, is skateboarding, says the group's leader. "It is an art form. It is about pushing the boundaries of human achievement and what you can do, not only on a skateboard, but with your mind."

Maybe you could happily live your whole life without hearing another operatic aria. Perhaps you wish daily that those cannon balling skateboarders would get off the sidewalk. Most of us will have an opinion on the best use of the space at the Southbank center. But arguing for one side or the other is not my purpose. Rather, I invite you to consider the importance of having something which takes you beyond yourself, something which engages you beyond the tasks of daily routine, something which keeps you from going dead inside. Our spirits are meant to stretch and explore the limits, whether that is mastering a Mozart flute concerto or executing a "fakie switch 360 shuvit" (yes, I confess I had to look that up).

Stretching is particularly important for us as disciples of Jesus. We don't want to just go through the motions. Our calling is to push beyond our comfort zone, exploring new ways to invest ourselves in the work of Christ. When the apostle Paul was pulled into a controversy at Corinth the issue was not practice rooms or skateboarding; it was whether Christians could eat food offered to idols. That might seem trivial to us, but it threatened to rip that community apart. His counsel, which serves us equally well, was "whether you eat or drink, or whatever you do, do everything for the glory of God." We can differ on how we judge the merits of one position or another, but if we are clear about our ultimate goal, we'll work through our disagreements.

Here is hoping that whatever you do this day stretches your spirit, fills you with passion, and gives you an opportunity to show Christ in your little corner of the world.

Mr. Happy

He had everyone looking at him – and if you have ever walked on Chicago's Michigan Avenue in the middle of the day you know what an accomplishment that was. In any big city, the wave of humanity swirls obliviously around just about any distraction. Past silver painted mimes, homeless folks slumped against the storefronts, street preachers announcing coming calamity; outrageously tattooed, dressed, and coiffed characters, the anonymous tide rolls on unheeding. But this little boy had everyone's attention. He screamed loud enough to drown out the siren of a passing fire engine, and his eyes bugged out so far I feared he would burst some capillaries. When his mother reached in to grab an angry arm, flailing like a buzz saw, I got a look at his T-shirt. On the front was a smiley-face over the inscription, "Mr. Happy." I laughed out loud at the incongruity.

Sometimes incongruity is no laughing matter. The speaker at the conference I was attending last week in the Windy City reminded us of something I have been reading a lot lately: Despite Christian self-perceptions, those outside the Church increasingly regard it as a bastion of intolerance. They perceive the saints simultaneously wearing a T-shirt that says "We are all beggars at the table of God," and checking IDs at the church door to make sure only the right kind of folks come in.

Check it out for yourself. Jesus reserves His harshest words for those who ought to know better, the people who have been incredibly blessed by God but insist on looking down on others. When you have received mercy, says Jesus, the proper response is to spread it around wherever you can. As Luke 7:36-50 suggests, when you really experience love, you can't help but show it.

That is not the same as having a squishy "anything goes" attitude which refuses to discern between what gives life and what causes pain. Jesus famously told a shady lady, "Go and sin no more." But it does mean that our lives should match our confession. If we believe we have received mercy, let's be merciful. Having experienced God's patience with our persistent failings, let's be patient with that annoying co-worker. As we humbly claim God's forgiveness, let's be quick to offer it to others.

So, a little exercise: This week imagine you are wearing a T-shirt emblazoned with a cross and the words, "Mr. (or Ms.) Grace." How many people would laugh – or cry – at incongruity between your shirt and your attitude?

Hole in the Water

Last week I was at the ELCA's pre-retirement seminar (No, this is not an oblique announcement of my resignation; when you became a "person of a certain age," you go). I was talking with a friend of many years. "So how much longer before you hang up your cleats," I asked him, "Are there things you want to see happen at the congregation before you leave?"

"I'll go as long as I feel like I am being effective. I have no illusions about how indispensable I am. The day I walk out the door, the good folks at St John's by the Gas Pumps will be on to someone else. You know what they say: Put your hand in a bucket of water, take it out, and see how big a hole you left."

A little bit of gallows humor, I suspect, to keep at bay the fear of irrelevancy which we all share. Yet often there is wisdom in humor, dark or otherwise. Perhaps the most important choice we make each day is how we will use our time. Will we hit the gym, read a book, write a paper, call a friend, plan a presentation, read to our child, go to a meeting, or opt for one of the hundreds of other possibilities we have? We want our lives to matter, but we do not want to be slaves to a schedule we hate. The choices are seldom straight forward.

So how do we make those choices? I've lived long enough to realize that sometimes the choices feel impossible. Do you spend time with your son or work the extra shift which means you will have the money to feed, clothe, house, and educate that same beloved child? We need to be gentle with ourselves when either choice provokes guilt.

That being said I think there is one principle worth keeping in mind: You are all the world to someone – or several people – for others, you are just valuable. When push comes to shove it is those primary people who should get the first bite of the apple which is your life. Yes, history is filled with people who sacrificed their families, their health, and their friends because they felt a compelling need to work for a cure, abolish slavery, or take the gospel to the far corners of the earth. If your work is truly that important, then go for it – and humbly ask forgiveness of those you use, abuse, and ignore. For the vast majority of us, that is not the case. More often we spend our lives sacrificing the important to the merely urgent, and then regretting it.

Pondering that bucket of water and the hole we do not make can be rather depressing – life as "a tale told by an idiot, full of sound and fury, signifying nothing." But it can also be liberating to realize that it does not all depend on us. God is acting in the cracks of life, has been acting long before we came on the scene and will be doing so after we depart the stage. Our task is not necessarily to change the world by ourselves, not to be perfect, not to work until we drop in a harness which some other mule will fill tomorrow. Sometimes it is enough to be the world to just one person at a critical moment. There is a difference between sloth and sanity; the better we learn to distinguish the two, the happier and more fulfilled we are.

Silent Saints

Grandma asks the comic strip heroine Agnes, "What do you want to be when you grow up?" Agnes replies, "It's not really up to me, now is it? There's fate…random accident… mistakes in judgment…all the obligations that will outweigh my personal preferences." Her long suffering guardian responds, "So you want to be a grandma."

I audibly groaned as I read that strip over my morning coffee and granola. Sometimes the comics make you smile and sometimes they evoke a pathos which breaks your heart. That little exchange called to mind twenty-five years of conversations with my wife, the kindergarten teacher. It made me think of all the surrogate parents Gail has told me about who hang tough against all odds, when they could easily just walk away. So this week's Bread for the Journey is a shout out to all

• The grandparents and aunts who reared their own children as best they could – and are now doing it all again because they refuse to abandon an innocent child to irresponsibly foolish parents.

• The brave spouses who anticipated trips and beaches in retirement, but gladly and tenderly care for their beloved as the tendrils of dementia choke the mind of their heart's desire.

- The men who dreamed of college but dropped out, working soul-crushing jobs to support a widowed mom and siblings.
- The women who have all the smarts to be whatever they want to be – and want to be totally available to a special needs child.
- The lawyers who could be pulling down six figures designing tax shelters and opt to speak for the battered kids who have no voice.
- The volunteers of all types who think scratching the surface of human need is more important than being a scratch golfer.

One of most formative myths of American life (in the sense of a lens through which we see the world) is that you can be whatever you want to be. That is true to a point – though it is amazing how one little clot going down the wrong artery curtails your options. But more fully expressed the myth might be, "You can be whatever you want to be, as long as you are willing to sacrifice everybody and everything to your vision." I admire those who overcome obstacles, but I admire even more those who defer personal preferences for the sake of the most vulnerable and the common good. Sometimes great accomplishment is just naked selfishness stripped of conscience.

So here's to all you solitary, silent saints who love something more than yourselves. Thanks for making our world a more humane place.

Rehab Reflections

I warn you that this week's Bread for the Journey may be a little less focused that some others. I am writing it from a recliner with a knee propped up following surgery. I am in that "two steps forward, one step backward" phase – and the drugs can give the illusion that you are more lucid than you are. Surgery imposes reflection time. You can't follow your regular routine because you can't get around. So a few random reflections as my knee ices:

In an effort to be semi-productive during this down time I have a stack of books next to the chair, books I have been meaning to get to for a long time. One concerns spiritual disciplines. I am not a patient patient, so I was in the grip of surly self-pity when I ran across these words about the discipline of gratitude, "When I want to practice thanks, I can start with toes…I can be grateful for working toes, then for working feet, then for mobile ankles…"

I realized I am so focused on the one part of me that is not working very well right now that I have forgotten all the parts that are. Isn't that the way it often is? We receive the good as our right and obsess about the less than perfect. Our basic attitude toward life is thus not gratitude but perpetual dissatisfaction. The world looks grayer than it truly is when we view it through a dark filter. Take just one minute right now and give thanks; I guarantee it will improve your attitude.

One of the gifts of this down time is that it has forced me to change my daily schedule. I have to block in time for therapy and rehabilitation exercises; that means something else has to go. That is not all bad. I am taking stock of whether all those old blocks in my schedule will stay put when I am back to 100%. Much of life is lived on autopilot and that is fine because we need a certain basic, stable structure when each day brings unique challenges. But every once in awhile we need to step back and ask, "Is this really getting me where I want to go? Does the time I give to this really reflect my values and what I want from life? Is this feeding my soul or sucking me dry?" Our datebooks are like peach trees; they need to be pruned periodically if they are to bear more fruit than leaves.

One final reflection: People are important. I am the chief of sinners when it comes to sometimes letting a task become more important than attending to the people around me. There is nothing like being unable to even pull on a sock to remind you that you need other people. There is nothing like having a friend, fresh from his own health issues, dropping by to give you a get well gift to remind you that riches consist in the people who surround us – which takes us back to gratitude...

Crazy Like Us

I haven't read the book, but the teaser for *Crazy Like Us: The Globalization of the American Psyche* by Ethan Watters, intrigues me. He writes, "In teaching the rest of the world to think like us, we have been, for better and worse, homogenizing the way the world goes mad."

I knew we exported fashion and blockbuster movies, hip-hop and democratic ideals (if not always the reality). I did not realize that our craziness was rapidly becoming as ubiquitous as blue jeans. I'm sure Watters has his own thoughts on what constitutes the distinctive American mental pathology which he sees spreading around the globe, but it got me thinking about what I would put on a list. A few of my nominations:

- Obsession with individuality at the expense of community, which often leaves us feeling depressed and isolated from one another.

- Deep fear of silence, so that we fill our world with noise and have no time for reflection on what is most valuable.

- Preference for novelty over quality, in both cell phones and relationships. We flit from one new experience to next, seldom savoring or investing in the present.

- Inability to value anything which is not material, so that, paradoxically, we fill our lives with things which do not satisfy but demand a great deal of our energy in the pursuit.

I invite you to think a little bit about what you would identify as symptoms of our distinctive malaise, not just as a mental exercise, but as a means of thinking about what we as persons of faith can offer to the world. How we talk about our faith should be influenced by what we perceive to be the needs of those we meet. What does the gospel have to say to people who are often isolated, depressed, and longing for meaning?

To make it a little more personal, do you see yourself in the list I created? As the summer winds down and our schedules fill up, let me suggest that you heed the words of the psalmist, "Be still and know that I am God." [46:10] Take a walk, with no tunes playing in your ears, and listen for God's voice. Let it invite you into caring more deeply for those around you. Allow yourself to rest in the awareness of God's love, no matter what stresses are howling on the edges of your consciousness. In short, sink a deep well into the aquifer of the Christian faith; allow it to refresh and sustain you when life gets hectic. It just might keep you from going crazy.

Poem of Presence

To experience such moments, when insight breaks like a sunbeam through a thunderhead, this is a big reason I do campus ministry! Gathered in a circle for our weekly Lutheran Student Movement meeting, our worship was focused on cultivating an awareness of God's grace in the midst of the busyness which crowds our days. The assignment was to create (in five minutes) something that celebrates God's presence and care. We shared our drawings, prayers, and a letter to God – all good. Yet Aaron's poem left me pensive long after the program was over:

We see the sunrise over the ocean,
> but not your face.
We hear a newborn's cry,
> but not your voice.
We feel the touch of our loved ones,
> but not your calming embrace.
We smell the coming rain,
> but not the majesty of your creation.
Help us
> to see your face,
> to hear your voice,
> to feel your touch,
> and to know that you surround us.

I wanted to hand-carry that poem to the man who was, at the moment Aaron wrote it, feeling terribly alone on the anniversary of his beloved wife's death. I wanted to pray it at the bedside of a friend who is feeling forgotten and worthless. I wanted to offer it to the family who is contemplating hospice care. I wanted to post it on my Facebook page, hoping that a certain despair-filled teen might read it, sense God's care for her, and decide to live another day. I wanted to e-mail it to the graduate who still has not found a job in her field and to the one who is on his first deployment. I did not do any of those things, but I share it here in thanksgiving for both a young man's discernment and the divine presence which lovingly enfolds us even in our greatest darkness.

Now you try it. Take a few minutes to make a list of how you experience God's care each day in the little things which you usually take for granted. Then create something to celebrate that care. I think you will be amazed at the result. I was.

On the Way

Some quotations speak to a variety of situations. In my reading, I came across these words from Martin Luther, "We are not yet what we shall be, but we are growing toward it; the process is not yet finished, but it is going on; this is not the end, but it is the road."

As I ruminated on those words I was taken back to a couple of conversations I had last week. The first was with a student who is questioning some of the religious beliefs and practices she was taught growing up. These interpretations are starting to sound to her like disco tunes at a hip-hop party – quaint, outmoded, and decidedly out of touch with the world in which she lives. Her implicit question: "Suppose I just can't accept A, B, or C, can I still be a Christian? Is it all or nothing?" We talked a little bit and I hope she discovered that many of the things to which she objects are not within the Church's core tradition in the first place. Lots of the saints before her have had the same reservations.

Sometimes, when we have faith questions, we just need

213

better information. But I wish I had remembered Luther's words when she was in my office, because they make a crucial point: To be a Christian is not to have all the answers nailed down, it is to be committed to following Jesus in asking the questions. Discipleship is not thinking you have arrived; it is deciding that Jesus will be your guide. The Christians I most admire – the ones who are most alive – expect to discover something new each day; they embrace having cherished assumptions challenged and modified. They make room for God's unexpected, slightly disconcerting revelations in their lives.

The other conversation was less theological than pastoral. He came in very depressed; as we talked, it became clear to me that a big part of the problem was perfectionism. He has set a high standard for himself, but there are just too many balls to keep in the air. They are starting to drop. The issue is more than just a few failures. At the ripe old age of no more than 25 he does not yet have a detailed plan for his life and he feels like he is behind the curve.

I think Brother Martin's words also speak to my depressed friend. In a high pressure world we need to hear the graceful word offered to us in Christ. We cannot expect perfection of ourselves. We will fall down, but God's love is constant to lift us up. We will not have an unobstructed view of the future – and that's okay (how boring that would be anyway). Like explorers on a glorious journey we are moving ahead – and the trip is as important as the destination. So be patient with your failings and your blind spots; God is not finished with you yet.

Maps

My beach reading included *Caravans*, James Michener's 1963 novel set in Afghanistan immediately following World War II. The plot pivots on the fate of Ellen, a young American woman who becomes enthralled with an Afghan studying in the United States, follows him to Afghanistan, and then promptly disappears into the untamed landscape far from Kabul. In researching her past, the young diplomat assigned to find her discovers this comment from a former teacher:

"Ellen Jaspar is sick with the disease that is beginning to infect our ablest young people. She has disaffiliated herself from the beliefs that gave our society its structure in the past, but she has found no new structure upon which she can rely for that support which human life requires."

This, I thought, is a dead-on description of our present crisis. As I read these words on the porch of our beach rental, the folks next door were slowly drinking themselves into oblivion, a sort of commentary and validation of the text. Many in our society – and young adults in particular – have decided that the language and vision of Christian faith, which have sustained and guided previous generations, no longer speak to them in a meaningful way. Musty doctrines answer questions nobody is asking. Worship options appear to be either hopelessly antiquated or excruciatingly trivial – so why invest a beautiful Sunday morning? The old map no longer seems a reliable guide, but no alternative through the chaos seems any better. So we just sedate ourselves as the ship drifts toward the iceberg.

Perhaps these seem to be dark thoughts from a glorious week at the beach. I do not mean to be despairing; rather, I want to urge compassion and hope. Nobody chooses to have their map fall apart. Be gentle with those who are on the road – even if it is yourself. Conservatives often bemoan the loss of what was, as though young adults desire to be at sea, struggling for joy and purpose. In my experience our young people are desperately trying to forge meaning at a time when the foundations are crumbling around them. The world is not more dangerous than it was in previous days, but it is certainly a lot more complex and the certitudes are much fewer. So if you are in relationship with a young adult who seems a bit sad and lost, try to see the world through his or her eyes. That is my call for compassion.

At the same time there is reason for hope. The first step in drafting a new map is seeing where it is inadequate. Just because we have allowed our Christian map to become outmoded, it does not follow that the Way of Jesus is wrong. More than ever we need to be bold in suggesting that love is better than polarization, sacrifice more life-giving than mad accumulation of things, and seeking the will of God more satisfying than drifting with the newest fads.

We are not the first people of faith to go through a crisis of confidence. God was faithful to Israel in exile and the church through many persecutions. God will be faithful to us if we dare to be pioneers who tweak the map of faith, gently but firmly bearing witness that Jesus does indeed offer direction when everything else seems tenuous.

Joy in Ministry

Last Sunday afternoon a group of our members saw a performance of *Clybourne Park* play at Virginia Tech; then we gathered at my home for refreshments and conversation about this provocative play. As we sat around, someone expressed appreciation to Gail and me for hosting the event. I heard myself say, "This brought together three things I love – drama, good food and beverages, and stimulating conversation with good people – it was no burden at all."

Later that evening I started reflecting on that statement. It was absolutely true. Though one might have seen the organizing and hosting as part of my job, it did not feel that way. It felt like a wonderful moment when something important – reflecting on the roots of prejudice and the difficulty of adapting to change – intersected with other things which give me great joy.

Our ministry in the world should not be just picking the low hanging fruit, doing only the things which we find fun. But neither should it feel like drudgery. When it does something is wrong. I wonder if one reason we sometimes lack joy in our identity as disciples is that too often we are doing tasks simply because we think we ought to do them, rather than because we have gifts and passion for the work.

If you are like me, each day your mailbox is filled with solicitations from very worthy causes and groups. Yet only one or two really speak to your heart and, therefore, get your contribution. Faithful, joyful discipleship involves paying attention to what deeply engages our heart, finding that particular place where we have gifts and passion which others may not have at that moment.

As Christians we share a single calling, to love God and our neighbor. But that calling is best expressed when we bring our unique interests and gifts to the task. What are your joys, abilities, and passions telling you about where God needs you this day? What is the work you might take up which would feel like more like a lark than a duty?

Bookmarks

Following the April 16 shootings at Virginia Tech our campus ministry received many thoughtful expressions of care and concern from around the country. All were deeply appreciated, but I treasure one in particular, because it keeps on giving. We received a box of hand-colored bookmarks from a youth event in the New England Synod of the ELCA.

All the bookmarks have the same printed front:

I am…Marked with the Cross of Christ Forever,
A Gift to the Students of Virginia Tech,
Hammonasset 2007 ELCA NE Synod.

The young people colored the bookmarks, sometimes with wonderful art work, and many wrote a message on the back. We distributed them far and wide after 4/16, but some were left over. I keep a stack in my office and use them whenever I need a placeholder – when I am writing a sermon, preparing a class, or just reading a novel. On a rough day it is wonderful to glance down and be reminded of whose I am through my baptism. On the back of the bookmark I keep in my devotional and study Bible a young person I will never meet wrote, "NEVER lose hope and keep strong, we together will endure."

It is a simple sentence, cast defiantly into the chaos following 4/16. That young person will never know how many times it has buoyed my spirits and reminded me of what it means to be in the body Christ.

My friends, never, ever forget how important your witness can be. Like a stone cast into a pond, the most humble word or deed can have an impact far beyond our dreaming, rippling out and touching others in ways which would amaze us. Your actions need not be dramatic or eloquent, just rooted in the hope of Christ and the desire to reflect his spirit in all you do.

Andrea

Andrea has already had more chaos in her brief six years that many people see in a lifetime. She's been assaulted, ignored, and shuttled from one pathological family configuration to another. The men in her house change faster than a gambler's luck. Loving, attentive parents are as mythical to her as unicorns and dragons. Hers is the kind of story that makes died in the wool opponents of capital punishment think, "Well, how about thumb screws for those who have done this...."

Given all that she has been through, it should come as no surprise that she has "issues" at school. She is not a great student. Her impulse control is nil. When crossed, she tends to kick first and ask questions later. Yet, if you look closely, you can see a real sweetie itching to come out. She is a beautiful doll whom thoughtless fools have thrown to the side of the road. You know that with a little TLC, some soap and water, and patience – lots of patience – she could shine.

It got pretty bad last week; her teacher had to sit Andrea down and have what we used to call a "come to Jesus" conversation with her: Either she improved her behavior or she would spend a lot of time by herself. Much to her teacher's delight the serious sit-down seemed to work; Andrea had several good days in a row. Eager to reinforce the trend, her teacher pulled her aside and gushed, "Andrea, I am so proud of you. You've been doing great." Obviously pleased with herself, the pixie pursed her lips, stuck out her little jaw, and with a matter-of-fact innocence which melts your heart she said, "Yep, I didn't hurt nobody today."

I tell you about Andrea for two reasons. First, it never hurts to remember what a heavy load some folks are carrying when we meet them. Sometimes words and actions which are barely civil reflect a heroic effort which would leave us in awe if we only knew. Phi Beta Kappa earned with all the advantages bestowed by affluence, parental support, good genes, and countless cultural opportunities is not be as impressive as a GED scratched out of a dung heap of adversity. Be gentle in your judgments and quick with your praise. Andrea needs all the support you can give her.

Second, as you drop off to sleep tonight and reflect on how you interacted with others today – with your children, your parents, the guy at the checkout stand, the idiot on the interstate with the cell phone, your students, or your roommate – ask yourself if you can meet Andrea's standard… "Yep, I didn't hurt nobody today."

Thou Art the Man

I was screaming at my radio. As I washed the evening dishes, NPR aired a story on the many unintended consequences of the draconian immigration law passed by the Alabama legislature: crops rotting in the fields due to a labor shortage, a rise in violence against Latinos, children afraid to go to school lest they be separated from their parents. At one point the interviewer asked an influential legislator, a man who identified himself as a Christian, if he thought Jesus would have voted for the law. The lawmaker paused for a long time and then, sounding like a Southern politician straight from central casting, he replied "No suh, I don't think Jesus would have voted for this law."

"Then why the heck did you vote for it?" I bellowed at the ceiling and flipped a wet bowl toward the dish drain. At that point I had one of those Nathan and David moments: "Thou art the man." If you don't know the reference, take a few minutes and read 2 Samuel 11-12. I'll wait....

I had worked myself up into frothy, self-righteous indignation. "Boy, if Jesus is so important to you, why do you act in a way contemptuous of His welcoming spirit? If Jesus is Lord, why do you treat Him like political window dressing? If you long to love as He does, why do you cave to the only barely veiled racism which has plagued our beloved South for too long?"

But then I saw the question coming back to me; if Jesus is your Lord, Bill, why...

- Do you so quickly hate the hater?
- Do you more fear offending the powerful than failing to speak the truth as you see it?
- Do you not care more about the plight of the poor when you make spending choices?
- Do you not more boldly bear witness to His way among your unchurched friends?

Siloing, compartmentalization, prudence – there are a lot of words for it, some more socially acceptable than others. But the reality is the same, we keep Jesus hermetically sealed away from 99% of our lives, sealed in a niche called "religion." We tend to confess Jesus a lot more than we allow Him to make a difference in how we spend our money, treat those with whom we disagree, or use our time.

I give that Alabama politician a lot of credit for honesty. At least he was able to 'fess up, admit the mistake, and begin down a new path – what the Bible calls "repentance." I hope you and I can be equally honest in our self-reflection. If we cannot imagine Jesus doing it...maybe we should not either.

Biscuit Card

He reached into a grubby pocket, flashed a gap-toothed smile, and held it out to me. "This card'll get you a free breakfast biscuit at Hardees. It was just the two of us sitting in that slightly chilly room. Luther Memorial was hosting To Our House, the thermal shelter for homeless men, and I was there to take whoever showed up to our campus center for the night. "I don't need this; you folks feed us breakfast every morning."

My immediate reaction was to refuse the card. I could certainly afford my own biscuit. It felt absurd for me, wearing a winter coat more expensive than his whole wardrobe, to take his biscuit. Sure, we feed the men who stay at the shelter each night, but he could hold his card for that day when he needed a little something extra to eat.

Then it occurred to me that this really had little to do with physical hunger. Rather, this was about another kind of desire, the need we all have to feel that we have something to share. Nobody likes to feel perpetually dependent. We all want to feel valuable, able to deposit into, as well as take from, the common stores of humanity. In that moment Adam (not his real name) was thankful for all that To Our House provides for him, but what he most needed was for me to receive, with some degree of graciousness, the small gift he could offer.

Far be it from me to romanticize poverty, to glibly intone that, "In some ways those folks are happier than folks with all the pressures of middle-class life." That is usually the desperate dodge of the justly guilt-ridden. But sometimes we forget that we can learn from even – especially – those with little. Abundantly blessed, we think our job is to be compassionate and generous with our material blessings – and we should. But even harder than parting with a few dollars is to blur that distinction between giver and receiver until we see the less fortunate, not as a separate species from us, but as children of the same Parent. That is even more important; when we do that, the material generosity follows.

So I took his card, because he needed to give it – and because I needed to learn how to receive. This is not a story of great pastoral care or uncommon sensitivity. On the contrary, it is a confession of how I like to keep the barriers up between "those people" and me, how easy it is to dehumanize others by seeing them as persons with nothing to give. And it is a story about the warm conversation we had on the ride to Blacksburg because a biscuit card had broken down a barrier.

As you encounter the materially poor, the emotionally bankrupt, the spiritually destitute, the intellectually challenged, and those overwhelmed by life's myriad challenges, may you be blessed with many opportunities to both give and receive.

Simple Kindness

You could tell from his posture that he was ready to go home. The sign said they were open until 7:00 – it was 6:59. Behind him, all of the shop lights were off, save one in the office. An empty lunch box was tucked under his arm; his stride had that languid look of someone who feels the demands of a long day on the job falling away. That's what I saw from the front seat of the tow truck.

Gail and I were returning from a getaway to Staunton where we had seen some wonderful drama at the American Shakespeare Center. As always, the time together had been refreshing, and in the darkness of the interstate we were basking in warm memories like two cats in front of a fire. Suddenly it sounded like a jet was taking off under our car; we pulled over and found shreds of steel and rubber where our front tire had been. I will spare you the gory details. Suffice it to say that in the space of thirty minutes I had two flats, the second coming a mile after changing the first.

With no spare left the only option was a call to AAA. The driver said that the only place open on a Saturday night was going to be the Merchant's in Salem, "I think they close at 7, but I'll try to get you there." All the way there I thought about how this truck was going to become a very expensive cab to Blacksburg if we were too late.

Now you can say that the guy at the tire shop did no more than his job, that he was there to sell tires and I gave him one more sale for the day. But he was an employee, not the owner; he had little skin in this game. I felt bad about hitting him at closing time, so I was watching his face very closely – and there was not a hint of resentment to be found. He was almost jaunty as he pulled the chain to open the bay door and started installing my new tire. Twenty minutes later we were both on our way.

On Thanksgiving Day we typically ponder the grand blessings of family, country, and the bounty of the land. I will certainly do that tomorrow. But I am also terribly thankful for the two people who stopped on a dark and dangerously crowded interstate to help me change a tire, the helpful tow truck driver, and the guy at the tire store. What we do – and more important, the spirit in which we do it – can make an amazing difference in the lives of others.

Our little efforts may seem so piddling, yet they can make a big difference to another person's life. We all have the gift of kindness, which we can give whenever we are willing. I think that is worth remembering as we enter the Festival of Conspicuous Consumption, when bigger price tags too often get equated with greater love.

Seven Reasons

I recently read an article in which Christian Piatt identifies seven reasons why many young adults don't go to church:

- College or adult life doesn't seem to mix well with church.
- Many activities compete for their time and attention.
- Their lifestyle leaves them exhausted.
- They are especially skeptical about people or organizations trying to get their attention.
- They don't see any relevance to the church.
- They've been hurt by the church.
- Churches don't know how to connect with mobile young adults.

As I read this list I had a couple of thoughts. First, most of what is on this list is not unique to young adults. Talk to anyone who sees little need for the church, and you will hear several of these reasons. Second, this list says at least as much about the stress of modern culture as it does about the church. We are over-programmed, over-stimulated, and over our heads in demands most days. The unfortunate thing is that we do not see the community of faith as an antidote to the pathology; no, the church is for many just one more demand in an already crammed schedule. As a pastor, that gives me pause.

There has never been a time when the work of the gospel "mixed well" with the dominant values of the culture, never a time when there were no competing activities, nor a day when folks were not exhausted (think about how many hours folks worked in fields or factories – and then went to church). We are not as unusual as we think. The change is how we prioritize – when it comes time to choose where we will put our first energy, it is not in feeding our souls or serving in Christ's name. We do not deem those as important as the other options.

Do not hear this as fussing about the choices we make. Rather, I am pondering why people identify the church with being bored and hurt (five and six in the list). What is going on when people who routinely talk about feeling alone, without purpose, and exploited in relationships do not clamor for the message and community we claim to offer? It makes as much sense as a man in the desert refusing to drink. The only possible answer is that we are not helping young adults – and their parents – connect their inner hunger to the bread which is Christ.

This Bread for the Journey is less an attempt at brilliant insight or pithy observation than it is an invitation to reflection. What is your hunger? Why does the church fill you up most days – or not? What do you most need from your community of Christ? What would it take for you to recommend your church to your friends with as much enthusiasm as you tell them about your favorite restaurant or movie?.... And since being a Christian is not just about consuming the Bread of Life, but also being in the distribution chain, how would you like to be part of a community which excites all who glimpse its life?

Not Nice

Can we stop being so nice? Perhaps that seems a strange opening for a devotion appearing a few weeks before a highly contentious election. With truth long since a casualty of ambition and the airwaves as toxic as a battlefield trench filled with mustard gas, any infusion of gentility into our common life is desirable. When we are at each other's throats and acting as though those with whom we disagree are obviously devil spawn, wouldn't dialing back the emotion seem like a good idea? Of course.

But I am not talking about civility or the virtue of assuming the good intentions, rather than the malevolence, of our neighbor. By all means, let's act as though the gentleness of Jesus forms us in all circumstances, even when we feel politically passionate and personally vulnerable. But civility and tolerance are different from the anemic, pseudo-virtue of "being nice."

- Nice never gets angry – because it doesn't care enough about anything to be invested.
- Nice purchases serenity with the coin of oblivion to the pain which surrounds it.
- Nice fears disagreement and momentary tension in a friendship more than it values the honesty which might prompt growth.
- Nice prefers gliding along the surface of superficial, but calm interpersonal relationships over digging deeply into the darker, yet rich places of another's life.
- Nice fears being rejected more than failing to offer the best it has.

Being merely nice costs us dearly because it keeps us from engaging others in any depth. It prevents us from acknowledging the pain we have given and received, and thus, from getting beyond the resentment which corrupts marriage, parenting, and friendship. Nice is a self- imposed armor which protects us from being hurt but prevents us from touching others at any great depth.

Loving and being nice are not the same thing. Love wants the best for another person, whether or not the word spoken or the action taken is well received; nice wants only pleasantness. Love wants to mend the cracks in our common life; nice wants only to hide them with a thin smile.

As Christians we always come back to Jesus. Jesus was never nice, but He was unfailingly loving: He spoke the truth even when it was painful. He sought healing not ceasefire. He invited people to change, knowing full well that substantive change is always resisted. He was bold in offering alternatives to the dead ends He saw others taking. But He did it all with a gentleness which could not be mistaken for pique.

So don't be so nice this week. Dare to offer yourself. Dare to speak the truth. Dare to share your experience of trying to follow Jesus. Dare to risk a little awkwardness for the sake of healing a breach or showing another the way. Dare to care more about being faithful to Christ than merely being liked. Don't be nice, be a disciple.

What I Really Said

It is always a revelation to find out what I said. During the weeks when I am privileged to preach I spend a lot of time reading, researching, and crafting a sermon. (I also spend a fair amount of time staring into space, positive that this is the week when the Spirit will deny me even the smallest inspiration and expose me as a pastoral fraud. But that is more about my insecurities than you want to know.) I write sentences, aspiring for depth and eloquence – then delete them as hopelessly turgid. I tweak the language, playing with the images, rhyme, and cadence. I boldly start down an interpretive path only to discover it is a dead end. Somehow a sermon emerges, my puny effort to explicate a passage of a scripture for the good of the community, and I preach.

Then I find out what I said. Perhaps in words of affirmation, sometimes in an angry challenge, maybe in person or via an e-mail, people tell me what they heard. I am often amazed. Like most preachers I get praised for erudition and insight beyond my wisdom and castigated for theological and political agendas I never intended. Each time I preach I am reminded that my words are like arrows shot into a dense forest; I may know where I aimed, but usually have no idea what I hit.

I am not complaining about this. The risk of being misunderstood comes with the turf if you dare to speak in a public place. I deeply value the feedback. I find it a helpful reminder of a basic reality with which we all deal, whether we preach or not: we cannot control how others interpret our words and deeds. We can try to be clear. We can try to be gentle. We can try to live and speak with integrity. But as therapists sometimes remind couples in counseling, "The message sent is not always the message received." We bring our filters to every encounter. We inevitably interpret the words and actions of others through our own experiences, fears, and assumptions.

I raise this because it seems to me that these days a lot of us are running around with raw nerve endings. Grief, economic insecurity, health worries – the list could go on and on – all make us edgy and prone to find offense where none is intended. Graciousness is a gift which Jesus' followers can give to each other and to those we encounter each day. In a world where folks are feeling besieged and threatened, how healing it can be if we assume the best intentions from all we meet. The Psalmist tells us that God is "slow to anger and abounding in steadfast love." Try cultivating that attitude this week in all your interactions and judgments.

Psalm 46

I am neither mystical by temperament nor skilled in the interpretation of dreams, but I knew what this one meant. I was sitting on a deck sipping a coke. This was one of those large decks found at restaurants, built so that trees grow up through the floorboards and shade the tables. But there was no shade on this deck. Instead, there were three massive, redwood-sized stumps where the trees used to be, and the sun was baking the deck unmercifully.

Last week three of my dear friends and colleagues on the national campus ministry team lost their jobs through absolutely no fault of their own. A familiar story these days: budget shortfall…you have to cut somewhere…they got the phone call. Between them I estimate they had over ninety years of experience in campus ministry; no wonder those stumps were so big. I've been feeling a lot of things since then: relief, profound sadness, a bit of anxiety, and a healthy dose of survivor guilt. The one thing I know is that my deck is going to be greatly diminished without those redwoods.

Many of you reading this "bread" are living the same story, not in campus ministry to be sure, but in your own context. You worry about your job. You rage at impersonal forces over which you have little control. You mourn for friends whose lives have been uprooted. The carefully crafted script you had written for your life is in for a major rewrite. You look around and see stumps – and wonder if you will soon be one.

I have little patience with those who, in the face of great suffering, glibly quote scripture as though it were a Flint-stones band-aid to be slapped on a child's boo-boo to make it all better. We dare not trivialize another's pain with cheap consolation. But neither should we forfeit the wisdom of the saints, those who have experienced upheaval and sorrow before us. When Luther confronted the destruction of all he held dear, the cleaving of certitude for which he longed, he found perspective and hope in Psalm 46:

"God is our refuge, and strength, a very present help in trouble,

Therefore, we will not fear though the earth should change,

Though the mountains shake in the heart of the sea;

Though its waters roar and foam, though the mountains tremble with its tumult."

From that encounter with scripture came Luther's defiant hymn, *Ein Feste Burg*, which has steeled the resolve of many generations. Neither one text nor one hymn magically banishes the pain of dark days. Yet I hope for my friends, I hope for myself, and I hope for you who read these stumbling words the grace to rest in the assurance that, even when mountains crumble or redwoods topple, God's love is sufficient – and that from the stumps new verdant life will arise.

Power to Bless or Curse

"The truth is that each of us is necessarily either a blessing or curse to those around us. How much better – both for them and for ourselves – to be a conscious blessing to another than a burden on the way." – Joan Chittister, *Listen with the Heart* –

As I read the above quotation during my morning devotions last week, I remembered an incident which occurred during the summer I spent in Clinical Pastoral Education. As part of my seminary training I served as the chaplain to several floors in a large general hospital. I visited patients, spent periodic nights on call for emergencies, and supported the nursing staff in whatever ways I could.

To tell you the truth I do not remember the exact circumstances; I just remember the nurse's words. We were sitting in a nurse's station on the orthopedic floor when she looked earnestly into my face and said, "Pastor King, I believe in you, I really believe in you." My immediate reaction was to be dumbfounded – and then to be consumed by terror. I really did not want that kind of power and trust given to me. I was just a callow young fool who was making it up as he went along.

Part of clinical education is debriefing critical incidents with your supervisor, and I could hardly wait to bring this one into Len's office. Len nodded as I explained what had happened and how I felt about it; then he said, "Bill, you don't have a choice. Whether you like it or not you have the power to bless and the power to curse. It comes with the turf."

Since then I have learned the truth of Len's words. Few are the people who listen to a pastor unquestioningly, but we who occupy the office of pastor do have wisdom and power imputed to us far beyond what we deserve. I hope knowing that means I weigh my words carefully, whether speaking from the pulpit or to a wounded soul sitting on the sofa in my office. Yet Joan Chittister points out something much more important: Every single one of us, not just clergy, has the power to bless and curse in ways we can scarcely imagine.

• A little child will remember whether or not you called him "stupid" the next time he is faced with a daunting challenge, and your blessing or curse may make all the difference in whether he succeeds or fails.

• Your patience – or lack thereof – may be the critical factor in whether a co-worker who is struggling through divorce dares to expose her pain and begins to heal.

• The telephone call which is just one among many things on your "to do" list may be the lifeline which gets a deeply depressed friend through one more day.

We simply have no idea how much power we have, how often another is waiting with bated breath to hear whether we will speak blessing or curse, whether we will ease the burden or add more weight to the load. Does that scare you? Good, it ought to. Unacknowledged power wielded in irresponsible ignorance causes a lot suffering. Yet don't let knowledge of your latent power paralyze you, rather let it prompt you to speak wisely and act gently. Someone you will meet today needs your blessing. Give it.

African Queen

In the classic film, *The African Queen*, Humphrey Bogart and Katharine Hepburn play a grizzled ship's captain and a tough-as-nails school missionary trying to make their way down an untamed African river at the start of World War I. They overcome German guns and treacherous rapids, but the marsh almost defeats them. The river disappears into a trackless sea of mud and reeds. Their engine dead, Bogart is reduced to pulling the boat along through leech-infested waters (The scenes of Hepburn plucking the little critters off Bogart's body still give me nightmares). Totally exhausted, they collapse on the deck of the boat to die. During the night torrential rains arrive, lifting the boat above the reeds on flood waters and revealing that they were mere feet from open water when they gave up.

We spend a lot of time in the reeds. Daily demands can seem so overwhelming. We do our best, but sometimes we feel like the cumulative weight of job, home, school work, sports, caregiving for aged parents, and church are just too much. In the middle of it all there does not seem to be much escape. It feels like the only path available is to keep slogging through the reeds until we literally collapse under the weight of all the demands. What can we do?

One thing is to ask ourselves whether we really need to be doing everything we are doing – or at least whether our time use reflects our priorities. It is easy for the merely urgent to crowd out the important. Are there things we can let go of? Are there things we should let go of, not because they are not valuable, but because they are not as important as the energy they demand?

Another thing is to be sure we take time to receive God's grace into our lives. In the movie, salvation ultimately comes as pure gift, water which carries them over the reeds. Yes, I know, "I don't have time for devotions; I have so much to do." But isn't that a bit like saying, "I don't have time to stop at the gas station because the journey is going to be so long"? When so much of our day is taken up with messages that say we are valuable only if we produce, it is important to take time to hear God's assurance that we are loved before we do a thing… And here is the odd truth, when we take time to listen to God's voice, we almost always discover that some of the stuff we thought was so very, very important isn't.

Jesus said, "I came that they may have life, and have it abundantly." So here is a question for the week: Does your life feel abundant? If not, what do you need to add or let go of to make sure it is?

Life's Not Fair

I downloaded an episode of Garrison Keillor's *News from Lake Woebegon* and was only half-listening to it as I puffed my way up the big hill near my house. Keillor was wryly talking about the lack of justice in the world: You go out and do all the hard work to put in a garden – tilling, planting, watering, and weeding. Then the deer, which have done nothing to create the abundance, come ambling in and "go at it like old men at a buffet." "Life's not fair," he opined. Then after a long pause he added, "But sometimes there is grace."

I stopped dead. Yes, that is exactly right: a fundamental insult of existence and the wonder which redeems it all. There are the great injustices. Just why does one person deserve to be born in secure affluence when, from day one, another's life is bitter competition with an army of rats for a grain of rice and some fetid water? Each day brings the small moments of unfairness such as someone sweeping in to take the parking space you were patiently waiting to claim. And most of us have known the middle-sized affront of losing out to the merely beautiful, oily, and well-connected. Take them all together and you realize that life is most assuredly not fair. We can strive for justice in our society, but only the most naïve would suggest that rewards neatly match up to deserving. Good people get sick. Drunken fools walk away from the carnage they create on the highway.

But sometimes there is grace. Sometimes we feel the touch of someone who loves us in spite of everything we have done to push them away. Sometimes the sun breaks through the clouds at sunset and bathes the forest path in an amber haze. Sometimes the steak and the Bordeaux go together perfectly. Sometimes, despite all the odds from a horribly stacked deck, the abused child finds a foster family or a loving teacher to heal her fearful spirit. And sometimes, out of nowhere, we have the sense of being enfolded in a love which will not let us go. We have done nothing to deserve it; we just know nothing will separate us from that care – come what may. Then, for a brief moment, perfect justice does not seem to matter quite so much...

"Blessed be the God and Father of our Lord Jesus Christ! By God's great mercy we have been born anew to a living hope through the resurrection of Jesus Christ from the dead and to an inheritance which is imperishable, undefiled, and unfading." – I Peter 1:3.

Jerk

It would be a lot easier if he were a jerk. Over the past few days I have been engaged in an e-mail exchange with someone over the issue of healthcare reform. I will not bore you with the specifics of our positions; suffice it to say that I am interested in a much more radical solution than he is. I think the patient is critically ill and needs extraordinary measures, stat; he fears a governmental cure more than the disease. As I said, I will not bore you with merits of our arguments, because the healthcare debate is not my main focus here.

Rather, think about how you tend to regard those with whom you strongly disagree. Perhaps you are a better person than I, but my great temptation is to attribute either stupidity or malevolence to those who are not instantly persuaded by my brilliant insights and stand unmoved by my eloquence. That is why it would be a lot easier for me (if not as growth producing) if Ed were a certifiable jerk, a callous bore who gazes with unmoved heart on the suffering of the uninsured. Then I would feel less need to take him seriously; after all "what can you expect from that sort of person." But I know that is not so. In point of fact, Ed is a genial spirit, respected in his church, and well known for his compassionate community service. So I dismiss his concerns only by creating a dishonest caricature.

It is extraordinarily painful when folks like Ed stretch us, a bit like having the physical therapist push muscles where they are not accustomed to going. But just as stretching tight muscles makes us stronger and healthier, so we benefit from being taken out of our comfort zone and forced to see the world through the eyes of those with whom we disagree – but still respect.

When we disagree with another our natural impulse is to regard them as an enemy. We have the choice to regard them instead as a holy gift which keeps us intellectually and spiritually alive. I am not so naïve as to deny that there is real evil in the world, but I increasingly believe that the greatest danger is imputing corrupt motives to those who simply see the world a little differently than I do. When we do that we create enemies where there were none, and sow rancor where there could be common cause in facing great challenges.

I make no apology for being passionate in talking healthcare reform with Ed, but I am trying to remember what the writer of Ephesians says about Jesus' work – and thus the spirit I am called to embody as his disciple:

"For He is our peace, who has made us one, and has broken down the dividing wall of hostility, by abolishing in His flesh the law of commandments and ordinances, that He might create in Himself one new man in place of two, so making peace, and might reconcile us both to God in one body through the cross, thereby bringing the hostility to an end." [2:14-16]

Exhibit A

I was not a happy camper. So fresh from thirty minutes of picking up soggy garbage, styrofoam shards, and assorted cans from the church's lawn, I took to Facebook and awarded Clemson my mythical "Iron Pig" award, given to the visiting school whose fans have made the biggest mess on our grounds when they parked here for football. CU was the worst in history. Now, I know that the squalor was not totally created by the Clemson fans (but there were a lot of tiger paws amid the biggest piles of refuse). More than that, I know that there were a lot of great Clemson folks parked in our lot. I know because I had some very friendly conversations with them. But, the fact is, it will be a while before I can hear "Clemson" and not immediately think of beer bottles, cigarette butts, and empty Bojangles bags. It may be from a skewed sample but I have a vivid, personal experience which powerfully colors my perception of South Carolina's land grant school. Just a few folks make a difference.

That is also the case when others form their perception of Christians. You can line up rows of historical facts to prove that Christians were essential in the birth of modern hospitals, colleges, and human service agencies. You can easily demonstrate that the gospel has inspired some of the most sublime music, profound thinking, and revolutionary social movements of past centuries. You can wax eloquent about the wisdom of Jesus. But finally it is how you and I live out the Christian faith that determines whether others give it any credence.

"I don't want that kind of responsibility," you say, "I don't want to be Exhibit A of what a disciple looks like." You don't really have a choice. Like it or not, friends, co-workers, and the guy next to you in the football stands [I blush as I write that one] are going to form their opinion about Jesus in large part by seeing how He affects you. Theology is the schematic drawing; you are the walking, talking demo model on the ground. If the Bible is the recipe, you are what people taste to judge the chef.

Little things matter. So as Paul wrote to Timothy, "Set the believers an example in speech and conduct, in love, in faith, in purity." (1 Timothy 4:12)

Instrument

I almost culled it. After my friend, Dave, died, his widow asked me if I would like to go through several cartons of his books. We all have our addictions, so I said, "Sure." If you have ever done this, you know the drill. You separate the collection into various piles: duplicates of books you already have, immediately identifiable pearls, good books which are more suitable for a library than your personal use, thrift shop fare, and those volumes you are not quite sure where to put. *Make Me an Instrument of Your Peace*, by Kent Nerburn was in that last category. I had never heard of Nerburn. I already had several books on the prayer of St. Francis. It was almost in the thrift shop box when I thought about Dave. I deeply respected him – thoughtful and gentle. If he had this book in his collection, maybe I ought to give it a read. I have been using it for my daily devotions over the past few weeks.

Nerburn's book is a good one. I don't agree with everything he says, but I would certainly recommend it to you as better than 75% of the religious books I have read. The merit of the book, however, is not my point. The only reason I am reading *Make Me an Instrument of Your Peace* is because of Dave's witness. Dave was a living example of the faith which sermons are supposed to inspire. Solely because of who he was, I took a chance on a book he valued enough to put in his library.

Sometimes we are afraid to speak of our religious faith because we are not sure we are smart enough, informed enough, or articulate enough to give a good account of the gospel. But in some ways those concerns are beside the point. If we inspire admiration and trust in others, we do not have to be brilliantly conversant in the intricacies of theology – and if we do not, it makes little difference how sparkling our command of biblical passages might be. The most effective tool of evangelism is our personhood. The most convincing testimony we offer is the one we give in the ordinary moments of life when evangelism is the furthest thing from our minds. Never devalue the impact you can have just by treating others as Christ would. Because they show the Lord alive in your life, small acts of kindness allow others to take the risk of considering Christ.

I Don't Know How You Feel

"We finally got that coon!" The word was as nasty and offensive thirty years ago as it is now. Watching the presidential inauguration, I was transported back to my high school the day after Martin Luther King, Jr. was killed. Some students ran up and down the halls hooting and hollering like we had just won the state football championship. Though not endangered, I remember feeling horribly alone in my grief and appalled by my classmates. Since then I have seldom thought about that day. But when I saw the mall filled with humanity and heard Obama take the oath I realized that, for me, inauguration day distilled into a national repudiation of that horrible day at Travelers Rest High.

But this Bread is not primarily a meditation on the significance of electing our first black president. The pundits and TV crews have run that horse around the track repeatedly over the past few months. No, my point is that even when we share an experience, the meaning is very different for each of us. As moved as I was by those moments on the Mall, they could not mean the same thing to me as to the eighty-year-old black woman who knew the sting of dogs and fire hoses first hand. The children my wife teaches in kindergarten find the Jim Crow South of my youth as incomprehensibly fantastic as a Martian landscape. They might have found the day interesting but hardly as historic as I.

In our sincere efforts to empathize with those in the midst of crisis we sometimes say, "I know just how you feel." But in fact we don't, not really. We do not know what this death, this loss of job, this C on an exam, this disintegration of a cherished marriage means to this particular person in front of us. One of the great gifts we can give to another is to listen while he or she slowly discovers what an event means.

Not imposing our understanding or feelings, we patiently wait until the particular pain of this person becomes clear — both to him or her and to us. Then, perhaps, we have something to offer. That was Jesus' approach.

Each of us has a complex and beautiful story; take the time to learn a little bit of another's this week. More important, learn what the events mean to him or her. You will be enriched and you will be a better conduit of God's care.

Grace Meal

I could hardly get the words out. The Virginia Synod assembly had been emotionally draining; eight years of deferred discussion on sexuality gushed forth onto the assembly floor like water from a long-kinked garden hose. Most spoke honestly, but respectfully, even when disagreeing on where the Holy Spirit is calling the church in matters of sexuality and ministerial practice. But there had also been words whose ignorance was matched only by their wanton cruelty.

These were words designed to dehumanize. Think Selma at the height of the civil rights struggle. I was more than ready to put a period to this chapter and head home.

I had one last task. I'd agreed to distribute the bread at one of the communion stations for the closing worship. The church long ago established that the value of the sacrament does not depend on the worthiness of the one who distributes it. Thank goodness, for I was hardly a paragon of piety as I moved to my place at the rear of worship space: angry at what I had heard, disappointed at my own less that Christlike response to those with whom I disagree, emotionally drained.

But a funny (or rather, grace-filled) thing happened.

242

Looking into the faces of those coming forward to receive a morsel of slightly stale bread from my hand, I saw a longing for wholeness, a hope that maybe at this place we could get beyond the bitterness. Wrinkled, leathery hands of farmers who do not feel qualified to adjudicate esoteric theological debates reached out for a sign that we could still be a community after all the harsh words. Soft suburban hands took and ate from mine, and the memory of floor fights faded. The ice encrusting my heart began to melt.

We were almost done when I looked up and stared into the eyes of a young woman I knew to be a lesbian. For two days she'd sat and heard herself called a "pervert" and an "abomination" by the council president of a Lutheran congregation. She listened to others say they would refuse to be part of a church which welcomed her. She was crying as she paused before me, but I could see these were tears of joy, tears of relief, tears that she was going to hear the words she longed for. And I was so overcome by emotion that I could hardly get them out, "The body...the body of Christ... given for you." There are days you could have my job for the change in your pocket. But at that moment I would not have taken a mountain of diamonds for the privilege of taking, breaking, giving, and speaking.

Some of you reading this meditation disagree most vociferously with me on matters of homosexuality. I do not ask you to pretend otherwise. But I wish with all my heart that you could have seen what those words and a piece bread meant to that young lady. Does her appreciation of the sacramental gift settle all the issues? No, but this I do know: The Church's most critical need is not debate on how God reconciles broken humanity to Godself, but people who are signs of that reconciling Spirit, not explanation but embodiment of God's gracious welcome to all. We will continue to struggle together with how we are to understand sexuality, but I hope we can at least agree that God desires for every single person to hear and receive those healing words, "The body of Christ, given for you."

"Question: How can eating and drinking produce such great effects?" [forgiveness, life, salvation]

"Answer: The eating and drinking do not in themselves produce them, but the words 'for you' and 'for the forgiveness of sins.'" (Luther's *Small Catechism*)

Elwood A. Fox

Walk over to the pedestrian plaza between Newman Library and Squires Student Center on the Virginia Tech campus. Take the little walkway that goes between the bookstore and the Graduate Life Center. Then look down and to the left in the flowerbed. There you will see a simple granite marker inscribed, "Elwood A. Fox, Groundskeeper, August 27, 1987."

I have no idea who Elwood A. Fox was or why someone put a marker in that particular place. But I like to imagine him as someone who loved plants and cared about this campus on which I have served these 25 years. I imagine him showing up without a whole lot of fanfare every day to do whatever needed to be done: mulching in the spring, weeding during summer, pruning in the fall, repairing the ice-damaged trees. While students thoughtlessly threw litter in his flowerbeds and professors, engrossed in discussions of world changing research, passed by his trees, I like to imagine him quietly doing what he did well. Most of all I like to imagine him blushing just a little bit (if that marker was not placed posthumously) when others recognized his dedication.

Imagine a little more with me. Imagine where you would place a marker to recognize someone whose faithfulness has marked your life. Would it be in the middle of the reading group where a teacher made the magic of books come alive for you? Perhaps it would be along your favorite hiking trail where an uncle filled you with wonder at nature's miracles. Maybe it would be over the Burger King fry vat where your first boss taught you about responsibility – and maybe a little about grace when you messed up. Perhaps it would be next to the phone of a colleague who gently absorbs the misdirected abuse of callers angry at a faceless bureaucracy.

Ministry takes many forms and one of Luther's greatest insights is that the baptized have a religious vocation; every occupation offers opportunities to live to the glory of God. There is incredible dignity in every task, if we do it in the right spirit. Most ministers don't wear clerical collars.

Much of your week will be consumed in performing rather mundane tasks; can you see them as places of ministry? Many you meet are struggling with a variety of burdens. For Christ's sake, can you give them at least a verbal marker of appreciation to lighten the load?

Can't Win If You Don't Play

"You can't win if you don't play." There are precious few times you will find me saying anything positive about the state lottery – a cynical, shameful way of trying to shift the burden of funding public goods to those who are very desperate, very bad at math, or usually both – but that promotional slogan does have a sliver of truth. Your odds of dying due to a flesh-eating virus are ten times better than winning Powerball, but you must participate to have even a tiny chance.

That little phrase came to mind last week when I heard someone bemoaning the failings of a certain community of faith (not Luther Memorial, by the way). Don't get me wrong, there are times when a congregation most assuredly does not live up to its calling of being the body of Christ, the embodiment of God's care, concern, and action in the world. We have to be willing to be self-critical if we are not to be complacent. But in this case I knew the person had not invested a great deal in his community. He complains about the lack of friendliness but seldom takes the initiative to reach out to others. He bemoans the lack of programs for his children, but never volunteers to chaperon an outing or makes driving his children to meetings a priority. He laments the lack of energy in worship, but stands silent if he does not care for a hymn. He says the church is "all show and no go" but is dependably on the golf course if there is a choice between that and a service opportunity.

I do not mean to fuss; people make choices for a lot of reasons and part of my job is make the gospel so compelling that they want to be engaged. Still, Christian discipleship is not a spectator sport and the life of faith is no different from mastering a sport, discovering the pleasures of wine, or cultivating an appreciation for a new musical genre – until you invest yourself, you cannot expect to find much which gives pleasure and fulfillment.

You can't win if you don't play. Jesus said it a little differently; He said that we experience God's love in the moment that we give it. We discover purpose in the hour that we invest ourselves in the vision of Christ which can heal our world. We discover a community to help us carry our burdens in the act of being willing to be burdened by one even more heavily laden.

"Play" today. Invest a little time and emotional capital in another person – it's likely to have a lot bigger payoff than the lottery.

Moving My Office

Over the past few weeks, after assuming new duties as pastor of Luther Memorial, I have been moving my office down from the campus center, where it has been for many years, to the first floor of the parish life building – one armful of books at a time. A few observations:

What once seemed essential may not still be important. Wisdom knows when to let go. As I pulled a book off the shelf for transport I sometimes reflected on why it is in my library. At some time I thought this theologian or that novelist offered an essential key to understanding the world in which I was ministering. Many of those books speak to me with as much resonance now as they did the day I bought them, but others feel as dated as the *Saturday Night Fever* soundtrack. The world changes and sometimes we need to let go of our past assumptions.

It is hard work deciding what is really important. In the best of all worlds, I would have taken each book, weighed its worth, and given it a valued place on my new bookshelf – or a less honored place in the recycle bin. In truth, I just wanted to get it done, so it was a lot easier to reach up and squeeze a row of books together and tote them down the steps. On my shelves there is still a lot of chaff among the wheat. Discernment is tough. Whether it is choosing books or choosing how we will spend the day, most of us just follow the path of least resistance. Lent is a great time to take a hard look at how we are spending time, energy, and money.

Some things are useful, and some things are simply precious. A few of the books I carried downstairs have limited practical utility for my daily work; I could easily replace or discard them. But I would never dream of chucking them: the much patched and underlined Bible my Dad gave me during college, the collection of vintage sermons a dear friend gave me, the literature anthology which reminds me of the time I discovered the magic of beautiful words and deep thoughts. It has been quipped that our society often knows the price of everything and the value of nothing. Take time this day to savor something that is not useful – except that it is deeply healing and keeps you connected with what gives you life.

Willfulness and Willingness

Lately I have been reflecting on the delicate balance between willfulness and willingness which we need to strike in our lives. The immediate reason for this pondering is that I am trying decide how hard to drive myself in the gym and on the tennis courts. In the past year I have injured a shoulder and had knee surgery; both have negatively impacted my never championship grade tennis. And the question is, "How hard do I push my almost 60 year old joints in an effort to get back to where I formerly was? How much discomfort do I ignore? How many hard shots do I not chase?"

Wiser (and older friends) have urged me to push hard, not to concede a thing. The minute you stop pushing, they assure me, you are half way to the rocking chair. You just need to exert your will in the face of the pain and the ominous pops of bone rubbing bone. This is the archetypical American attitude – gut it out, strap it up, and get it done, no matter what stands in your way. I have had enough challenges over the years – physical, academic, and professional – to know that sometimes all that separates success and failure is sheer force of will, a decision to persevere against all odds. The habit of sheer willfulness in the face of adversity is usually much to be admired.

But then I have this vision of becoming a walking cliché, the aging Boomer who refuses to believe he cannot do what he did when he was 18. Even if I devoted hours upon hours of effort to rehab (which might raise serious questions about my priorities) the reality is that my body really can't do what it did 40 years ago. Isn't part of maturity being willing to acknowledge, with a certain grace, that life really has changed, that the past is not going to be the future?

The line between determination and delusion, between passionate and pathetic, is often very hard to draw. When do you try to stop trying to shape reality and admit that the new reality is not what you would have chosen – and begin to deal with that?

I share my reflections on this, not because I think you have any great interest in my joints or my tennis, but because the ability to discern between when to be willful and when to be willing to accept change is necessary in many spheres of life.

- When stresses come, a marriage survives only by sheer force of will. But sometimes, despite our best efforts, the relationship dies, and we need to move on or be forever unhappy.
- Achieving our goals almost always demands a certain

stubbornness, but wisdom may lie is recognizing that the goal is not worth achieving in the first place.

• A regular prayer life is not achieved without ruthlessly imposing our will on the schedule and carving out time for devotions, but a deep prayer life is impossible without a willingness to sit in patience until God draws near on a timeline different from our own.

As we seek to find that sweet spot between willfulness and willingness one of the questions we might ask is, "Why? Why is this thing – this sport, this job, this relationship – so important to me?" Sometimes we push too hard and hang on too long because we have too much invested in something which has died. We dare not let go because there will be a gaping hole in our identity and self-concept. Here, if we are willing to hear it, the gospel has a freeing word for us from God. "You are mine; I love you, no matter what." It is easier to make wise decisions on what to pursue and what to release when we realize that, whatever we decide, our whole being is not hanging in the balance.

Communities

"The communities to which I belong are a measure of myself. They tell me what I care about, what I consider important, how I relate to the rest of humanity. Take an inventory of the groups to which you belong and you learn a great deal about yourself that no psychologist can tell you."

(Joan Chittister, *Listen With the Heart: Sacred Moments in Everyday Life*)

If you are ready for an enlightening experience, try Joan Chittister's suggestion right now. Take out a sheet of paper and start making a list.

To what organizations do you give money (that makes you a member); to what are they dedicated? To what things do you buy season tickets, have a subscription, or pay dues? Do those communities of shared interest make the world a better place? Do they enrich your mind and spirit? Are they centered on something that matters in the great scheme of things – or just in amusing the members? Do they expand your vision or cause you to bunker down complaining about "them"? Is the value they give the world commensurate with what you pay?

Pull out your calendar. What are the regular meetings and gatherings of like-minded people, the ones you seldom miss? Do the people with whom you share that time reflect the sacrificial love of Christ? Can you imagine Jesus applauding the values on display in the jokes, the economics, and the attitudes of those you meet at those gatherings? Is the time well spent or do you often think, "That's an hour I'll never have back." What draws people together into those communities of common purpose; would you say it is hope or fear?

Someone once observed that life is what happens while you are doing something else. In like manner, spiritual formation is what takes place while you spend your time and financial resources. Our communities help define who we are and how others will see us. If we habitually give ourselves to the trivial, the selfish, and the mean-spirited we will have a hard time becoming the fully formed human beings God longs for us to become, reflecting the image of Christ. Pay attention to your communities; they tell you who you are and who you are becoming.

Cloud of Witnesses

"Since we are surrounded by so great a cloud of witnesses, let us also lay aside every weight and sin which clings so closely, and run with perseverance the race which is set before us…"

I am convinced that the best sermons (and meditations) are found at the intersection of the biblical witness and life's most intense experiences. So I hope you will indulge me if I use this "bread" to reflect on how the above words from Hebrews came alive for me in the days of my mother's recent illness and death.

Of course these were days of thankful reflection on the race my mother had run, the life she had lived in God's service. But such thoughts almost immediately took me to the lives which formed Mom: her gentle father and resolute mother, the hymn writers whose words permeated her soul, the innumerable teachers, coworkers, and friends who molded my mother – and thus me. One of the most absurd and pernicious myths in our world is the idea of the "self-made man," a concept both myopic and arrogant. In truth, there is no such thing. We are all products of the people who give us their wisdom and care. When we pretend otherwise we set ourselves up for loneliness and miss out on the life-giving opportunity to say "thank you" to those who have invested themselves in us.

We usually think of the "cloud of witnesses" in the same way as does the writer of Hebrews, as the saints who have lived and died before us. But in these last weeks I have been keenly aware of how the cloud of witnesses can be very much alive. I am profoundly grateful to the nurses who treated my mother with infinite gentleness during her last journey, the pair of old men who shoveled my Dad's driveway after one of South Carolina's rare snow storms (I am so glad we did not add another funeral to the queue that day), and my brother, whose demeanor and words at Mom's funeral embodied the graciousness of Christ. We call them a "cloud of witnesses" because such persons are living testimonies to the Love which enfolds us in every moment of existence. As clouds bring water in the midst of drought, so such people refresh us when our spirits are parched and our reserves are exhausted.

I often end my "breads" with an exhortation. This time I end it with an affirmation: In the past week I have experienced the care of God and the communion of saints. In thanksgiving I bear witness to you that I have been surrounded by that cloud of witnesses and found the love of God to be as real as the deli-trays, calls, cards, words of scripture, funeral liturgy, and hundreds of acts of kindness which buoyed me during this time of sadness. Much of that care was offered by those reading these words. Thank you.

Unholy Juxtaposition

The worship service began with the minister making it clear that though the Lord's Supper would be celebrated, the table was not open to all in attendance. Those who were not members of his particular Christian tribe (we will omit the name here) were expected to remain in their seats during the distribution. Having made that necessary announcement he invited the congregation to join in the gathering hymn:

One bread, one body, one Lord of all;
One cup of blessing which we bless,
And we, though many throughout the earth,
We are one body in this one Lord.

Some stories don't need much commentary, the point as subtle as a brick in the face, but let me offer just a bit. It is easy to shake our heads at the absurdity of this situation, to "tut-tut" at the blatant hypocrisy on display. "Those people," we smugly think, "just don't get what it means to follow the Lord of love." But though this may be a particularly egregious example of a mixed message, it is hardly unique. I shudder to think how many times a day I, who say I am a follower of Jesus, belie that confession. I know very well that Jesus calls me to be patient in adversity, gentle when falsely accused, and generous when proven right. In reality it does not take much to make me impatient, testy, and sarcastic – for example, one political ad.

If someone were watching me closely, I am sure she could cite a juxtaposition of word and action every bit as excruciating as the one with which I opened this reflection. And that's the point; people ARE watching us closely. Precious few folks know or care about how pure our theology is, but they do care about our congruence, how closely our lives and our confession match up. We can assert that God is love until we are out of breath, but if others do not see it in our daily actions they will never believe it.

St. Francis famously prayed, "Lord, make me an instrument of Your peace." As a devotional exercise, let me suggest that you pray that tomorrow morning and attend to making it a reality in all that you do throughout the day.

Cost/ Benefit

Today I am thinking about cost/benefit. Earlier this week I met with a consultant to talk about ways to improve the energy efficiency of our house. If you have ever done this, you know that the question is not whether there are things you can do (there always are), but whether it is worth doing them. Seal the edges of the attic? Wrap the water heater and the lines? Put insulation rolls between the joists? Put in LED bulbs everywhere you can? Seal off the fireplace? You can trim a little off the gas bill, but at what up-front cost? Do you change out the old windows for triple thickness thermopanes if the breakeven point is 30 years out?

And the question is even more complex than that. Even if the pay off is not immediate savings, there are moral, non-economic reasons for doing good. Perhaps you do some things just because, on principle, you want to reduce your carbon footprint or do your little bit to reduce destruction of the planet.

Everything has a cost, and the question is whether we want something badly enough to pay the freight. That is true in weatherizing your home, and it is true in managing your emotions.

In *Wishful Thinking*, Frederick Buechner writes, "Of the Seven Deadly Sins, anger is possibly the most fun. To lick your wounds, to smack your lips over grievances long past, to roll over your tongue the prospect of bitter confrontations still to come, to savor to the last toothsome morsel both pain you are given and the pain you are giving back – in many way it is a feast fit for a king. The chief drawback is that what you are wolfing down is yourself. The skeleton at the feast is you."

At some point we need to phrase the question as baldly as we can: "Is my anger in this situation worth it? Who is really being harmed when I stay in a stew over everything from unsynchronized traffic lights to those idiot pundits on TV, to my son's unwillingness to dump his loser girlfriend? Is the pleasure I get from feeling smug and superior worth what it is costing me?"

We can ask the cost/benefit question purely out of enlightened self-interest. There is plenty of research to suggest that reducing chronic rage improves our general health. But Christians have a special mandate to learn how to let little things – and the things we cannot control – go. As Jesus' disciples, we try to live in the world as He did, aware of what is wrong but not dominated by it. Our Lord was often passionate, but never bitter. He saw the ugliness of the world with more clarity than we do, but gave His energy to transformation rather than pointless resentment.

We only have a certain amount of psychic energy to spend each day. Where are you spending yours? Is the benefit worth what it's costing you?

Tennis Group

It would embarrass them to read this, but some of the people I most admire are in my tennis group. With a colleague's retirement, I've just become the longest serving campus minister at Virginia Tech, but at 56 I am a mere babe compared to virtually all of the guys and gals in that tennis group. Forget age; they are some of the most alive people I know. I want to be like them when I grow up.

Of course, I admire anybody who is still playing tennis (and pretty good tennis at that) into his eighties – you have to get points for pure survival. Yet that's not what is most amazing about these folks. I look forward to talking current cinema and books with one of them. Another gives untold hours cutting wood for the poor. Another burns with a passion for social justice while maintaining an incredibly gentle spirit. Yet another pushes me to live the gracious theology I espouse. When injury or chronic illness makes one unable – if the truth be brutally told – to hold up his end on the court, the group always finds a way to carry him: shots not hit to a wide open court, an occasional volley (deliberately?) dumped in the net, a serve hit at half speed. In every way my tennis friends are not just playing out the string. They grow and give of themselves each day. Someone has said, "If you are not busy getting born you are busy dying." My friends are perpetually pregnant.

The apostle Paul reminds us that growth in Christ is not a once and done affair. Near the end of his life he wrote, "Not that I have already obtained all this, or have already been made perfect, but I press on to take hold of that for which Christ Jesus took hold of me. Brothers, I do not consider myself yet to have taken hold of it. But one thing I do: Forgetting what is behind and straining toward what is ahead, I press on toward the goal to win the prize for which God has called me heavenward in Christ Jesus."

How might you be busy getting born this week?

Marion's Mom

She was sitting on the other side of the dining room, and I decided to go over and speak to her. My father lives in his own home in a retirement community. However, the food served to those who live in the assisted living apartments is excellent, so when I visit him we often eat a meal at the community center. As we finished our meal, I noticed Marion's mother. Marion is one of my oldest friends from college, and I thought it would be nice to greet his mom.

I introduced myself and reminded her who I am. She smiled, yet the vacant look in her eyes told me that each day Alzheimer's claims a few more precious connections in her brain. I think she remembered me, remembered how close Marion and I were at Furman. Yet twice in a single minute she asked the same question, "Now where are you living these days?" We chatted for a bit, and I told her to give Marion my regards. Walking back to my Dad I was pretty sure she had already forgotten our conversation and that Marion would never hear my greetings.

"Well, that was pretty useless," I thought. In retrospect I am not so sure. We usually value deeds based solely on tangible results: Did my actions make a difference? Did they substantively change anything? By such a standard, speaking to that dear woman was pretty pointless. I certainly did not alter her dementia, and I am not sure I even gave her more than a very fleeting moment of happiness. My lasting impact on her was like a knife blade cutting through water, gone the moment it passes. You may say that I can never know what impact our conversation had, that maybe she remembers more than I think she does. That is true and I certainly hope our brief talk brightened her day.

Yet whether it did or did not something important happened, not necessarily to her, but to me. Much of life is beyond our control. If we only invest in people and things we can be guaranteed of changing, we become increasingly turned in on ourselves. Small acts of compassion, done for their own sake, are for the soul what stretching is for our bodies, a discipline which keeps us flexible and ready to embrace life. Marion's mother did not particularly need my greeting, but I needed to speak to her. I needed to experience our common humanity. I needed to be reminded that, even when our actions seem to change very little, showing love is valuable because it reflects how God deals with our broken creation and makes us partners in the healing.

Next time you are tempted to flee from a death bed because you cannot stop a friend's pain, don't. When you are ready to give up on a child who repeatedly has broken your heart, don't. When you are tempted to abandon politics to the shrill and the selfish because it seems so futile to care, don't. Love is sometimes just about showing up, about staying engaged – for the sake of others, to be sure, but also for our own spiritual health.

Flashlight Hammer

Do you ever feel like you're a flashlight trying to drive a nail? By that I mean do you sometimes feel that your skills and the demands of your day are mismatched? Few things are more spiritually draining than spending a lot of energy on things for which we have neither passion nor ability. If you meet people well, but spend your day in a cubicle doing data analysis, you are likely to be very dissatisfied. Conversely, if your idea of hell is "grip and grin" small talk at a party you will probably hate a job that is all about networking and relationships. It's not a matter of one personality or set of gifts being better than another. The issue is whether we think our abilities and passions match up well with what we are asked to do. We want to make a contribution; when we swim too long against the stream, depression and a feeling of failure often follow.

Of course we cannot spend our days doing only what is deeply meaningful and comfortable – there is a reason they call it work. But neither should we assume that the best we can hope for is grinding away at something we hate. God wants more for us than that.

When I start getting that square peg in a round hole feeling, I examine my call. No, I don't mean I wonder whether I ought to be a pastor at Luther Memorial (at least not most days). Rather, I take time to reflect on whether the gifts I have are being best used to serve God in this place. Are there challenges I need to take up because I am well-suited for them? Are there tasks I need to pass on to someone else because he or she will do them better?

Calling is not just for clergy. In I Corinthians 12 the apostle, Paul, reminds his readers that all Christians share one call (to glorify God), but each of them has unique gifts to live out that call. Each of you reading this devotion has gifts and cultivated skills which God needs. So two questions:

Have you thought about what your gifts are?

Are you using those gifts well – or are you a flashlight driving a nail?

If you answered "no" to either question, I invite you think some more about your calling. God desires our calls to be sources of joy and satisfaction. When they are not, something is out of whack.

Results

"Your system is perfectly designed to yield the results you are getting."(management saying)

"In the same way, every good tree bears good fruit, but the bad tree bears bad fruit. A good tree cannot bear bad fruit, nor can a bad tree bear good fruit." (Matthew 7:17-18)

One of the gifts of the summer, at least for those of us whose lives are driven by the academic calendar, is the opportunity to step away from the routine to relax, retool, reenergize, and reflect on the bigger picture. For me part of that is plowing through the stack of professional books I backlogged during the school year. In one of those books I ran across the first quotation. I can't tell you where it originally came from (the author did not provide a citation), but I have been chewing on it for several weeks. Though the saying primarily pertains to business analysis, it strikes me as an interesting way to think about a life, to engage in that personal reflection which the summer invites.

So what results are you getting these days? Are you excited about the way you spend your days? Does it give you fulfillment? How well are you balancing the various elements of life such as work, family, personal growth, and relaxation? Are your relationships in good repair or are some fraying from abuse or neglect? In short, is your life one you can be proud of, one which gives you joy, and on balance, charges your battery more than depletes it?

Just as important as thinking about your results is thinking about what is causing them. Are your priorities in order? Are you actually spending time, money, and energy on the things you tell yourself you value most? It's easy for the system to get out of whack, for your life to become a Rube Goldberg machine of on-the-fly adaptations which lacks a unifying vision. Do you know what you want from your life?

Long ago Jesus made essentially the same point as the management guru. A life that is properly focused on what is most important produces that which is deeply fulfilling. Conversely, a nagging sense that something is wrong should be a tip off that we need to check out our basic values, assumptions, and daily choices. We are meant to be lusciously fruitful. God desires that our lives be filled with joy and fulfillment; is yours? What change might you make to your "system" this week?

Renate's Choice

Sophie's Choice, a film starring Meryl Streep and adapted from William Styron's powerful novel, pivots on the decision a mother is forced to make at Auschwitz. Arriving at the death camp, Sophie is told by a Nazi officer that she can save only one of her two children. She must pick one for execution. If she refuses to pick, both will die. That scene is one of the most excruciating I have ever watched in a theater. But that was fiction painted on a background of history.

Let me tell you about Renate's choice. During campus ministry's recent spring break trip to Germany we met her. Renate spoke with our group in Wittenberg to give us a sense of what it was like to be a Christian in the GDR (East Germany) during the Cold War. She did not tell of dramatic oppression, á la Sophie. The pressures, she said, were much more subtle. You could be a Christian; there would just be costs to pay – promotions denied, educational hopes blocked, applications for better housing lost. In her case it came to a head over a divorce. After years of marriage she discovered her husband had been unfaithful. Because he had spent much of their married life working far from her and the children, she assumed little would change; she would continue to have the responsibility of raising her children alone. Then her husband suggested he wanted custody. "What are you thinking," he taunted, "what will you say when the judge asks you if you intend to raise the children in your faith? Will you lie? Do you think they will give you the children then?"

Your children or your faith? What would you have done? Cling to the fruit of your loins or to the main thing that gives you hope in a grey world? Renate spoke with tears in her eyes as she told about her anguish in contemplating that court room scene, but I must admit that I did not hear everything she said because I was still pondering that choice. What would it be like for confession of the faith to be more than a slightly unfashionable intellectual choice? What would I do if it became a matter of risking what I love most in the world?

Every culture presents its own challenges to the life of faith. I could even argue (as I have heard citizens of the GDR do) that the affluence and materialism of the USA are more corrosive of discipleship than communist oppression ever was. We don't need to play "my struggle is worse than yours." The point is that Scripture is very clear about the cost of faithfulness and the inevitability that following Jesus will mean often swimming against the stream. This day, be thankful that you do not have to make a choice akin to Sophie's or Renate's. But also choose to follow the way of Jesus in all the little encounters you have.

And in case you're interested, Renate ultimately did not have to make the choice. Her husband withdrew his challenge, which she regards as an answer to prayer…but that is another story.

Zucchini

To illustrate the vibrant productivity of the gospel word Jesus told several stories about wheat. Let me humbly suggest that he missed it – he should have used zucchini. At our house, we are way beyond grilled with balsamic vinegar, sautéed with onions, zucchini bread, and assorted squash casseroles. How about a little zucchini sorbet or squash mousse? Please don't be alarmed if your dog starts barking at 3:00 a.m.; it's just me leaving a plastic bag of squash on your doorstep. Yes, our garden has flourished. In words from the parable of the sower, "some seed fell into good soil and grew, and yielded a hundredfold." Two observations:

It is wonderful when your biggest problem is how to dispose of abundance. I make jokes about being sick unto death of squash, but in fact many in our world are simply sick unto death. War, famine, drought, and corruption conspire in many places to make those big, tough zucchini which I carelessly throw into the bushes look like a family feast for a week. The electronic gizmo which is so "yesterday" for you will still be a dream for most of the world's population ten years from now. If you are reading this online, you own a computer; by definition you have been extravagantly blessed. How can your abundance bless others?

One of life's greatest joys is sharing. As I noted in an earlier Bread for the Journey, our garden is totally Gail's – she planted it, she weeds it, she picks it – I just show up to enjoy the harvest. No doubt she enjoys eating the beans, squash, and other veggies, but what Gail obviously enjoys the most about her garden is sharing what comes from it. Her face lights up when she starts planning how we will share the wealth. All too often we unconsciously think that the great goal is accumulating as much as we can for ourselves; I can attest that there is no great joy in having zucchini coming out of your ears. A squash glut just illustrates a much broader truth: the only way to find continuing joy in abundance is to pass it on. How much joy are you getting from a closet full of shoes or a shelf of once read books? So treat yourself –

share your time, your money, or your gifts with someone this week.

The Right Gift

I had been looking forward to this evening for several weeks. One of my closest friends from seminary and his wife were going to be at our home for dinner. Because of where they live, I have often enjoyed their hospitality when traveling on business, but she had never been in our home. After some thought Gail and I planned a Low Country Boil – shrimp, sausage, corn, and potatoes boiled together in Old Bay and dumped in the center of a table covered with newspapers – a South Carolina sacrament so good that it will curl your toes.

As we munched on the appetizer and sipped a cool beverage I told them about the coming attraction. "That sounds great," she said, "but I won't be eating it – I'm a vegetarian." She said it with gentleness and absolutely no edge in her voice, but we felt terrible. She assured us she would be just fine with the hummus, vegetables, green salad, fruit salad, and lemon ice cream we also had on the menu. Still, we are good cooks (the pastor said rather immodestly); we could just as easily have prepared a delicious vegetarian meal. We were so eager to bring out our best that we never thought about asking whether it would be suitable.

There is a minor parable in this little story. As we deal with others, one of our first duties is to be attuned to what they want from us. We can be so eager to give and please that we forget to discern what is most needed and appropriate. More than what we do for folks, the greatest gift we offer people is to take time to know them, so that it is their real need which is being met, rather than our need to be needed. Sometimes we have a wonderful gift to offer another, but it is not the right time or place to offer it. Discernment, patience, and restraint are often as important as generosity of spirit in giving the right gift at the right time.

Prayer Infirmary

Take route 11 west out of Dublin and just before you enter Pulaski you will come to a old cinderblock building which has been painted pink and bears the sign, "Prayer Infirmary." Maybe it used to be an old gas station or country store, but I am guessing that these days a small church meets there, a little fellowship which understands praying for those in need to be a big part of its ministry.

I would never disparage that small community of faith or make fun of its ministry, but I confess that the sign always prompts a little whimsy as I pass it. I imagine a scene straight out of ER, complete with tubes, gurneys, and IV bags:

Pulse?

Faint and tacky. Respiration shallow – we're losing this prayer, doctor.

What happened?

He was out of shape and then got hit by a major crisis – heart just exploded under the stress.

Okay, we gotta get this prayer stabilized and buy some time…Major infusion of scripture and start a central line of the sacraments…. Come on don't give up; don't die on me now… Bag him…and start regular petitions. We're not gonna lose this one.

Yes, I'll admit I have a weird sense of humor, but sometimes our prayer life could use a checkup. Our spirituality, like our bodies, can get sick or flabby. Our praying becomes purely rote. Our prayers get ingrown to the point that all we are doing is creating a big shopping list for God to fill. Instead of making space in our busy day for prayer, we let it slip into whatever leftover time might be available just before we fall asleep in front of the ball game. Like a once precious friendship which we have allowed to languish we discover our relationship to God is more memory than present reality. It'd be great if we could take our prayer life to the infirmary.

As anyone who has ever lost weight or laboriously gotten into shape can tell you, getting healthy is seldom about big, dramatic actions. It's about little things done dutifully and daily: a few more veggies, a few less Doritos, and a little more time carved out for exercise. So right now, take your prayer life to a mental infirmary; give it a quick workup. What little thing can you do – this week, this month – to renew your spiritual life and your relationship to God?

Pillars and Perspective

My summer reading list included two massive tomes by Ken Follett, *The Pillars of the Earth* and *World Without End*. For two thousand pages I was immersed in the world of medieval England, an age of both grandeur and horror. This was a time when the great gothic cathedrals were built and life for the common folk was usually, in the words of Thomas Hobbes, "poor, brutish, nasty, and short." I am a fairly slow reader, so I do not often choose such big books. The slower pace of summer allowed me to linger in another era.

One of the gifts of a well-researched, epic novel is perspective. Do you despair that the rich crush the poor in our land?

There was a time when serfs cowered before their Lords and rape was the right of a knight. Does the church seem to be a cipher for one political ideology or another? Kings used to appoint bishops, cardinals raised armies, and a monastery was often the richest landowner (and slumlord) in town. And if human suffering seems massive in our day, consider what it must have been like to live in the time of the Black Plague, when whole towns simply ceased to exist.

We are about to enter the season of hysterical hyperbole (if we are not already in it). Political campaigns will imply that opposing candidates are demon spawn, the other party the minions of Satan, and governance by the wrong party the first step to the apocalypse. Make no mistake – there are important choices to be made. Persons of faith should weigh very carefully how confessing discipleship to the Lord of compassion, nonviolence, and justice might impact their vote.

But there is a great difference between prayerful discernment of alternatives and yielding to vicious idolatry. For it is idolatrous – literally setting up a false god – to suggest that any political or economic program is the solution to the brokenness of our world. It is wicked to yield to hatred of another, as benighted as you may think he is. It is foolish to lose a sense of perspective and forget that generations rise and fall, governments wax and wane.

Anyone who knows me well knows that I have fairly strong political opinions, usually expressed in unequivocal dogmatism. So this Bread is written first and foremost to myself, as we enter into a time of temptation, a season when we easily become so passionate in invoking Jesus that we forget His spirit. Just because we are entering a political campaign we do not have an exemption from Jesus' command,

"Be merciful as your Father in heaven is merciful."

Our country needs for Christians to thirst for justice and righteousness, but even more it needs for us to bring the same passion for reconciliation which our Lord taught and modeled.

Farewell to Jennifer

Last Sunday we bid farewell to Jennifer. There was great weeping and gnashing of teeth, particularly in the choir, where her beautiful voice has anchored the sopranos for a few years. Standing behind the altar, as my colleague Joanna conducted the brief Order for Farewell and Godspeed, I felt the intimations of a familiar nightmare. The dark fantasy which haunts most campus pastors each fall is that this is the year nobody shows up. That students leave is a given – as graduates, transfers, or drop outs, they inevitably leave – but maybe this is the year that no first year students replenish the community. You work so hard to know students. You get close to them. Then they leave. It is hard to imagine starting over again, building relationships and developing that emotional intimacy anew.

How does a congregation deal with the loss of a Jennifer or a campus ministry with the graduation of its leadership? With thanksgiving and hope. Rather than focusing on what has been lost we do well to give thanks for gifts freely offered, the miracles of daily grace which we have received from those who depart. At the same time we remember that God is faithful; God lifts up new people who enrich our lives and ministry. It is not that someone new comes along to simply fill a slot (as if anyone could); it's much more exciting than that. We never know what new gifts will be added to the mix, how a new relationship will change our perspective or ministry.

Of course, it is the same on the personal level. We come to know and love people, jobs, and places – and then they are taken from us. The challenge is to avoid getting stuck pining for what will never return. Surely we mourn; that is the price we pay for love. But if we are wise we then focus our thoughts on thankfully savoring what we have received and opening ourselves to the next chapter unfolding in the shadow of what we have lost.

Dietrich Bonhoeffer put it well, "I believe that God can and will bring good out of all things, even the most evil…I believe that in any trial God will give us as much power to resist as we need. But in order that we rely on him alone and not on ourselves, he does not give it ahead of time. Such faith must overcome all anxiety about the future."

Thank you Jennifer for what you gave to this congregation. I can hardly wait to see how you will bless another community – and what unexpected gifts God has in store for Luther Memorial.

King Lear

First a commercial: If you have not been to the Blackfriars Playhouse in Staunton, Virginia, http://www.americanshakespearecenter.com/, for a production of Shakespeare, you are depriving yourself of creative, world class productions of the Bard (and the chance to eat at some killer restaurants, too). Now back to our regularly scheduled Bread for the Journey…

For me the beginning of August means two things are drawing near: a wedding anniversary and the start of Fall semester. To celebrate the former and savor one last fling before the latter, Gail and I treated ourselves to a *King Lear* getaway. I love live theater, but I'd never seen a production of Shakespeare's most majestic and agonizing play. This was a real treat. I do not know how you were taught *King Lear*, but I came to the production regarding Goneril and Regan (Lear's eldest daughters) as cardboard villains, no more complex than the wicked step-sisters in Cinderella. When you read the play they come off (or they did to me) as merely conniving daughters who abuse and betray their father. Certainly, they do heinous things, but the gift of live performance is nuance. The gestures, inflection, and pacing of talented actresses made the sister's duplicity comprehensible, even perversely reasonable.

My primary intention is not to give you a theater review but to share an insight which the production prompted: nobody is as uncomplicated as we like to pretend. Something within us longs for simplicity. Maybe it is the undeniable fact that life usually presents us with less than ideal choices, that each day we feel forced to choose the lesser of two evils and make grudging compromises. Whatever the reason, we tend to seek simplicity as a thirsty woman longs for water. We like to split the world into black hats and white hats, heroes and cads; the saintly, sage politicians who share our enlightened perspective on the world and the incompetent tyrants who must be stopped.

It's seldom that simple. To be sure there is genuine evil in the world, and we should name it, confront it, and work against it when we can. But more often, in my experience, what I am tempted to call evil is fear, ignorance, misperception, and deep woundedness. Unless we at least consider the possibility that the other's actions are not the result of malevolence but a different understanding of the situation, we will always be boxing with shadows and raising the emotional ante to destructive levels.

When Jesus met Zacchaeus he could have dismissed him as simply a crooked tax collector. Instead Jesus chose to understand him as a man literally up a tree spiritually and unable to find a gracious way down. Looking a little deeper into Zacchaeus' pain Jesus healed a breach and increased justice in Jericho. Is there an "evil" person in your world on whom you might look with greater compassionate understanding and forbearance this week?

Gail's Garden

I figure the cost is $10.00 per tomato or zucchini and dropping daily. Gail and her friend, Karen, have a garden in Karen's backyard, and it is looking fine. If the thing produces to its potential, by mid-October we should recoup the cost of seed, fertilizer, bedding plants, stakes, tarps, mulch, fencing, and having the plot tilled. Almost every day Gail goes over there to water and pull weeds, and it's the weed pulling I want you to think about.

Why do you pull weeds? It's hot, boring, often back-breaking work. Pulling a weed does not create a bean plant or tomatillo. You can pull weeds until you have a huge pile and that won't put a single hot pepper into the salsa. You know the answer; this isn't a trick question. You pull weeds to create space for what you value. You pull weeds to free up nutrients for the good stuff. Left to itself a garden quickly gets overgrown and choked by grasses which rob you of what you want.

Now think of basic spiritual disciplines as weeding your

garden. Folks have asked me, "If I want to be a Christian, is it absolutely necessary to go to church every week, to pray daily, to read my Bible regularly?" That puts the question the wrong way. It's like asking if you absolutely have to weed the garden. In both cases the answer is, "No" – but you will soon have a plot or a Christian life that is overgrown, and neither will be terribly productive. The reality is that lives are at least as likely as garden plots to get filled up with stuff which is ugly and life-sapping. Spiritual disciplines such as worship, prayer, and study are ways we hack away the mess and carve out some space in our days and in our inner life for the Holy Spirit to renew and transform us.

Make no mistake, we Lutherans have basically got the main thing right: God's love comes to us unconditionally, abundantly, and totally unmerited. Grace showers us like a refreshing summer rain on a parched garden. It's just that failure to receive that love in prayer and worship effectively puts a big tent over the field.

Something Rotten

What do a Broadway show and Rudy Giuliani have in common? Stay with me for a minute. I recently saw *Something Rotten*; that's not a judgment, it's the title of a musical playing in New York City. Set in Shakespearean England, the play's premise is that an aspiring young playwright is searching for the next big thing. He consults a soothsayer, who tells him the next big thing will be something called "a musical," a theatrical experience where the dialogue suddenly stops and characters break into song. The young man is incredulous, and becomes increasingly so when the soothsayer starts talking about dance breaks and production numbers. Of course, it's one big inside joke, a musical about all the tropes of musicals. The serious point (if there is one) is that there was a time before musicals. This art form which we take for granted, and many love, was once strange and brand new.

The day after I saw *Something Rotten* former New York City mayor Rudolph Giuliani was in the news, roundly condemning all Arabs and Muslims as a danger to America. I wondered what he would say to someone asserting that all Italians are filthy criminals, that they refuse to learn English and are a dishonest, violent people who harbor Mafioso thugs, that their immigration to American threatens to water down the pure Anglo-Saxon bloodlines, that they are a political danger because they owe allegiance to a foreign sovereign (the Pope)…Wait, actually that's exactly what Nativists said when waves of Italian immigrants hit Ellis Island in the late 19th Century. The irony of a Guiliani in New York City spouting such vitriol would be hilarious if the blindness were not so sad and the potential consequences so dire. I guess all it takes to get your xenophobe card is a few generations of assimilation, the decades needed to move from feeling like an outsider to joining those who revile "them."

Something Rotten and Rudy Giuliani, in their own ways, remind us how hard it is to envision and accept change to what we take to be the constants of our lives. We instinctively react to changes with disbelief, resistance, fear, and anger. But that is finally a losing proposition. The world does change, with or without our consent, and our task is not to stand like guards at the fortress of the past but to be scouts which discern new possibilities on the horizon. The world is too dangerous, the challenges too complex for us to think scapegoating is an effective strategy. More than that, it is antithetical to the gospel, assuming we care about that…

274

Convergence

This morning two things converged in my consciousness. The first was a podcast featuring author Walter Mosley. He began a story he was telling on *The Moth* (themoth.org) by saying, "I am absolutely convinced at this point in my life, in my 60th year, that the older you are the more you live in the past." He goes on to say that we are all moving through the decades, but we keep being driven by ideas and perceptions which are no longer true; our present keeps being filtered, influenced, and perhaps contaminated by phantoms from our past. When I got to the office there was a newsletter from my healthcare provider offering me ten strategies for coping with stress. Number four: Focus on the present moment, not the past or the future.

Permit me two quick observations about this convergence, one on the process and the other on the content. I am not one of those folks who sits down with a Bible, randomly opens it, plops his finger down, and assumes that whatever it hits is his personal text message from God, his marching orders for the day. But I am just mystical enough to believe that if we pay attention we sometimes get the word we need in our daily experiences. The voice of God may well sound in a devotional text, but sometimes it is in children's laughter in the park, a friend's observation, a character's speech in a novel, or the podcast we are listening to on our daily walk. The point is to be paying attention, to notice when we seem to be hearing the same thing in different voices.

The word I got today was apropos for me, and I suspect it might be for you, too. I began the week with a vague sense of being overwhelmed; the specifics are not important. I realized that a big part of my uneasiness was the weight of some past experiences and the felt need to solve several months' demands in a few days. I needed to let go of the past and ration the future. That is not just pop psychology; it is at the heart of what it means to be people of grace. If we truly believe we are loved "as is," we are free from the need to be super achievers. If we can accept that forgiveness is real, we need not let the past enslave us.

I don't know if my convergence is exactly the word you need to hear today, but I am guessing – if you pay attention – you can indeed discern one that is.

My friend, Frank Honeycutt, puts it this way, "These spiritual disciplines are not the things we do to get God to love us more than God already does; these are things we do that give Jesus room to work in our lives."

Confronting Evil

Few things are harder than knowing when to confront evil and when to deny it the oxygen of being taken seriously. This Saturday there will be an Alt-Right rally in Charlottesville which will bring together true-believer haters and some folks who probably don't know the history of when and why all those statues of Confederate soldiers were erected (If you don't, stop reading, go to the wonderful podcast *Backstory*, and click on "Contested Landscape: The Battle Over Confederate Monuments," http://backstoryradio.org/episodes). My bishop and other religious leaders will also be there at a different rally, as a silent witness against the divisiveness. I could not be prouder of them. But I will not be there – and it is not for the noblest of reasons. I just think being ignored is more painful to bigots than being actively confronted.

Long ago when I was in grad school at LSU, David Duke, the blow-dried Klansman, was a regular feature on our campus. Duke was not the stereotypical bigot – Brooks Brothers suits and PR smarts instead of hogwashers and a plug of Redman. He and his crew spouted their bile on the drill field, and it being the early 70's in south Louisiana, he could gather a few like-minded people to listen. The vast majority of students, however, ignored him and you could tell it drove his cadre nuts. They were all set to rumble; being dismissed as merely ignorant, silly, and irrelevant took the air out of their bombast. Ever since then my default has been to deny such idiocy the dignity of acting as though it needs to be rebutted. The Alt-Right deserves the same intellectual consideration that you would give astrology in a science class or leeches in a hospital.

As I said, it is hard to know when we need to be more active in confronting hatred. When the vulnerable are in direct danger we cannot simply ignore the ignorance. Whatever our strategy there should never be any doubt about where we stand. So let me be clear: The Alt-Right rally in Charlottesville is not about politics; it is the cynical, wicked manipulation of fear and resentment.

I will be praying for the folks who have made a different choice than I regarding the best way to respond to this hatred. I affirm their conviction and their witness. I invite you to stand for reconciliation in whatever way seems best to you. Pray for those who are being manipulated – and for those who are doing the manipulating. If we are trying to follow Jesus, we don't get to exclude anyone from our care.

Calling in Daily Life

I have no idea whether he would call himself a Christian, but his actions illustrate living out a disciple's calling. Few things are more difficult than working with families as they deal with end of life issues for a loved one. Emotions are fragile. The choices are seldom black and white. Exhausted bodies and minds, pushed to their limits by long hours of worry, strain to do the right thing when nothing can really be "right." It must be very hard to be a doctor in those moments.

I have observed a lot of these conversations over the years. Some doctors march in and dispassionately lay out the options like a stockbroker offering the cost/benefit analysis of buying a new public offering – and make their exit as quickly as possible. He didn't. He began with their pain, acknowledging how wrenching it is to sit in their chairs. Then, with infinite patience, he shared some possible courses of action and the probable consequences. More than that, he offered himself as one who would honor the difficulty of their decisions and work to ease the pain of both patient and family. Maybe he would not say it this way, but from where I sat he was not just doing a good job; he was offering a ministry.

One of Martin Luther's great theological contributions is his bold assertion that every work, from the most obviously religious to the most socially lowly, can be a place where the holy breaks though into the world. It is not just preachers who have a calling; every Christian has the privilege of serving the gospel through the mundane tasks of a typical day. There are few actions which cannot be imbued with deep dignity if done to reflect love of God and neighbor.

Think about the most difficult or unpleasant task on your agenda today. How can you make it a moment when the love of Christ is shown to those around you? How can you live out your baptismal calling to be a minister in the service of Jesus Christ?

Dead Lines

If you have recently passed by Luther Memorial's property you know we are in the middle of a massive project to solve water infiltration issues in the main building's foundation. We are excavating all around the walls – and we keep hitting stuff. We've cut water and cable lines and we almost took out the gas. I am confident that our contractor has been very careful, but locating the various utilities was complicated by a lot of dead lines – old pipes, wires, and conduits.

There is a parable here. When we meet people each day we usually assume that what we see is what we get. But sometimes the most important knowledge is well-hidden. Sometimes there are "dead lines" lurking to complicate our encounter. We experience her as stand-offish and do not know that any intimacy conjures up long ago memories of unwelcome touch by an uncle. He has a hair-trigger temper and we do not see the hours of bullying which warped him. A song plays in the background on TV and we find ourselves crying. Only later do we realize it was our mother's favorite.

William Faulkner wrote, "The past is not dead, it is not even past." It is good to be aware of how the past – both our own and that of others – continues to affect the present. There are "dead lines," fragments of our past which continue to complicate our interactions. Just remembering that can help us bring more grace to our relationships.

Copying the Answer

A recent article in the *Christian Century* sent me searching for the short stories by James Runcie which are the inspiration of the PBS series, *Grantchester*. Both feature Sidney

Chambers, an Anglican priest in 1950s England, who finds himself pulled into various mysteries. I like both the stories and the show because they offer thoughtful reflection on the clerical vocation and the challenges every Christian faces in forming and following a religious vision,

In one of the stories Chambers is asked, "Do you know that line of Kierkegaard's… 'There are many people who reach their conclusions about life like schoolboys: they cheat their master by copying the answer out of a book without having worked the sum out for themselves.'" Those words got me thinking about how easy it is to live a second-hand life.

We can go to church and mouth the creed without ever asking exactly why these words have been chosen for our corporate confession. We say the Lord's Prayer and do not even tremble at the reckless boldness of saying, "Thy will be done on earth as it is in heaven." We trust that someone else has already "worked the sum out" and this is what you say if you are Christian. Of course, these are profound words, but until they are our words, embraced from our hearts with some semblance of intentionality, they will be neither anchor nor guiding star in our lives.

If the danger of second-hand living is big for religious folks, it is just as great for those who claim no faith. There are plenty of people who think religious faith is bunk and Christians are intellectual sheep, but who never think to question whether their political or economic orthodoxy actually reflects reality – or is just lazy, unthinking buttressing of self-interest. Christians may accidentally live second-hand lives, but is it an improvement to be driven by whatever raging click-bait hits your Facebook feed?

Kierkegaard speaks of cheating the master, but I sure he

would be the first to say that it is really ourselves whom we cheat. To live fully and with meaning we have to do the hard work of deciding what we most want from life, what we are willing to pay to have it, and how our priorities will be rearranged to reach our goal. What sums do you need to work out this week?

Congruent Confession

Oliver Wendell Holmes is quoted as saying, "I might have entered the ministry if certain clergy I knew had not looked and acted like undertakers." It is unfortunate that he traded in a derogatory stereotype (those who work compassionately with the bereaved at the most horrible moments of life exercise a hard and noble calling), but we understand his critique. All too often there is a disconnect between the joy which the gospel is supposed to give and the affect of those who proclaim it – and the problem is not confined to church professionals.

There is much hand-wringing these days about the church's loss of influence in our culture. A lot of factors are in play, but one is certainly this disconnect between what we Christians say and what we do. We say the gospel spans all divides, but 11:00 is still the most racially segregated hour of the week. We assert that God is gracious, "slow to anger and abounding in steadfast love," but those outside the church often perceive Christians as seething over lost privilege and quick to judge anyone different from themselves. We assert that Christ is the center and the source of all truth, yet many Christians are terrified of science which challenges their ignorance and prejudice. We proclaim Christ as the hope of the world, but many of us are lukewarm in our passion and reluctant even to invite a friend to worship.

Why should others take Christians seriously when the example of Jesus seems to have precious little impact on our actions? Why should they believe in a God who cares about peace, the hungry, and the creation, when those who say they are Christians are the most reliable defenders of bellicose foreign policy, reduction in aid to the poor, and the plunder of the creation for short- term profits?

What we say may not be as important as how we say it. Our witness is a combination of words, attitudes, and actions. My worship professor made this point in discussing hymn selection. "The music should support the words," he said, "and when it doesn't, the text is weakened." Then, to illustrate, he pulled out a hymnal and read the text of a well known Easter hymn, "The Strife is O'er, the Battle Won." Read the words yourself; they are joyful and triumphant. Then hum the ponderous dirge which usually accompanies them. They do not go together; indeed the music sucks the life out of the words.

Words are important, but the music of our lives needs to fit them if the world is to hear a confession of joyful hope.

Baseline

I can breathe. Maybe that doesn't sound like a big deal, but for me it is. For a couple of years I have struggled with congestion, coughing, sneezing, and raspy throat. I have seen an ENT, had sinus surgery, been tested for allergies, refitted my bedroom, pulled out the rugs, turned on the humidifier, run an air filter, and swallowed, squirted, and puffed various medications in multiple combinations.

I do not want to get too cocky (maybe it is just a temporary reprieve because some allergen count is extra low), but today I am not having to wonder if I will get through a sermon without coughing (and I don't think I am keeping my wife awake at night, sounding like a moose giving birth). Looks like we have found the solution, and I am thankful.

I give you this brief window in to my respiratory health only to emphasize that this saga has taught me not to take breathing for granted. The wonder of our body is that, for the most part, it operates on automatic pilot. Eyes see color and shapes, blood cells deliver nutrients and oxygen to cells and take away the waste, muscles respond on cue, and in each moment our brain generates millions of commands, calculations, and integrations of data without conscious thought.

We easily take such wonder as our right, assuming a baseline of health which is actually pure gift. So we focus on what goes wrong in our day rather than giving thanks for blessings received. We gripe because we have to sit through a boring PowerPoint presentation rather than being thankful that we have the strength to sit in the chair, the vision to see the graphs, and the intellectual acuity to be bored in the first place.

And it's not just health. We complain about politics and forget millions whose idea of a great day would be having enough food to keep their baby from starving and not being bombed. We take our most intimate relationships as givens and fail to treasure those most near at hand because – well, because they are near at hand, as constant as the picture which has hung on the wall for 25 years.

Some would define deep spirituality as mindfulness, as the ability to notice every moment and appreciate it as an explosion of blessings erupting all around you. Today, study

283

your hand's movement, notice how your lungs work, give thanks for your spouse's smile, rejoice in the phone call from a friend. As poet Elizabeth Barrett Browning wrote,

Earth's crammed with heaven,
And every common bush afire with God,
But only he who sees takes off his shoes;
The rest sit round and pluck blackberries.

Wildfire

It's not the lightning; it's the tinder. During the wildfire season in the West, we often hear a news story about why fires are getting bigger and hotter. Most wildfires in remote areas are caused by lightning strikes. The number of strikes has not radically changed in recent years. Lightning has been setting forests and plains on fire since long before there were humans to see it.

What has changed is what's on the ground when the strike hits. Drought, logging practices which leave a lot of debris and combustible small plants on the forest floor, along with our reluctance to let smaller fires burn, have ensured there is abundant fuel when lightning strikes. Formerly, lightning might strike a tree and cause a fire. But it usually burned itself out fairly quickly because there wasn't enough fuel to sustain a wildfire. Now those random strikes decimate whole forests and the communities which border them. Forests are increasingly receptive to becoming an inferno.

It's not the lightning; it's the tinder. Surely, what we hear daily from political candidates is appalling and should not be ignored or condoned. I have not personally heard such naked appeals to racism, bigotry, and fear-mongering since my South Carolina high school was desegregated in 1970.

Candidates slander one another and appeal to our most base selves. We dare not minimize the culpability of those who manipulate the fearful. We need to take them seriously – as seriously as you'd take a cranky toddler with an Uzi. It's not that he has anything intelligent to say, but he can cause a lot of harm. However, when you get to the heart of the matter, these muck miners are not the problem.

There have been and will always be those who incite to hatred. We can no more stop them than we can stop lightning from striking the forest. The most terrifying reality is not those who spew fire, but that they are finding tinder eager to be inflamed in our country. We cannot wish the lightning away, but we do not have to be welcoming fuel for firebrands. That we can control. Christians can say in no uncertain terms that we follow the one who said, "Let not your hearts be troubled" and "Love one another as I have loved you" and "Come unto me all who are heavy laden and I will give you rest" and "Love your enemies."

If we do not want to do that, then let's at least stop claiming our goal is return our country to a mythical Christian Eden – because clearly we hold in contempt all that Jesus taught and died to proclaim.

Rejecting rage tactics is not enough. We must accompany our firm condemnation of prejudice with an equal measure of compassion for those who are hurting so badly that scapegoating makes perverse sense. We make little progress if we simply hate haters.

All the evidence says that we are in for a lot of lightning strikes in the next few months. We can't stop that. But perhaps we can make sure that our little corner of the forest is so soggy with the waters of our baptism that the fire does not take hold in our lives or in the lives of those we have the power to influence. It's hard to burn with hate if you are awash with the awareness of God's love.

Relay Race

I read a lot – newspapers, magazines, professional journals, web sites, e-mail, novels. Most of the many words I scan each day become part of a grey haze of verbiage, hardly marked and not remembered. The paradox of the information age, it is often noted, is that we have exponentially more data with less ability to separate wheat from chaff. We are drowning in words, often unable to distinguish profound from trivial. But every once in awhile something makes me stop dead and ponder, such as these words in a column by Ellen Goodman: "When we're young we think change is a 100-yard dash. As we get older we think it's a marathon. Eventually we see it's a relay race."

I don't know how Goodman's words will affect you; maybe they (and this meditation) will be part of your "grey haze of verbiage" today. In me they inspire a profound sense of thankfulness for the diversity of people who strive to make things better. We need different gifts at different times from different people.

We need the impatience of the young. Too naïve to know that nothing will ever change, they impetuously invest themselves in what they believe in, crazy enough to attempt the impossible because they don't know any better. Their fire lights the torch by which we envision a better tomorrow.

We need the faithfulness of those who are steady rather than spectacular. Like a sculptor releasing beauty from a slab of marble one chip at a time, they refuse to be discouraged when the results are slow in coming. Daily they tap, tap, tap

286

until the new day takes shape.

And we need those with the wisdom of perspective, those who readily confess that the task is not done – but bear witness that great strides have been made. In these scary days of financial melt- down, niggling wars, and globalization which challenges our sense of security, I notice that the old generally seem much less anxious than others. Their experience makes them concerned, to be sure, for they know what can happen. Yet they also have a serenity which comes in having surmounted great challenges.

Ultimately, it seems to me, the art of living joyously, particularly for Christians who long and hope for God's gracious reign in a world that is decidedly not as God intends, lies in embracing all three "ages of humanity" which Goodman lifts up. Simultaneously to have passion, patience, and perspective is to live abundantly. Find something worth investing yourself in today. Commit yourself for the long haul. Yet finally allow yourself to find serenity in the knowledge that the baton you carry today will be picked up by another saint tomorrow. Your mandate is not necessarily to cross the finish line, but only to run your leg faithfully, remembering that the race ultimately belongs to God. Paul puts it well, "So let us not grow weary in doing what is right, for we will reap at harvest time, if we do not give up. So then, whenever we have an opportunity, let us work for the good of all…" (Galatians 6:9-10a).

Bumped

So there we sat, trying not to make eye contact with the flight attendant or one another, the cold Chicago air bathing our faces from the open door, de-icer dripping from the wings. Oversold and overweight…until three people got off the plane nobody was going anywhere. And did I mention we'd already sat in this Mexican standoff for thirty minutes, it was late at night, and there would be no more flights to Roanoke this day?

I'll spare you the suspense. I finally got up and took a flight the next morning. But this is not a story of nobility and sacrifice. The calculus was more complicated than that: I got a free ticket and hotel. It was so late I would have felt crummy the next morning anyway – so why not sleep later? And since most of the seats were filled with a lacrosse team from the University of Oregon the prospects of anyone else leaving were pretty low. I had images of sitting on the tarmac for another hour until they booted somebody anyway. Better to jump early before getting pushed late. So don't hear this as a story of selflessness: enlightened self-interest is closer to the truth.

My point is just the opposite. As I sat there I realized we were all thinking pretty much the same thing, "They can't take my seat. My priorities are much more important than anyone else's on this plane. I have a right to this seat." How quickly we move to thinking about our rights when the least little stress is put upon us. "Rights" is the way we tend to frame any conflict.

Concern for rights is fine – I like fairness as much as the next guy – except such focus on personal privilege is not the primary principle which is supposed to govern the lives of Christians. Love is, and the only right which love has is to give itself. Looking back I think I did the right thing; I had some flex in my schedule. I just wish I had done it with a less sour attitude. I wish I had embraced that moment as a chance to let the mind of Christ make a difference in how I met what was, compared to the suffering of millions, a very petty annoyance indeed.

"Think of yourselves the way Christ Jesus thought of Himself. He had equal status with God but didn't think so much of Himself that He had to cling to the advantages of that status no matter what." (*The Message*, translation of Philippians 2:5-6 by Eugene Peterson)

Bring the Heat

"Bring the heat." You can count on one hand all the innings of baseball I watch in a year, but I was clicking through the channels (on my way to Home Shopping Network to pick up a diamond encrusted dog collar) when I caught a bit of a game. The pitcher was behind in the count and the sportscaster said, "When you're in trouble you just have to bring the heat." Sure enough, the next pitch was a fastball.

I write this several days before the election (and it will appear after November 4) and this Bread is only secondarily about politics. Still, I am struck that as the campaign winds down we have seen the social equivalent of that baseball truism: When in trouble, bring the hate. I'm not talking about just, or even primarily, the presidential campaign. Pick a race and you will see that the tighter it got the more venial and primitive the instincts to which the rhetoric descended. Consultants clearly know where the sewer of the soul runs – and adeptly make it the feed line for their message.

But, as I said, this BFJ is not really about politics, and certainly not an effort to parse partisan transgression. It's about us. Ninth grade civics idealism aside, parties are in the business of getting folks elected. Until men and women are angels some will always choose the low road. Unfortunately one can no more expect a party not to bring the hate than expect a scorpion not to sting. Campaigns "bring the hate" for one simple reason – it works.

And that is the theological truth reflected in our politics. Sin is alive and well; we are broken and need to be transformed. Our politics are merely a mirror of our faces and a window into our souls. Successful bigotry says at least as much about us who respond to it as about the candidate who is only reading his electorate's personality. The man who warns that microwaves are really UFO-thought control transmitters is hooted down in derision. But the equally absurd politician who appeals to our fear of the stranger, the faceless fat cats, or a minority of any sort – who "brings the hate" – is quite likely to be elected. We like to think we are generous, gentle, and reasonable, but a little reflection on our campaigns, like stepping on the scales after an indulgent weekend, makes us confront rosy illusions about ourselves. The beast is crouching in the dark corners of our psyche waiting to be summoned.

Whoever has won the election when this BFJ appears will confront great challenges. We are still facing many problems. The campaign is over, but there will still be plenty of folks eager to bring the hate. Expect it. Disappointment demands scapegoats. Uncertain economic times tempt us to act like a dog protecting its bone. But even in the best of times there are always those who will bring the hate to get what they want. We cannot stop the appeal to our lowest instincts.

But those who claim Jesus as Lord can refuse to respond to fear. We who seek to follow His way can stop the cycle of recrimination by returning good for evil and gentle truth telling for sweaty prejudice. Discipleship is beyond Democrat and Republican; it is about loyalty to the reign of God in Christ Jesus.

Unexpected Acceleration

Last week I was working out and listening to a podcast which concerned the "Toyota unexpected acceleration" controversy. You may remember when this hit the headlines a few years back; cars were reported to accelerate for no good reason and could not be stopped. Hysteria is not too strong a word for what followed: law suits, investigations, dire warnings – and denials from Toyota that anything was wrong.

If you are interested in the full story you can hear it on the *Revisionist History* podcast. Cutting to the chase: Brakes override throttles very well and the explanation for sudden acceleration is almost always drivers getting confused and hitting the gas instead of the brakes. When people get distracted and frightened, they make very human errors, sometimes repeatedly. They say they did the right thing but the "black box" in newer cars, which records use of brake and throttle, tells a different story – in virtually all cases of reported sudden acceleration the brakes were never applied. Still, in the Toyota case, folks wanted to believe the car was the problem.

My primary point is not automotive but relational. It is very human to resist taking responsibility. When things go wrong we want to blame something "out there" rather than admit any fault of our own. This tendency is not a moral failing; we are not lying. For the most part we really do think the problem is external. Fear easily distorts our perceptions and actions.

So, our marriage or friendships go south because the

other person is so unreasonable. The economy is in the tank because "those people" are not working hard enough and others are shipping jobs overseas. We can't get ahead because the system is rigged, and we can't catch a break. The problem is everywhere but within ourselves. The demonic thing about this is that the angrier we get – the more fear is in the driver's seat – the less likely are we to see how we are contributing to our problem.

Of course there are times when external factors are indeed at play, but not nearly as often as we assume. We are much more likely to look for a scapegoat than to do the hard work of self-examination. Next time it feels like things are spinning out of control, pause for just a second and consider whether there is anything you can do to throttle down the fear. I am guessing you will make better choices and see the world more accurately.

Traveler or Tourist

Are you more a traveler or a tourist? In a recent issue of *The Christian Century*, Peter Marty discusses the historical difference in the two. In previous centuries travelers were people who were interested in expanding their horizons and taking risks to do so. They ate local food, ventured off the beaten path, and expected to be challenged and disoriented by strange experiences. They actively engaged the places they went, trying to meet new people and see the world from their perspective.

Today, tourists are much more common. Tourists want to be insulated from the places to which they venture. They go sightseeing, but end the day in a hotel which serves familiar dishes. They collect pictures but few new ideas or perspectives. Their goal is be in a place without dealing with its smells, language, or customs. They have little interest in being changed by new experiences. They are much more likely to remember the day the air-conditioning on the tour bus failed than amazing tapas from a street vendor.

I suspect there is a little traveler and tourist in all of us. I am much bolder in exploring new ideas than in venturing into the hinterlands of a distant country. Our risk tolerance varies from one context to another. Still, the biblical preference is clearly for folks to be travelers rather than tourists, when it comes to the journey of faith.

The life of faith calls us to bring what we know into conversation with what is unfamiliar. It invites us to ask how seeing a new way might change our understanding of God. Being a faithful Christian traveler means taking seriously a new context and trying to find language which speaks in fresh ways.

Some years ago I was at a conference in Phoenix. A colleague, who served in the area, and I were standing on a mesa looking out over miles of cookie cutter homes. "You know," he said, "most of those folks have absolutely no interest in what this area has to offer. All they want is to create a bubble of Wisconsin in a warm place." I wonder if the church is too often like that, more eager to create a bubble of familiar holiness than to be changed and invigorated by new challenges.

Traveling always carries a certain risk, but doesn't anything which gives life?

Values and Fear

I had already written this week's Bread for the Journey – then Orlando. As I write this 49 persons are confirmed dead with others in critical condition following the shooting at a gay nightclub. The politicians have mounted their respective ramparts, using the incident to emphasize positions long in place: We need gun control; everyone needs to be armed. Secure the borders against Muslims; stop anti-GLBTQ violence. We are at war with an international conspiracy; the greater danger is home grown intolerance. Each will tend to favor one position or the other, but parsing the politics is not the point of this Bread. Rather, I invite you to think about a more fundamental issue.

Writing in the aftermath of this tragedy Karen Tumulty observes, "It has always been true that the toughest issues pit our values against our fears." Our values are supposed to be the gyroscope which keeps us balanced when the world is spinning. They are the North Star by which we steer when we feel lost and disoriented. That's why we call them values; they are what we hold dear, the convictions we will not sacrifice to expediency. It is precisely at the moment when we are most afraid that we must reflect on what values we will not compromise. Nothing is easier than affirming unfettered free speech when hateful rhetoric presents no real danger or glibly calling for greater security when we believe we will not feel the burden of irrational prejudice. We prove we hold our values precious when they drive our actions at inconvenient times.

My goal this day is not so much to tell you what you should value as to invite you to seriously reflect on what you do in fact hold dearest. Just as important, think about what is making you fearful this day. Fear is most powerful when we do not acknowledge it, for then it steers us without our conscious consent. When we name our fear we can better assess its reality and the cost of letting it drive our lives.

To prime your pump I offer two quotations, a prudential observation attributed to Benjamin Franklin and a timeless promise from our Lord:

- "Those who would give up essential liberty, to purchase a little temporary safety, deserve neither liberty nor safety."
- "Do not be afraid, little flock, for it is your Father's good pleasure to give you the kingdom." (Luke 12:32)

Soon Be Over

It will soon be over. As the bile in our political climate grows, perhaps you, like me, have been taking some consolation in the thought that it will all be over on November 8. Except, of course, it won't. There will be winners and losers. The winners will claim an outsized mandate and the losers will mount a rear guard action to keep anything substantive from happening. Some will gloat and others will be reinforced in their belief that the country is going to the dogs. Though the campaign is over, the reasons for the acrimony remain.

Long after the yard signs come down, the issues which divide us will continue to stand. We have been treating ourselves to a bender of bitterness, throwing down shots of scorn for those with whom we disagree, but we will awaken on November 9 with a political hangover and the awareness that all that bile has not gotten us any closer to solutions. We will still have to decide how to both ensure our security and be people of compassion. Manufacturing jobs will not magically reappear. Like it or not the demographics of our country are changing and we have to find a way to live together as one people – or admit that the American claim to weaving one culture from many strands is just a fiction.

We like to think that things will work out. But that is just the point, things don't work out. People work things out by hard effort. We start to make progress by admitting that the problem is not out there, but fundamentally within ourselves. We say we want civility, but rage at the guy who cuts us off in the parking lot. We expect our leaders to give us solutions to complex problems, but can't be bothered to listen, really listen, to those who do not see the world as we do. We would rather silence than acknowledge the pain of another.

Christians do not have policy answers which nobody else possesses, but we do have a mandate to be people of peace, people who are more concerned about building understanding than winning arguments. That is the contribution which followers of Jesus can offer. Whether we are liberal or conservative our call is to be persons who strive for reconciliation when division is at its worst.

To the church at Thessalonica Paul wrote, "Be at peace among yourselves. And we urge you, beloved, to admonish the idlers, encourage the faint-hearted, help the weak, be patient with all of them. See that none of you repays evil for evil, but always seek to do good to one another and to all." [I Thess. 5:13-15] Some words are timeless; perhaps these are ones for this political season.

Bear One Another's Burdens

Nick's parents died suddenly. Last week I got the e-mail from the national office in Chicago telling me that both the father and mother of a campus ministry colleague had been killed in a car accident. In the wink of an eye he is an orphan. Nick and I are not particularly close friends (though we have shared plenty of laughs), but the announcement had a special poignancy for me because Nick has been doing very good ministry for some folks I care about on the campus where he serves. More than that he has sent me regular e-mails, letting me know how those friends are doing. He's been everything a good pastor should be. So as I read that e-mail I offered up a silent prayer, "Please Lord, give Nick someone as kind and compassionate as he has been to support him through the tough days ahead."

How quickly we can move from being the one who gives strength to desperately needing to feel a comforting hand. Many are embarrassed by their sudden weakness, but the reality is that this is the nature of life: sometimes we have much to give and sometimes our knees buckle in agony.

One of the consolations of life in Christ is that we are called into a community where we do not have to be embarrassed by moments of weakness and one of the great joys is the privilege of carrying others when they are out of strength.

One of my favorite pieces of "Christian art" is a simple line drawing in the *Good News Bible* (*Today's English Version*). It illustrates Galatians 6:2, "Help carry one another's burdens, and in this way you will obey the law of Christ." The picture shows a line of people walking across the page, each holding a heavy bag, basket, or jug. When you look closely you see that each person is reaching up to put a hand under the load of the next person in the line. Nobody is toting a burden alone.

I hope Nick has lots of people with a hand on his bag. Sustained by God's unlimited love may each of us take a place in the line.

Are you the Chaplain

"Are you the chaplain on call?" She looked up at me with hopeful eyes from her seat in the nurses' station of the ICU. "No," I replied, "I'm just here to see a couple of my members. But what do you need?" Glancing toward a darkened alcove she said, "Mrs G. is dying, and she asked to see the chaplain. We put in a call, but she's tied up. She said she'd be here as soon as she could…" The question hung in her statement.

That's how I ended up in a lonely little room beside the bed of an old woman I had never met. She was barely conscious. An array of wires monitored her swiftly fading vital signs. Mrs. G. mumbled something, and I bent close to her dry lips to hear. "Sins…want to get right…" Her hair was pulled straight back in the style of a country woman who has lived a hard life, and I gently cupped my hand on her dry, pale forehead. I have no idea why there were no family members there; maybe they did not realize the end was so near. But as her life ebbed it was I and a nurse who tried to convey that she was not alone. Putting my lips to her ear I prayed as fervently as I had in a long time. I spoke of the God whose mercy is always greater than his condemnation, of care that never lets us go, of the love that calls us into being and welcomes us at the end. In silence we held Mrs. G's needle-punctured hands, that nurse and I, for a few minutes more. Then I slowly left that holy ground to make my other visits.

Two observations: First, there is a bracing clarity which comes in sitting by a deathbed. Many of us are uncomfortable around death; that is entirely natural. We do not enjoy contemplating our own non-being in the world as we know it. But nothing reminds us of what is most important like confronting existence stripped to the bone. When we run from the reality of death we also run the risk of living a life built on distractions. More than that, in being with others in death we discover what a holy gift it is to give and receive care. Yes, it is painful to sit by a deathbed, but what a privilege it is to be in that place, the incarnation of God's unfailing care.

Second, I was deeply moved by the ministry of that nurse. She was not just doing her job, punching the clock and collecting a check. She deeply cared for a single old woman in danger of dying alone. She went out of her way to meet her spiritual needs. She saw her work as more than pushing pills and checking charts; she gave herself as a sign of care when healing was impossible. One of Luther's great insights is that any occupation can be an expression of our vocation, our calling, to be signs of God's love in Christ. Perhaps this week will not present you with the dramatic chance to sit by a deathbed; be assured, you will have the chance to let your daily work reflect the care you have received from Christ. It will be a holy opportunity; take it.

Home Center

I felt like taking it back. Gail and I had been considering the possibility of sometime, maybe, perhaps getting a new television. The prospect of our nephews coming for Thanksgiving caused us to take the plunge. We figured they would enjoy the time more if they could play their games in a distant part of the house away from the adults. (Okay, I really do hate letterboxed movies, and that was a factor too.) I picked it out, lugged it into the house, turned the box over to unpack our new purchase, and there it was, printed on the side, "Make this the center of your home."

Not "center of your house" – where you might think of it as merely some sort of pivotal design element – the "center of your home!" I was being invited to make a television the focus of my most important space, my locus of security and renewal in a busy world. What a thought: a bunch of LCDs and plastic, the anchor of my emotional and spiritual well-being.

Now you may think you know where this is going. But this is not a preacherly rant against either technology or consumer purchases (I did buy the TV after all). We do spend too much money on electronic gadgets we probably don't need, we certainly should ask hard questions about our stewardship of our personal and planetary resources. But that is not my point here. No, my point is a question. If not the TV, what is going to be the center of our homes – and our lives?

The absurdity of making a TV the center of life is ludicrous; a little thought tells us just how pathetic it is when the piped in reality of the boob tube defines our existence. But there are more subtle temptations, potential centers which are socially much more acceptable, if not necessarily more life-giving. Work, children, hobbies, service, social causes, all are worthy of our time. Are they a sufficient center; can they hold everything else together? Each has the potential to become pathological. We can neglect relationships in pursuit of career. We can become so invested in our children that we smother them, so impassioned for justice that we turn hard and bitter.

So this is today's question: What is at the center of your life? What does everything else orbit around? What is highest priority which you serve before anything else? If that seems like more than one question, it's really just a restatement of the big one: What is your God?

Polish Silver

"Polish silver?" I worked that crossword clue for a solid twenty minutes, trying to find the right verb. Burnish? Rub? Clean? Detarnish? I tried everything I could think of, but nothing fit. And to make matters worse, several intersecting words gave me a very strange consonant combination. If you do these puzzles you may know the answer was "zloty" – a currency from Poland. I did not know that word anyway, but the bigger problem was my false assumption. Thinking I knew what I was looking for, I was not even asking the right question, not seeing what was right in front of me, and ignoring the capital letter.

We are prone to the same problem in dealing with other people. We see the spiked hair and the pincushion cheek and do not recognize that this person knows a great deal about bond markets and leveraged buyouts. We assume the perfectly coiffed woman in front of us is a walking blonde joke, not seeing that behind the perfect makeup is a very incisive brain. We get fooled by the swagger of the guy whose marriage is falling apart and don't hear the crack in his voice or see the glisten in his eye. We miss what's right in front of us.

One of the great gifts we give to one another is the willing suspension of assumptions. To listen to the person in front of you – really listen without presuming that you already know what they believe or feel – is a precious offering. Jesus did this often and two wonderful things happened: His ministry was effective because He understood the real, deep needs of the people He met. The persons with whom He interacted felt valued and affirmed, even when He said hard, challenging things to them.

Is there someone with whom you are constantly at odds? Just for today, try looking at him or her without previous assumptions. If you let go of "polish" maybe you'll discover "Polish."

Golf

My golf game has begun its annual descent from numbing mediocrity to ludicrous ineptitude. It's like this: My father-in-law is a very good golfer and we play on our annual family beach trip. I am loath to be that dork (if you're a golfer, you know this guy)) who holds up everyone's play by topping the ball five feet off the tee, spraying multiple shots into the trees, scaring the fish on every water hazard, and generally making his way around the course thirty feet at a time. So about two weeks before the beach I hit the practice areas, desperately trying to remind my body what a good shot feels like. I'll never cause Tiger any sleepless nights, but for about a week, on a short, easy course, I can break 90. Then the plummet begins.

The fall schedule heats up. New priorities arise. I decide that my body would get more cardiovascular good out of four hours on a bike than on the greens. My game goes in the tank, ignored until about two weeks before next year's beach trip…

The status of my golf game is unimportant, but I realize there is a constant danger that my spiritual health will have a similar up and down pattern. In times of crisis we are keenly aware of our need to draw on resources bigger than ourselves. We pray daily, read our Bible, and take time to reflect on what is most important. We commit to whipping our spiritual lives into shape. But when life is going smoothly or when the daily rush sweeps us along like leaves in a river, we often neglect the things which keep our spirits whole and our lives centered.

"It's show time," said one of my campus ministry colleagues last week. The students are back. Public schools are open. Whatever mellowness the summer brought is fading like a sweet dream when the alarm goes off. Before you feel your spiritual life deteriorating like my golf game, resolve to reserve a little time daily to "keep in practice."

Safe Zone

My office is a "safe zone." I have the rainbow triangle on my door to prove it. I filled out the paperwork and got certified by the appropriate office at Virginia Tech; my space is officially "[an] inclusive, accepting, and understanding environment for members of the lesbian, gay, bisexual, and transgender communities and their allies." I am proud of that designation. I embrace it by personal conviction and because I think it reflects our congregation's commitment to be "Reconciling in Christ." GLBTQ persons experience daily turbulence in their voyage through life; I want my office to be a safe harbor.

But when I ponder that triangle a little more I wonder if the sofa across from my desk really is a "safe zone." Do the people who do not share the political sympathies of the cartoons tacked next to that triangle on my bulletin board feel safe to speak their minds? Do theologically conservative students enjoy the same slowness to judgment from me which I studiously cultivate when dealing with those whose concern is sexual orientation? Am I as patient with those in a muddle over questions of faith as I am with those struggling with their sexuality? I worry about how many conversations don't even get started because someone is afraid of receiving a flippant or biting retort from me. Gentleness of spirit is a virtue few attribute to me, but I deeply value it in others. That disconnect gives me pause.

Some might say that I should take down the cartoons and have less to say on the religious and political issues of the day, if I am serious about creating a safe zone. They may well be right. But if the price of a nominal safe zone is silence concerning what are literally matters of life and death for millions, thus consigning the gospel to an insipid "spiritual" sphere where it never touches, much less challenges or consoles, people in the midst of their daily lives, I find the cost too dear.

Yet Jesus did it. Somehow, Jesus managed both to create a safe zone for all people and make that space an incubator for growth. Nobody who listened to Him very long had the slightest doubt concerning His passion and convictions, yet all felt welcome in His presence. From Nicodemus, a card carrying member of the ruling elite, to a desperate father with an epileptic son, they all felt free to lay their confusion before Jesus. How did He do it? I think it comes down to His attitude that loving folks was more important than persuading or coercing them. Jesus never apologized for His disconcerting vision, but He never lost sight of His purpose – to be the very embodiment of God's acceptance. Unlike me, Jesus never demanded that others mirror His beliefs in order to enjoy His respect, and so people were often changed, not by the force of His arguments, but by the relentlessness of His welcome.

Most of us find it pretty easy to create a safe zone for people with whom we fundamentally agree. Today, take the step of discipleship and create loving space in Jesus' name for those with whom you feel less kinship.

Araby After Nine Months

We turned off the still rubble-strewn road which runs through Araby, Louisiana. Nine months after being on this boulevard every day for a week during our Katrina relief trip, I was returning to show my friend Chris this area just east of New Orleans and some work we did in it. The stop lights work now. You can buy a po-boy without having to drive 20 miles. The porta-johns are gone from the median because most of the sewers work. But you could easily believe a hurricane hit only a few weeks ago: twisted signs hang in front of abandoned strip malls, half- submerged boats still dot the marsh, and through the windows of innumerable homes you can see the fetid mixture of soggy drywall, furnishings, and clothes left after eight feet of water surges through your house and then recedes. The lack of activity was eerie as we drove into what was once a thriving blue-collar neighborhood; I was reminded of the high noon scene in an old western movie when the townspeople abandon the street. Block after block the only sign of life was a stray dog or a lonely FEMA trailer homesteading amidst the desolation. I was looking forward to showing Chris a house we mucked and gutted. In the midst of all this mess, I would point to at least one definite sign of progress.

But when we pulled up in front of the school we used as a landmark to find our work site last March, there was nothing to see. More precisely there was a vacant lot on the site where we carried load after wheelbarrow load to the curb, where Mark had gently picked through piles of debris to find the owner's prized china, and where we lost pounds of water in hazmat suits. All that effort wasted!

Then I thought a little more. That effort was hardly wasted. Our campus ministry team discovered a bond in working through the muck. The woman who owned that house experienced care from a bunch of college students who gave a week to help someone they'd never see again. We all learned something about human suffering and the fragility of affluence which we will never forget. I suppose all of us on that muck and gut team imagined our efforts ending in rebuilding. But it was not to be, and that's okay. The point was never meeting our need to be needed. Love worthy of the name has only one right, the right to give itself. As Christians we do what we can, as faithfully as we can, and try not to let our need to be appreciated or to "make a difference" get in the way of giving ourselves in service. Paul puts it well, "So let us not grow weary in doing what is right, for we will reap at harvest time, if we do not give up." (Galatians 6:9)

Sister's Wrong

Reality is annoying. Just about the time I have everyone and everything in my world cleanly categorized and placed in a nice little cubbyhole, along comes a flesh and blood person to upset my neat system. I get people covered by sweeping generalizations, and then along comes someone who pokes out from under my assumptions like a foot from beneath a too short blanket: a pleasant prejudice wrecked on the shoals of experience. I hate it when that happens; ignorance is a lot more blissful than accounting for the complexity of the world. But I'm not the only one to have those troubling moments.

In her book, *In Search of Belief*, Joan Chittister tells of the day she came home from parochial school with a problem. Sister had told them that only Catholics go to heaven, and that was very disconcerting for a young girl whose step-father was an elder at the local Presbyterian church. Her mom, a wise woman, asked, "And what do you think about that, Joan?"

"I think Sister's wrong."

"And why do you think Sister would say a thing that's wrong?" her mom probed.

"Because sister doesn't know Daddy."

One of striking things about Jesus is that he always saw the person in front of him. He did not see a leper, he saw a man who had leprosy. He did not see a tax collector, he saw Zaccheus, a man with a deep need who made his living as a tax collector. Each of us easily dismisses whole sections of humanity out of hand: men, rednecks, blondes, Yankees, students, UVA grads, fundamentalists, soldiers, Democrats, Republicans, Muslims. We have different lists based on our upbringing and experiences, but each of us has one. It is so much easier to act on our prejudices than to see an actual person. For then there is no need to account for the fact that this gay man is the kind of person you'd be proud to call your son or that this Republican stalwart values the Constitution as much you do. Yet, if we are serious about following Jesus we must be serious about seeing each person we meet, not as one more example of our stereotype, but as an amazing child of God who might just wreck all our tidy categories.

In what personal encounter is the Spirit challenging you to open your eyes today and trade complacency for compassion and blind certitude for wisdom?

Spigot

Do you ever feel like a spigot with no pressure? Every year about this time – when the new program year cranks up, a fresh crop of students hits campus, and all the summer-deferred projects come due – my energy dissipates in multiple directions, so that I don't bring much verve to any one task. I turn on the psychic tap, and all I get is a dribble.

I am no civil engineer, but it seems to me that you can do three basic things to improve water pressure: increase what's going into the pipe, decrease the number of open spigots, and look for leaks in the line.

So right about now I always have to take a deep breath and do those three things. In the crush of the new year I am prone to forget that I can't give what I haven't got, which is to say I decide I am way too busy to take time for the devotions and reflection time which feed my spirit, give me some perspective, and provide the energy out of which I have something to offer others. When I feel the dribble I try to attend to what I need to be taking in.

It is easy to get over-committed with too many worthy pursuits, so many terribly important demands: Soccer for the kids. Grant proposals due in a month. Speeches to write. Inventory to order. Committees, like the poor, we have with us always. The list goes on and on. All worthy of our attention. But at some point we have to learn the discipline of saying,

"No." The reservoir goes dry if we keep all the taps open. Having energy for what is most important probably means not doing some other things.

Which is why it's doubly important to look for the leaks, the hidden drains on our time and emotional energy which are neither productive nor life-giving. Time management experts might focus on meetings and work patterns which get nothing done as leaks, but I am talking about something else. It takes a lot of energy to worry, to harbor resentment, to obsess so much about the possibility of failing that we virtually assure that we do. Plugging those leaks is one way to focus our energy on what really matters and what we can influence.

I don't know which of these three things you most need to do: increase the input, decrease the outflow, or plug the leaks. But if you are dribbling, my guess is that some attention to one or more of these might be helpful.

Precious

Last week I was participating in the review of another campus ministry. We were meeting with the student leadership and I asked them, "What do you think this ministry tries to communicate to people who come here?" There was only a brief silence before one young woman replied, with obvious joy, "During my time in this group I have learned that God values me very much and thinks I am very precious. And because that is true I can value myself and should treat everyone else as very precious too." That is not a full systematic theology, but it is awfully good for off the top of your head. If students in our own ministry at Tech gave the same answer I would be delighted.

In the popular mind religion is first and foremost about ethics and rules. If you are religious it means you do certain things and don't do others – primarily because God has laid down the law. I am all for ethics; we need a clear moral center from which we make decisions. Likewise, it is abundantly clear that the scriptures suggest God's desires for our life together. (Though it is interesting how we tend to be far more scrupulous regarding the counsels on sex than ones pertaining to economics and justice to the poor.)

But rules and social control are not the primary concern of faith, certainly not of the vision embodied by Jesus of Nazareth. In this Lenten season, when we ponder the mystery of a God who loved us enough to endure shame and suffering, sharing our struggles, we dare not forget that the cross says God regards each of us as precious, and thus invites us to see the value in every person we meet. No exceptions. None.

Feeding 5000

I could think of a hundred ways I'd rather spend a few days than reading through 162 reports. But that's what I needed to do, condense the year-end reports of all the ELCA campus ministries into some bulleted highlights. I was plodding along, eyes glazing over, when I came to one colleague's comments on hospitality, "Jesus' feeding of the five thousand is presented as a miracle. After 21+ years in this call & after some careful tallying…I figure that I'm well into my feeding of the 2nd five thousand. A miracle?"

I threw back my head and laughed out loud. At one time or another every campus minister wonders if the time given to studying church history or theology would be better spent in "Introduction to Food Service." I could hear Jane's gentle, self-effacing voice in the humor, and I imagined 162 campus ministers nodding in smiling recognition if they read her words. It would have been so easy for her to concentrate on all the impressive things happening in her ministry (and there were some), but she put in that little zinger to say, "Yes, though what we do is important, it's not always exciting. Sometimes you just do the most mundane of tasks with a joke and a twinkle in your eye. Those called to speak the Word of God just as often dish up uncountable pans of mac and cheese."

One of humor's great gifts is that it joins us with a community of all those who recognize a bit of life's absurdity in the gap between the ideal and reality, and thus we feel a little less alone. We realize that though life is serious it need not be grim. The ability to laugh at our pretensions saves us from feeling that the fate of the whole world – or just our little corner of it – depends on our perfection. It saves us from tyranny over self and boorishness toward others.

Jesus knew the value of a little humor. Confronted by folks who were "oh, so very concerned" about the behavior of others, he commented, "You might want to take the log out of your eye before you start helping others with their contacts." Okay, so that's a loose translation. The point remains: Season this day with some laughter and you may discover that whatever is on your plate is a lot more appetizing.

Seeing the Particular

Life would be simple if it weren't so complex. Perhaps that sounds like a Yogi Berra quip, but that was my thought as I walked away from a little café in the Indianapolis airport.

Gail and I took a few days last week to visit our son, Scott. We ate some good food, visited a museum, toured Scott's office, and met coworkers at the new job he took a few months ago. And it was with a few of those colleagues that delayed flights gave me several hours of conversation.

God must have a sense of humor. I have been known to thunder about the superficiality of the consumer society and the advertising industry which supports it. So, of course, I have a very talented and thoughtful son who writes advertising copy. As long as his work does not involve a felony, I would be proud of Scott; that's just parental bias. I do not have such bias concerning his coworkers, but as we chatted about a variety of topics, from books to the different flavors of Lutheranism, I realized how much I like these men who are Scott's new friends. They are everything I hope my son is: thoughtful, intellectually curious, courteous, friendly, witty, serious about their work. Heading for my gate, I was glad he has such friends.

My point is not terribly profound: We dare not lose the particular in the general. I still have concerns about the consumer society, our inability to distinguish wants from needs, and the temptation to think technological toys can substitute for deep relationships. But henceforth it will be hard for me to think about advertising without also thinking of Scott, Uriah, and Trevor, three young men who are neither malevolent nor stupid. Life is simpler when we dismiss whole blocks of people as the "enemy," but much less rich. We become prisoners of our prejudice.

When Jesus met someone He always saw the person, not the category. He saw Zaccheus, not a crooked tax collector; a faith-filled Centurion, not the Roman oppressor, a woman longing for love, not a prostitute. What class of folks are you tempted to dismiss today? Whose gifts are you missing? Who is waiting to enrich your life, if you will let them?

Rugged Individual

"...I owe such happiness as I have had to one Source – namely, the sheer grace of God as it is mediated through the lives of other people...I had set out to write about my own life, but what I discovered through the plain task of chronologically recounting my own story was that most of the time I was actually writing about other people." (Douglas John Hall, in his theological autobiography, *Bound and Free: A Theologian's Journey*)

The great American icon is the rugged individualist, making his way into an untamed frontier. With only grit and determination he subdues a savage land and creates a life for himself and his family. It is a powerful myth, encapsulating the competence, optimism and confidence we like to impute to ourselves. But it is historically inaccurate: Absent from the picture are the government subsidized railroads, armies, land grants, and mineral giveaways which made the great westward expansion possible. Absent are the small communities into which settlers gathered and the comfort an individual gained in knowing someone was just over the next ridge. (Absent too is the genocide and injustice perpetrated on the Native Americans, but that is another story.) Our lives are connected to others by a web of dependence, joy, frustration, and necessity. We need other people. We are the product of our interactions with others. Our most intense pain and deepest contentment are almost always connected to a particular face.

Today, think about some of those faces which mark your

journey. Give thanks for those who have given you life. Decide if you want others to keep on haunting your heart and stealing your vitality. Gratitude for past gifts and the willingness to let go of old hurts are two of the most healing attitudes we can cultivate on those days when it feels like "me against the world."

Bears

Some people go a whole trip without seeing one. More than once during our vacation to the Grand Tetons and Yellowstone National Parks, Gail and I narrowly avoided an accident as cars screeched to the side of the road and people poured out of them to see if the little black speck on the far side of the valley was a boulder or a bear. We, however, saw one within 30 minutes of entering the park.

We were on a short trail to an alpine lake, and as we rounded a switchback, I looked up and saw a furry bowling ball barreling down the trail toward us. That in itself was not terribly scary; it was only a little cub which quickly moved over into the brush. But as they never tire of telling you in bear country: 1) Most attacks occur when you get between Mama and her cub. 2) Where a cub is, there ye shall also find Mama close at hand. As you probably guessed, Mama did not eat us; we never saw her and after waiting a few minutes we finished the hike.

The experience did, however, mark the rest of the trip. I am sure more than one hiker we met wondered why we were scuffing our feet on the trail and yelling, "Coming through" to a bushy hillside – we were not going to surprise another bear. We loved the hiking, but constantly scanned the edges of the trail for bears. Looked so hard, in fact, that we sometimes weren't looking where we were going, and Gail almost took a tumble. With a sheepish smile she said, "I guess the rock on the trail is more likely to cause you trouble than a bear in the bush."

So what's your "bear in the bush"? What's that shadowy fear which occupies your thoughts much more than it should? Life has many potential pitfalls, some of them significant, but most of us exaggerate our fears way out of proportion to their probability of occurring. It would have been a horrible shame if Gail and I had missed the grandeur of the Tetons because we were overly afraid of bears, and it is sad when we allow vague anxieties to rob us of daily joy. Much better is to embrace each day as it comes, receiving its gifts and facing its challenges. You walk the path, noting the wildflowers, stepping over the rocks – and dealing with the bear only if and when it appears. Or as Jesus put it, "Therefore, do not worry about tomorrow, for tomorrow will worry about itself." (Mt. 6:34)

Trees

It's not how I planned to spend the day. After a deluge my driveway was a mess, so I called the gravel company to drop off a load. I knew I might have to spend a few minutes raking it smooth, but then it would be off to the office to get some work done in the quiet of the July 4th holiday.

What we had here was a failure to communicate. I assumed he would drop part of the load at the bottom of the driveway, lower the bed, and drop the rest at the top. He thought I was telling him to just raise the bed and "git'er done" up the hill – right through all the overhanging trees. I spent the rest of day, not in front of the word processor, writing something like this Bread for the Journey or a sermon, but with a chainsaw, trimming, dragging, and stacking all the arboreal carnage which results when a dump truck hits multiple heavily leaved branches.

I never would have chosen to spend the day as I did or undertaken landscaping in this way, but the trees are healthier for the pruning, and the decreased canopy gives the yard some much needed sunlight. Much of life comes to us unexpected and unbidden – accidents, deaths, layoffs, divorce, disappointments of all sorts. Part of spiritual maturity, and indeed happiness in general, consists in adapting with good cheer and wisdom to the unexpected and unwelcome events of life. The trees needed to be trimmed and what initially felt traumatic ended up being very positive; a dump truck got me off dead center.

The biblical witness is filled with situations where people confront unpleasant challenges which lead to insight and growth. We like the security of the familiar; it's important to be ready to grow when life gives us the opportunity, through an event we never willingly would have chosen. The key, I think, is to cultivate the attitude of the apostle Paul, finding ministry opportunities in his imprisonment:

"For I have learned in whatever state I am to be content. I know how to be abased, and I know how to abound; in any and all circumstances I have learned the secret of facing plenty and hunger, abundance and want. I can do all things in Him who strengthens me." (Philippians 4:11b-13)

Sophie Scholl

I hope you saw *Sophie Scholl: The Final Days* when it was at the Lyric theater; it's a movie both uplifting and horrifying. Most of the film concerns the arrest, interrogation, and execution of a young woman who distributed banned literature in Nazi Germany. But in contrast to the solemn tone of what follows, the film opens with Sophie and a friend lying in front of the radio singing along with the latest top 40 song. The scene's exuberant innocence effectively sets up the rest of the movie. Sophie is no superwoman; she is a typical teen who giggles, dreams of boys, and listens to pop music like giddy girls everywhere – which makes her extraordinary courage later on all the more moving.

Too often we allow ourselves to think in terms of "super saint" and "bench warmer" Christians. The super saints are the ones, we think, who really live out the Christian calling. They have special abilities, a mystical closeness to God unavailable to mere mortals, and a higher calling because they are really "into religion." We assume the rest of us cannot (and need not) aspire to such lofty spiritual heights. We just plug along trying to live good Christian lives, and by that we mean being reasonably nice, generous, and honest.

In fact, Scripture knows nothing of such a division between those who play the game with passion and those who just wear the uniform and cheer the stars from the bench. Jesus approached people in many ways, but He ultimately asked the same thing of each person, "Follow me." It would be a lot easier if we could convince ourselves that only an elite few have the capacity to follow; we'd at least have an excuse. But, as the Bible documents with monotonous regularity, God calls the most ordinary and unfit to extraordinary places. Braggarts, cheats, boys, adulterers, farmers, hot-heads, persecutors, and ordinary fishermen – God calls them all and fills them with the power to do what needs to be done.

Perhaps you will not be asked to display the courage and sacrifice of Sophie Scholl today, but it's not because you and she are of different spiritual species. Each of us can answer the call to deeper discipleship – if we are willing. Where is God calling you to deeper obedience and discipleship today?

Tarshish and Nineveh

Are you spending your life wishing for Tarshish? Unless you are a Bible baseball all-star you probably don't recognize the reference, but Tarshish is where the prophet Jonah was headed when he had his famous encounter with the fish. In a wonderful book on vocation (*Under the Unpredictable Plant*), Eugene Peterson says many pastors waste a lifetime and a ministry longing for Tarshish. God called Jonah to go to Nineveh; Tarshish was the exotic, semi-mythical Spanish city on the other side of the Mediterranean. Nineveh was going to be hard, probably unappreciated work; Tarshish looked like fun in the sun. If he could just get to Tarshish, Jonah thought he would be happy and fulfilled. So too, says Peterson, many pastors miss the holiness of the present by dreaming of an ideal that never was and never will be.

Of course it's not just pastors who disparage the present possibilities in the tragic assumption that real life begins later – when I get married, when I get tenure, when my business takes off, when I make senior management – tomorrow and tomorrow and tomorrow....But in the words of the old Creedence Clearwater Revival song (which some of you aging Boomers will recall), more often than not "someday never comes."

As my son, Scott, has been looking for his first job after grad school, I have been thinking a lot about Tarshish and

Nineveh, and how hard it can be to tell them apart. Until we are some years down the road it is hard to know an exciting byway from a missed fork in the road. Without the benefit of hindsight it is hard to discern crushing setbacks from providential doors opening into exciting places. And perhaps the great teaching of Scripture is that virtually all of life's events and circumstances can be either wasted days or hours filled with meaningful, fulfilling pursuits – depending on whether we are willing to see and serve the presence of God in each moment.

Not for a moment would I suggest that you abandon the dreams which beckon you forward, but every once in awhile ask yourself whether you are missing the very real and present joys and opportunities of Nineveh while you await passage to Tarshish.

Being a Contemplative

I'll be on sabbatical during the summer. As I have pondered how to make that time most productive (Note the irony of talking about a "productive sabbatical" – we really don't trust the idea of Sabbath do we?), I have done some pre-sabbatical reading. I ran across these words from Parker Palmer in *The Active Life*, "Life makes contemplatives of us all, whether we want to be contemplatives or not. The only question is whether we can name and claim those moments of opportunity for what they are."

We tend to think of contemplation as the purview of super-saints or those of a particular temperament. We imagine contemplatives as a special breed which luxuriates in being inside their heads, or in our more jaundiced moments, we suspect they are folks who are in full retreat from the world. Palmer reminds us that humans are by nature mean-ing makers and persons who long for purpose. We cannot help looking for connections and common themes in our lives. We are all contemplatives; the issue is whether we will do the reflection well or poorly.

We are happiest when the various pieces of life – family, faith, work, leisure – feel integrated into a coherent whole. Yet often our lives are like a golf bag filled with mismatched clubs. The various pieces do not complement one another. We have tasks and commitments, habits and priorities which we have just jammed into the bag because we have not had time to consider their value. And so we hack our way through life. Periodically we need to pull out all the clubs and very deliberately ask of each, "Do I really need this one anymore?" That is the kind of contemplation that Palmer is suggesting, a pulling back from merely reacting to life to considering what kind of life we actually want.

As I write this, a big box from Amazon has just arrived, my reading stack for the sabbatical. I have an agenda for this time away from regular duties, studying what I need and want to do. But I also plan to spend a lot of time listening to my body, thinking about how I spend my energies, and re-flecting on what you, the persons I am called to serve, most need from me. I am keenly aware that I have been given a great gift in this time away. Thank you. But even if you cannot take a formal sabbatical I invite you to claim a little time for yourself. Take a long walk. Write one paragraph on what you most want out of life. Think about what gives you the most joy – and be sure you are doing it regularly. I am willing to bet it will be the most "productive" time of your day. God needs us to be contemplatives because God wants us to savor each day and be vibrant testaments of what a well integrated life looks like.

Context

Context is everything. In preparation for preaching, I was reading through the appointed lessons for an upcoming Sunday and came on these words from Paul, "…from now on, let those who have wives live as though they had none." [I Corinthians 7:29b] For one brief, whimsical moment I imagined hoards of husbands, eager to spend yet another weekend either out in the woods hunting or plopped on the sofa watching football, scurrying to their spouse's Bible and bookmarking this verse with a fluorescent stickie. "Don't blame me, honey, that's what St. Paul said!"

This is not the text I would pull out in the middle of a marriage counseling session. But I might well cite it (and the rest of the chapter) to illustrate how the early church expected a quick return of the Risen Christ. Context is everything.

Context is also important in weighing how we will respond to an angry word, a hurtful action, or a seeming snub. More often than I like to admit I give others good reason to be angry or disappointed in me. Other times, however, I realize that the lashing out directed toward me has very little to do with anything I have done. Maybe they are facing the loss of health. Their children did not make it home for the holidays. They feel devalued on the job, as younger workers come on board. They are frustrated because others do not share their passion for a cause. The list could go on, but the point is that sometimes it is not about us – even when the attack feels very personal and pointed indeed.

A gift we can give to others is to see their actions in as broad a context as possible, compassionately trying to see the world through their eyes. That does not mean we become emotional punching bags, tacitly approving hurtful actions and words, but we respond out of a desire to heal rather than hurt. We make understanding a higher priority than delivering a zinger. In short, we try to model the graciousness of our Lord.

Host or Bouncer

Are you more likely to be a host at God's party or the bouncer? Last week a group of us gathered for the explicit purpose of "Christian conversation," and by that I mean talking about what our faith has to do with the ordinary worlds of education, work, and relationships. I had the best intentions; I really did. I hoped to create a relaxed, safe meeting, a place where we could enjoy a beverage and explore what God might want us to be about in the world.

But as we walked away from the local watering hole at the end of the evening I had the distinct feeling that I had been more the bouncer than the welcoming host. The host invites people in; the bouncer checks IDs. The host puts people at ease; the bouncer forces people to prove they belong. The host regards guests with openness; the bouncer, with suspicion. The host assumes that all people bring something valuable to the party, the bouncer that only the "right" people deserve respect. The host stands with arms wide open; the bouncer exudes dismissive judgment.

The conversation did not get nasty, but I realized that in my eagerness to share my insights I had been deaf to the perspectives of others. I was much more interested in being right than in building a sense of community in which we can support each other in the often confusing way of discipleship. I am afraid I shut down conversation by an imperious attitude toward dissenting – or maybe just probing – perspectives.

The fastest growing religious preference in America is "none." Those who identify themselves in that way say it is, in part, because the church is intolerant. I'd love to think I and my community of faith are being unfairly tarred by the poor witness of "those other Christians." But if I am honest I realize that I can be a bouncer, every bit as much as they are – I just use different standards to determine who can come into my club.

When we look around and see folks believing things we regard as foolish or acting in ways that seem destructive, we may be tempted to think that God needs us to step up and enforce some standards, to be a bouncer. Sure, speak the truth as best you know it, but do it with gentleness and humility, with a willingness to at least consider that you might be mistaken. Never forget that God needs hosts at the welcome table a lot more than bouncers at the door.

Two Messages

I heard two messages last week and right now I am trying to decide what to believe. While we were on our service trip to Glade Spring, VA, I did something very foolish – nothing terrible, just the kind of bone-headed mistake that makes you want to give yourself a virtual dope slap. Instead, Alex gave me a big smile and assurance, "That's okay, Jesus loves you anyway."

The other word was not so pleasant. For some years I have been drifting away from an old friend. There was no harsh parting, just progressively less communication. Out of nowhere he changed that. He sent me a bitter email laying out my profound failing as a friend, ending with an expletive regarding my character. He would happily wear a T-shirt I once saw, "God loves you – the rest of us think you're a jerk."

As I reflected on the two messages I realized a few things: Alex's word is true, but my ex-friend, Robert's (not his real name), seemed infinitely more real when I got it. I believe in, teach about, and preach God's unconditional love for all of us – including me – but my friend's rejection made me question my value as a person and friend. I can glibly say that God knows my inner being and still loves me; that's theologically correct. The fact remains: Robert knows me very well and does not like what he sees.

At first I thought I had to choose between the two messages, accepting one as true and the other as false. But, in fact, I think they both might be true. My relationship to Robert is complex and I may well have failed him in some significant way. If that is true then I need more than ever to understand that Jesus does indeed love me, in spite of that failure. I share this because I suspect that most of us have a condemning voice sounding in our heart, which is usually louder than the gentle word of grace which God offers us: We've made a big mistake. We've caused someone untold pain. We've disappointed those who trusted us.

Forgiveness is not permission to ignore the consequences of our mistakes, but it is an invitation to believe we need not be bound by our past. When the voice of condemnation is loudest – and perhaps most deserved – listen especially hard for that promise, "Jesus loves you anyway." In it you will find the courage to turn from the past and make a new start.

Baseball and Energy

The cartoon on my office door perfectly captures my attitude toward the game: A feisty old woman stares out from behind her sunglasses and states her dilemma, "Decisions, decisions…watch baseball on TV or watch socks dry on a clothesline?"

Few things match baseball for sheer, mind-numbing tedium: the one pitch per hour pace, the spitting, chewing, and pacing about the mound, the endless, perfunctory attempts to pick off a base runner, the unctuous announcers opining about "strategy" (hit it, catch it – this ain't D-Day we're planning, guys), the absurd importance of knowing whether this ump's strike zone is "high" or "low" (as though the distance between knees and shoulders is an ever changing twilight zone), the annoying reality that as often as not the critical run is scored on a fluky miss-hit ball. As far as I am concerned the best thing about watching baseball in early summer is that there is so little to distract you from the good friends, hotdogs, and beverages nearby.

Give me that same summer day, and I'll head for a hiking trail or call up someone to set up a tennis match. Maybe I'll sit on my front porch and read a tale set in Victorian England, work a crossword puzzle, or take my bike out for a ride down in the valley. I might do any of those things because they reenergize me in a way that watching baseball doesn't.

And that is my point, not that baseball is a lousy way to spend time (I know my opinion is a distinct minority among most who like sports), but that it is absolutely essential that we know what replenishes our batteries and what drains us dry. God has not cranked us out on an assembly line, needing exactly the same fuel to function at optimum level. We are custom creations and we do well to know our own specs.

Some need a lean mixture of solitude, others roar to life with a rich mixture of people. Some like the comfort of a routine; others need novelty to feel fully alive. Some thrive on live theater, and yes, some come back from a baseball game ready to do great things for the kingdom of God. We are wondrously made, and no two alike.

During the holiday season we are often running on empty, draining our spiritual, emotional, and physical reserves. Make sure you take time out to replenish the tank so that you have something worth giving to those around you.

Scorpion Nature

The story has many variations, but one goes like this: The Indian holy man was sitting in meditation. When he moved his leg he touched a scorpion, which immediately stung him. The holy man slowly and gently nudged the scorpion to the edge of the clearing and went back to meditation. An onlooker witnessed the incident and asked, "Why did you not just crush the scorpion?" The holy man replied, "It is the nature of the scorpion to sting; he cannot help it. I choose to be merciful, that is the nature I choose."

There are a lot of scorpions in the public square these days. You pick up the paper and see the kind of naked hatred which brings to mind Selma and Little Rock. It's dressed up in the borrowed garb of patriotism and appeals to national security, but it's the same old scapegoating that always goes on when people get scared. It takes way too much energy and thought to work through complex issues and distinguish genuine threats from irrational fear, so we just demonize "them" – the gays, the Hispanics, the Muslims, the people who for whatever reason are not just like me.

I could wish it would all go away, but the sad truth is that there will always be scorpions. It is the nature of some persons to appeal to our basest instincts. As any political scientist will tell you, they do it for one reason – it works. Scorpions know where the sewer of the soul is located, and they make it the feedline for their message. Until we stop responding, they will keep feeding us bile. We can pray for their conversion, but until that happens, it is the nature of some to sting and spread poison. These are scared people; they need our pity and our compassion. But they also need our witness.

Christians have a choice. We can respond as expected or choose a higher nature. The truly embarrassing reality is that these hate-mongers are disproportionately likely to be sitting in a church on Sunday, praising Jesus and despising many of His children. I cannot make them stop hating, but I can choose not to hate. I cannot stop their stinging, but I can try to gently reject their appeals to my selfishness and my fears. I cannot stop them from sounding the siren songs of simplistic solutions rooted in bigotry, but I can choose not to respond like a Pavlovian dog to their prejudice.

The call to discipleship is an invitation to choose a new identity, to make the way of Jesus more important than whether I am Democrat or Republican, native born or alien, white as an arctic landscape or black as a cavern at midnight. If you are trying, as I am in my own halting way, to grow into the image of Christ, I commend to you these words from I Peter,

"Rid yourselves, therefore, of all malice, and all guile, insincerity, envy, and all slander. Like newborn infants, long for the pure, spiritual milk, so that by it you may grow into salvation – if indeed you have tasted that the Lord is good."

Prayer Before Travel

The mood was pretty grim. Two weeks ago I was in Chicago for some meetings related to my duties with the ELCA's churchwide organization. As we gathered, everyone in that conference room knew that a massive reorganization of the Churchwide office was in the works. Nobody had any idea what the changes would look like or what principles were driving the process. All we knew was that some of us in that room would probably lose our jobs on October 11. It made for a lot of awkwardness: Do you say good-bye to the guy across the table? How much effort do you put into greeting the new secretary? Why do strategic planning for an entity which may not exist in two weeks? Looking closely into the faces of those around the room, you could see that slightly pop-eyed expression which is a sure tipoff of anxiety.

The last thing we did before heading home was worship, and a dear friend led us in reciting together one of the great prayers of the church.

"Lord, you have called your servants to ventures of which we cannot see the ending, by paths as yet untrodden, through perils unknown. Give us faith to go out with good courage, not knowing where we go, but only that your hand is leading us and your love supporting us; through Jesus Christ our Lord. Amen."

I tell you this story for a couple of reasons. First, I invite you to rediscover the incredible treasure which is the church's liturgical tradition. Sometimes, as the apostle Paul says, we do not know how to pray. Our hearts melt. Our tongues grow thick. Our minds freeze. Others have walked similar paths before us and left us a legacy of psalms, prayers, and songs. We can borrow their words to express our deepest emotions and remember whose we are as God's beloved.

Second, as I recited those words in Chicago I thought of those in my life who are facing challenging days and I felt a kinship with them: a classmate who is waiting to see if the treatment worked, the colleague whose call became intolerable, the senior whose job prospects are uncertain, and the multiple members of Luther Memorial whose burdens I know in part. We sometimes have the illusion that we can nail down all the tent pegs once and for all, but in truth, there is always a piece of fabric flapping in the winds of change. We need one another. Being part of the body of Christ is all about the willingness to speak a word of hope and be its incarnation when a brother or sister is looking into the darkness of uncertainty.

As I write these words I have no idea what October 11 will bring for me personally, but I want to bear witness that I have been incredibly blessed by Christ and the community which bears His name. God has been faithful and will be still. If you are facing transition, uncertainty, or anxiety, linger with the church's classic "prayer before travel," which I quoted above. May it give you assurance as you take the next steps.

Peer Review

I spent several days last week serving as the peer on a campus ministry review in another state. I value these reviews because I get to appropriate good ideas from other campus ministries. That was particularly true this time; the ministries we reviewed are doing some creative things under difficult circumstances. Yet in the midst of much that was laudable I felt the need to offer a few pointed comments to one of my colleagues.

It happened that he was the one charged with transporting me for my return flight to Blacksburg. We shared a cordial lunch on our way to the airport, but I could not help wondering how he had received my less than unconditionally affirming observations. We pulled up to that hectic drop-off lane which, at major airports, feels like pit row on a NASCAR track. As I was jumping out of the car he grasped my hand and he said, "Bill, thanks for being part of this review and especially thanks for your loving candor; without honesty, reviews are not very helpful."

I share this incident, not so that you will see what a wonderfully pastoral and astute reviewer I was (I may have been way off base), but to lift up the truth of his general point and the graciousness of his spirit. Most of us have no shortage of people surrounding us who share our opinions and reinforce our way of looking at the world. Rarer are those people who care enough about us to say the hard word we do not particularly want to hear. Rarer still is the ability, when we receive loving critique, to embrace the words as signs of care rather than attack.

This Thanksgiving week we will offer our gratitude for many things: material abundance in a world of want, the gathering of family when many are separated by distance or deployment, health when friends face the specter of illness. My guess is that there will be a little tension around some of our Thanksgiving tables; there usually is. Maybe some of the words we find awkward are not intended to be an attack, but are rather a genuine effort to "speak the truth in love." Think how your response might be different if you chose to view words of challenge as opportunities to grow. Christian love is not sappy sentimentalism. Love desires the best for the other. Love is caringly honest. Love risks rejection. Along with offering thanks for food, family, and freedom I plan to offer thanks for those who care enough about me to make me slightly uncomfortable. Such persons are to be highly valued because they accept us as we are but long to help us be better.

Packing For Two Climates

I am on vacation. One of the challenges of this particular vacation has been packing. During the first half of our time away we will be hiking in Glacier National Park; the ten-day forecast shows crisp temperatures ranging from a low of 25 to a high of 68 degrees. In contrast, 68 degrees in July would be an arctic blast for Lake Charles, Louisiana That's where we will spend the second half of our time away, visiting my brother in south Louisiana, where you need a snorkel to breathe and even the gators have enough sense to just loll in the mud this time of year.

So, in one carry-on bag how do you pack for both alpine meadow and tropical swamp? Of course it can be done and, unless we hit a freak blizzard, I suspect that a little smart layering will keep me warm in Montana and – just maybe – cool enough on the bayou.

Simultaneously packing for two very different climates is a metaphor for what life demands of us. In any given week we experience both highs and lows. We get a promotion – and then discover our child is in for a year of busing to a distant school. We enjoy date night with our spouse and return to a message that Mom has fallen and busted her hip. We bring our big work project to a successful completion on the day the cholesterol test says our diet is going to be a lot less exciting. It's a challenge to maintain equilibrium amid emotional peaks and valleys.

The apostle Paul knew a little bit about highs and lows. His preaching wowed them in one place and started a riot in the next town. He knew what it was like to inspire great devotion and snarling contempt, to transform lives today and face utter apathy tomorrow. He enjoyed all the prestige of Roman citizenship but spent his last days shackled in prison.

Near the end of his life he wrote to the church at Philippi, "… I have learned to be content with whatever I have. I know what it is to have little, and I know what it is to have plenty. In any and all circumstances I have learned the secret of being well-fed and of going hungry, of having plenty and of being in need. I can do all things through Him who strengthens me."

Paul learned to take his cue from something deeper than the uncertain highs and lows of life. Whatever life brought him he received it in the spirit of one who knows he is profoundly loved by God. He received joys with thanksgiving and setbacks as opportunities for growth. Life does indeed blow hot and cold; our identity as God's beloved children, claimed and called by Christ, is a garment for all seasons. It gives comfort when adversity chills us and fits us for service like a favorite pair of work jeans. Put it on daily.

Welcome to My World

"Welcome to my world." It was scary to be in Blacksburg last week. A desperate criminal was on the loose, a man who had already killed two people. The worst part was not knowing where he was. He had a gun. He had little to lose. They couldn't find him – and he could have been anywhere. Suddenly, the sleepy little town, where the worst thing you usually have to worry about is a drunken college student stepping in front of your car on Main Street, felt unsafe. The idyllic trail where you go for a refreshing walk was a homicide scene. For most of a day the hallowed halls of learning were a locked down security zone. You couldn't presume the normal rhythms of waking, working, eating, and sleeping.

And that's when I heard the little girl's voice, the little girl from South Central L.A., or Darfur, or Kabul, or southern Lebanon, or from a hundred other places around the world where you can take nothing for granted when you wake up each morning – including that you will wake up each morning. "Welcome to my world, a world where it is not just a remote possibility that someone will die violently in front of me today, where going to school is an act of courage, and gunfire is the backbeat of my life's soundtrack."

I like to think I am a somewhat compassionate person who is reasonably aware of suffering in the world. I write checks when there is a disaster. I vote against my own economic interests if I think it might be good for the poor and vulnerable. But last week taught me that I have absolutely no idea what it is like to live as millions do, counting a day without bloodshed, hunger, or stomach-churning fear as a precious gift of grace. I discovered that my sympathy is usually exercised the same way I view lions at the zoo – from a safe distance. That's not all bad; it's better to see something rather than nothing. Even limited awareness holds the possibility of action. But viewing from a safe distance means I often take it as a grievous offense when life denies me small pleasures, and I am likely to impose middle-class standards on the decisions of those who are probably doing the best they can to just keep it in the road.

Next time you see the news footage of women holding

the twisted bodies of their children after a bomb blast or of boys playing hoops in front of a graffiti-scarred wall, take a moment… pause…remember what it felt like to be insecure. Try to imagine what it would be like to live a day, a month, a lifetime in chronic fear. Then say a prayer of thanksgiving for all that you take for granted, resolving, at the same time, to be gentle in your judgments of those who daily labor under burdens most of us can hardly comprehend.

No Time Machine

Two people said essentially the same thing last week.

She was a cute little girl who showed up each morning to be part of our Vacation Bible School. She must have had a great time. At the end of the week she gushed to one of her teachers, "Oh, I wish I had a time machine so I could go back and do this whole week again." [VBS staff – any doubts now that it was so worth it?]

He was a man in his twenties on the edge of despair. The accumulated legacy of many bad choices brought him to a crisis. He sat on the sofa, staring into space, surveying the wreckage that was his life and wondering what might have been. "I wish I could be young again, before all this happened."

Two very different people, in very different circumstances, yet each wanting to freeze time and go back to a pristine moment. We cannot go back; time moves inexorably on. Still, we wrestle with the twin temptations of trying to live in days which will never come again or of letting the past hold our future hostage. Part of the art of living is learning how to deal with our past. Can we receive the good with thanksgiving, rejoicing in the people and events which have enriched us, without constantly rejecting our present? Can we confront our mistakes, reaping wisdom rather than merely self-contempt?

We Lutherans talk a lot about "grace." It seems to me that embracing grace is at the heart of living with hope and joy. A gracious spirit is wonderfully aware that God's unmerited, extravagant love fills each day; it receives past signs of that love with thanksgiving and looks to the future with expectation of continuing care. At the same time, when we make a hash of life, a grace-filled spirit trusts that God's mercy can open the shackles which bind us to a dead day. The psalmist understood the nature of grace, may we also...

1 Bless the Lord, O my soul, and all that is within me, bless his holy name.

2 Bless the Lord, O my soul, and do not forget all his benefits –

3 who forgives all your iniquity, who heals all your diseases,

4 who redeems your life from the Pit, who crowns you with steadfast love and mercy,

5 who satisfies you with good as long as you live so that your youth is renewed like the eagle's. (Psalm 103)

Dr. Bass

I hated Dr. Bass in the fall. When I was growing up our yard had a bunch of pines and a few small ornamentals my Dad planted. My fall leaf raking should have taken ten minutes – except for Dr. Bass, our next door neighbor.

Our yard was all but devoid of deciduous trees; his was covered (quite literally) by mature oaks. Because he loved birds, his landscaping consisted of making his yard a natural habitat through benign neglect. He didn't mow the grass. He didn't trim bushes. And he certainly didn't rake leaves. Our lot was down the hill from his, so every fall I watched in dread as the massive yellow, red, and brown army mustered on the ground in his yard, knowing that the first big wind would march it down the hill, where I would have to spend some glorious fall afternoons (much better devoted to backyard football) doing battle with rake and tarp – while he watched his bird feeders. It just didn't seem fair.

That was my introduction to the reality that our lives are inextricably bound up with others'. I can try to teach my children well, but the poor parenting their friends receive may impact my children's choices. I can drive as carefully as I know how, but if another guy has an extra beer or two, tragedy may be unavoidable. We can turn our nation into fortress America, curtail civil liberties, and do all the right things to promote a vibrant economy, hoping to create a little island of affluence and security, but hunger, rage, and desperation on the other side of the world are likely to breach whatever barriers we erect.

For good or ill we are bound together. We can regard that fact with resentment and fight to seal ourselves off from others, a course both futile and lonely. Or as Christians we can embrace our connection to others as an opportunity to share their burdens and rejoice in the gifts which they can offer us. By embracing our connectedness we open ourselves to receive many blessings and live out the way of service and compassion to which Jesus calls us.

I had to rake Dr. Bass's leaves, but looking back, I realize I saw a lot of beautiful birds, more than most see in their manicured subdivisions. Dr. Bass was a gentle man who indirectly taught me something about what is really important.

336

I guess that lesson was worth a few lost football games.

Fraternity

I've joined a not so elite fraternity over the past few weeks. No Greek letters. No frat house. No kegs (though, as you will see, that might be a good addition). This is most assuredly not a fraternity I wanted to pledge – folks rehabbing from knee surgery. We have our chapter meetings several times a week at Blacksburg Physical Therapy. You can spot the brothers and sisters of "Gotta Gotta Cry"; we're the ones who regard staircases with the affection generally reserved for rattlesnakes and telemarketers.

Being in physical therapy is the epitome of vulnerability. What we once did unconsciously is now painfully difficult. We feel awkward, so we don't gawk at one another. But out of the corner of my eye I see the young girl doing the "quad sets" which mark a weak knee on the mend. I note the guy in the soccer shirt trying to get just five more degrees of motion in a joint which acts splinted. I see the avid biker's eyes cross in agony every time the trainer's pedal comes around.

I guess we have similar work schedules because I often see the same people when I go in for my appointments – and I find myself rooting for them. Slowly we've started to greet one another. We exchange gallows humor about our "torturers" (though I have nothing but the highest regard for the folks who work with me). We give each other a thumbs-up when the knee finally holds on a "step up" exercise. Just knowing others understand my "ice pick in the knee cap" helps me keep going.

I am sure you have had a similar experience – the community of chemo, the fellowship of the bereavement, the company of the laid off. You develop a special kinship when you share a struggle. It's good when we are able to give focused support to others because we know a lot about their pain. But why does it take trauma to wake us up to the struggles of those around us? The reality is that we do not meet a single person in the course of our day who is not laboring under some sort of burden. Our challenge is to be as sensitive to another's need as a feather responding to the gentlest breeze.

There is a wonderful story in Mark 6:24-34. Jesus is in a crowd. Everyone is pushing and shoving, but one single woman, hoping for healing, sneaks up to touch him. Jesus says, "Who touched me?" The disciples say, in essence, "You're in a mob; lots of folks did." But Jesus sees deeper; he feels one woman's need in the midst of the chaos. Calling the woman forward, He gently engages her.

Today, try to sense the need of those around you – in the downcast eye, the deep sigh, and even in the testy attitude which makes compassion hard – and then respond with grace and care.

False Witness

Earlier this week I heard a wonderful lecture by Amy-Jill Levine, an orthodox Jew and eminent Biblical scholar. Her topic was the many ways Christians (and particularly preachers) often misunderstand First Century Judaism, and thus, inadvertently, misread the Bible and contribute to anti-Semitism. Sometimes the problem is lack of information, and sometimes it is sheer thoughtlessness. Concerning the latter, she said that for many years she brought her small son into her classes, dressed in a way which identified him as unmistakably a Jew. Then she would say to her classes, "Anytime you are preaching or teaching about 'the Jews,' imagine you have this little boy on the front row and do not say anything which might be hurtful to him or cause him harm…and if that's not enough, imagine me on the back row, because I won't let you get away with that stuff!"

We all know that one of the Ten Commandments is not to bear false witness against our neighbor. In truth, we seldom tell a bare-faced lie about someone else. But we bear false witness every day when we allow our ignorance to outpace our tongues. We bear false witness when we assume the worst of another's words or motives. We bear false witness when we accept stereotypical images of other groups because it just takes too much energy and time to begin understanding them in any depth. We bear false witness when we impute malevolence to those who simply disagree with us.

Dr. Levine is a brilliant, articulate scholar, and I think imagining her on the back pew when I'm preaching would indeed put the fear of God in me, but as she herself suggested, imagining that little boy on the front row would be even more effective. It is just much harder to tell lies – about gays, Tea Party members, Liberals, or members of the NRA – when you imagine yourself looking into the eyes of someone for whom Christ died instead of a faceless cipher. Try putting a face on any group which you are tempted to dismiss and demean this week. It might lower your blood pressure and be a small step toward greater understanding.

CMS

Okay. It's official. I am undeniably a geek. I can't say this came as a total surprise; I've suspected these tendencies for years. But this weekend, with the rain echoing in the gutters outside my living room, I cuddled up with…*The Chicago Manual of Style*. I could plead professional motivation; my editorial duties with the ELCA often require consulting an authority on punctuation and usage. But that would be only partially honest. In truth, I enjoyed working my way through the rules governing whether the question mark goes inside the parentheses. I found a certain satisfaction in having what often seems arbitrary, or at least obscure, laid out in clean, logical prose. I felt a sense of control in understanding exactly why complex sentences are punctuated as they are.

That sense of control helped me see why so many people read the Bible as though it has the precision of a chemical formula rather than the evocative power of a Shakespearean sonnet. When the world seems dangerous, confused, and out of control, there is a seductive sense of security in pretending discipleship is reducible to rules as logical and precise as *The Chicago Manual of Style*'s prescriptions on the use of commas. It is uncomfortable to admit that, though the direction of our Christian journey is clear, many steps are shrouded in fog. Uncomfortable? Yes. But also honest concerning the messy world in which we live. Reality seldom conforms to simplistic explanations.

Even in the precise world of *The Chicago Manual of Style* the rules are not always clear or complete. The 14th edition (the one I was reading is the 15th) says very little regarding how to reference electronic media, and these days it is a rare research paper with no Web citations. Life evolves; clarity gives way to flux. Life presents us with challenges unheard of a generation ago. There are no simple answers. But there is the person of Jesus. There are few precise prescriptions, but there are His promises: "Peace I leave with you; My peace I give to you." "I am the vine you are the branches. He who abides in me, and I in him, he it is that bears much fruit." We don't need a rulebook; we need confidence in Him who rules with love.

Bean Plate

"What have you to do with us, Jesus of Nazareth?" (unclean spirit to Jesus, Mark 1:24)

I always prayed for partitions on bean day. Our high school cafeteria had two kinds of plates: standard and those which divided the plate into three sections. If you got one with the partitions, your square of corn bread was safely protected from the pink wave, formed by a mix of navy bean juice and pickled beet seepage, sloshing across the plate. A regular plate meant the bottom of your cornbread was a gloppy mess. I preferred my cornbread untainted by the "red tide."

Of course it was no great tragedy if the beet juice touched my cornbread, but it is a much bigger deal when we try to partition off little segments of our lives from the influence of the gospel. The first challenge Jesus gets in His public ministry is from an unclean spirit suggesting that maybe there are areas that really don't concern Jesus, personal places beyond His purview and power. Mark devotes a lot of time in his gospel to showing there is absolutely no sphere of human or natural existence outside Jesus' interest and sovereignty.

Maybe we don't worry too much about bean juice and beets turning our cornbread pink, but we certainly like to partition off little pieces of our lives and say, "Lord, there are some things on my plate I don't want you touching. This care for neighbor is fine most of the time, but you aren't going to make much money unless you keep the gospel at a distance from the bottom line....I can forgive everyone except my ex; let me treat that relationship as a special case... I'm a busy man, Lord; you can't really expect me to take time for prayer...Money, time, abilities – you can have them all, Jesus – but my sexuality is of no concern to you."

What we decide regarding the complex issues each of us faces daily is a matter of careful, prayerful discernment. Equally faithful persons can make different choices. What we cannot do is bracket-off spheres of life, pretending Jesus has no place there. Two things I believe: Beet juice should not bleed into cornbread. The blood of Christ must color every choice and relationship in the lives of the Baptized.

Kitchen Renovation

We're renovating our kitchen. I have deliberately avoided talking much about this in sermons and meditations because I can see how folks might quickly become sick unto death of hearing about the joys and sorrows of this endeavor. Projects such as these are like baby pictures – of much more interest to those responsible for them than to others. But there have been some insights. So, a few things I've learned in the past weeks:

• You can't avoid the mess – Life itself is unsettled; nothing endures forever. If you want to move forward there are times when the old lies broken all around you. It is disconcerting and inconvenient when familiar things disappear. But letting go and living with some measure of good cheer in the between times is part of welcoming new possibilities.

• You can do with less – Gail and I have been living in two bedrooms and two bathrooms (try washing dishes in the tub!). It is not the way I plan to keep living. I look forward to the new kitchen. But I am mindful that we are not suffering – and many in our world would love to have the option to wash their dishes in a tub like mine instead of a ditch or river doubling as a sewer. I say, "I need" less these days. But...

- You need other people – I never know who is going to be clopping around in my house as I prepare to leave for the day. We have a great general contractor who has coordinated the parts like a symphony conductor. There is a steady stream of people bringing their gifts to molding beauty out of the chaos: carpenters, electricians, painters, dry wallers, cabinet installers, supervisors, and assorted other craftsmen. I need them all and am thankful for the different skills and passions they possess. I appreciate that they care as much about their art as I do about structuring these sentences.

- You need hope – I truly am learning from this experience, but make no mistake I will very glad when it is over. My ability to endure is directly related to my capacity to tick off one more day on the schedule, one more completed step in the process. In the moments when the air is filled with dust, and I am tired of confining my culinary adventures to what can be cooked in a microwave or crock pot I remember, "This too will pass." How much harder for those who wake up each morning with few prospects of seeing a better job, decent health care, or housing which is not cold and drafty.

Here is where we preachers usually spell out the implications of our thoughts. But you readers of BFJ are smart folks. You don't need me to make the applications. May you find in the above a word to lift or challenge you this day.

Old Friend

I went by to visit an old friend today. There was a time when we saw each other almost daily, but times changed. He took a different job. I got busy. Our paths did not naturally cross and we did not make the effort to make sure they did. It's a familiar story. He's had some health problems lately, and it was a lot easier for me to go to him than vice versa. So I stopped by. Despite his pain he received me warmly, and it was like old times.

I'm working on a project, and as we talked I remembered that he has a long interest and expertise in the area. I thought he might appreciate a chance to reengage, might like an invitation to put his oar in the water. So I asked him if he would be interested in helping me. I saw his face darken a little and then he said, "Now I know why you came by to see me; you wanted me to do something." He said it without much edge; the smile never left his face. Still, I realized he suspected it might be true. He did not need a project; he wanted me to be a friend. The visit lost a little of its sparkle after that.

Driving away I thought how terribly important it is for us to feel valued just for who we are and not for what we can do for someone. Most of our personal interactions are about greasing the skids, establishing a working relationship, setting up the context for getting something from the other. We rarely interact with someone who does not have an agenda. So it is all the more precious when we feel that genuine warmth which says, "I want nothing from you except the pleasure of your company."

God's baptismal gift to us is to value us when we have precious little to offer in return. God delights in us just because we are who we are. Is there someone to whom you could give a similar gift today? Who could use a moment of grace, the experience of being cared about, no strings attached? Take a moment to be the love of Christ for another. You can probably do a better job than I did.

My First iPod

I got my first iPod last week. Half of you reading these words are saying, "Whazzat?" and the other half are asking, "What took you so long?" For the first group, an iPod is a small device that allows you to transfer and play music and other digital files from your computer to a portable player.

Which brings me to the crucial question: What music do I transfer? If you have a ten zillion gigabyte iPod, there's no issue; you can put the holdings of the Library of Congress on the thing and have room to spare. But mine is relatively small; it only holds about 500 songs (and a symphony takes up multiple "song" spaces). So what do I choose? Do I put on the drug-soaked rock anthems of my youth (you gotta have the Stones, Zeppelin, and the Doors don't you)? Do I admit that I am officially over the hill and give John Denver and Neil Diamond some bytes? Given limited space do I want the Motown slide and glide of the Temptations and the Supremes or the more intellectual, angst ridden music of Paul Simon and U2? And that's just soul, pop, and rock. My kids can attest that I am woefully ignorant of contemporary music (say the last 20 years). I don't have to worry about finding space for rap or (with the exception of Willie Nelson and Johnny Cash) country, but it's amazing how quickly the space fills up. What about the jazz, blues, and classical that makes up two-thirds of my collection?

In fact I have discovered that this forced choice exercise

tells me a lot about myself. I am realizing what music really is my favorite, of course. But more than that I'm remembering how music has moved me at various points in my life. I'm discovering what musical emotions resonate within me, what words I borrow to speak of my own longings, hopes, questions, and affirmations; which composers move me into places I cannot even name, but in which I am uplifted and healed.

If you have an iPod, what's on it? What does it say about who you are and what you value? What does it say about your fundamental attitude toward life and other people? "Hey, it's just music," you might say, "it's no biggie; I just like the beat." But allow me to suggest that what you force feed into your ears both reflects and forms who you are. It matters whether you fill your diet with veggies or Twinkies. It matters what you listen to. The whole concept of liturgy is premised on the conviction that we are changed by repeated exposure to a certain way of thinking, seeing, singing, and speaking. It's no different when we walk outside the church doors; we are changed by the words we hear and repeat. Even if you don't have an iPod, you can play this game. What would you put on it, if you did? What would it reveal about you?

The point is not that there is one "Christian" playlist or genre. I've shared some of my tastes and preferences, but I hardly claim them as the norm. In a complex world we do well to cultivate eclectic tastes in order better to sample the diversity of life. Rather, the point is that we need to be aware of what we consume – intellectually, emotionally, musically – because it does affect our spiritual health. Does something feed your soul? Tell me about it. I've still got some space on my iPod – and I can always delete "Staying Alive."

Reconciliation

A quick question: In the past week, if you listened to more than an hour of NPR news, how much Fox News did you watch; if you watched more than an hour of Fox, how much NPR did you hear? I am going to go out on a limb and predict that the answer will be close to zero for most of us. As any media expert will tell you, we usually listen to news programs which reinforce our view of the world rather than challenge it – and of course we defend our choice on the grounds that it truer, less biased, and more balanced than the alternatives. From there it is a short step to imputing ignorance and malevolence to those with whom we disagree.

As I read the New Testament I am struck by how hard the gospel witnesses work to understand the perspective of those to whom they speak. They do not flinch from saying what needs to be said, but they make an effort to see the world through the eyes of their audience. John casts the preface to his gospel in the language of Greek philosophy. Matthew frames his witness within the Jewish tradition, even as he shows how Jesus challenges the status quo. Paul says "I have become all things to all people, that I might by all means save some." These witnesses understand that until others believe we take their concerns seriously, they are not willing to hear us.

Few would deny that the tone of discourse grows more strident every day. Everyone is desperately concerned to "win" on the issues which confront society. But is that really the primary goal for Christians? Are we not charged with a much more difficult task? In II Corinthians 5:18-20 Paul reminds us that we are entrusted with the ministry of reconciliation, that is, the ministry of bridging the chasms which divide God from humanity and people from people. Being an agent of reconciliation takes patience and a willingness to be abused and misunderstood by those between whom we stand with arms outreached. Before that it takes listening and understanding.

This week make an effort to take seriously a perspective with which you violently disagree. It will not be comfortable, but it might fit you more effectively to witness to Christ.

Troy

I depend on Troy. I don't know if he knows my name, but over the years I have gotten to know his. Troy's the plumbing specialist at Heavener Hardware, and when you have an older home as I do, he is a good man to know. Over the Thanksgiving holidays we had a little incident involving my small nephew, a clog, a worn out commode flapper, and enough water to fill a bedroom (I know because it did). So Monday morning I was off to see Troy.

Troy knows his stuff, but I particularly appreciate him because he understands that I don't speak fluent plumbing. I am sure when he sees me coming he thinks, "Here comes that guy with the all the smarts of a cast iron drain cover." But whether it's a leaky commode, a worn out lavatory valve, or a sink trap oozing foul odors, he patiently – and often repeatedly – walks me through the project, being sure I get the piece I need and that I won't hurt myself putting it in.

I suppose I have learned a little bit about plumbing over the years, but those little forays to the store have also been another form of continuing education. They remind me of something I need to remember every day: What seems easy to me is very hard for somebody else, and a little patience is deeply appreciated when you are feeling stupid and vulnerable.

Notice, as you read Scripture, how Jesus never talks down to people. If questioners think they are smart He takes them on at that level, giving them all the verbal jousting they want. But if someone comes to Him weak, confused, and needy He is gentle and patient. Jesus deals with people as though they are valuable and teachable. Whether we sell plumbing supplies, preach sermons, or just meet people each day, that is a model worth imitating.

Gotta Lift Him Up

Fruitvale Station is one of the most humane movies I have seen in a long time. It tells the story of events leading up to the tragic shooting of a young black man by BART police at a transit stop in Oakland. Not the least polemical, the film gently shows the complexity of racial relations in America and how small events can have tragic consequences.

When Oscar, the 22-year-old center of the story, is shot, he is taken to the hospital. The anger of Oscar's friends is palpable as they gather in the ER waiting to learn whether he will live or die. But Oscar's mom, clearly a person of faith, repeatedly exhorts them, "We gotta lift him up y'all, we just gotta keep lift'n him up." Those words moved me on multiple levels and lingered in my mind long after I left the theater.

They were oil on troubled water. At the moment when she could have quite understandably yielded to hate for a totally senseless act, she modeled something deeper. She could have stoked the fires of a brewing riot, but she focused on what she and those who loved Oscar might be able to do to bring him through. How much time do you and I waste just being angry?

They were a confession of faith. If you have never been privileged to be in a black congregation when the community gets serious about prayer, you have missed one of life's great worship experiences. You feel the power flowing from folks who are speaking boldly to a God they fully expect to be listening. The will and the love of many get funneled together, becoming a great wave of confession and intercession. Consider how often our own prayer, public and private, is pro forma. We expect little and are not surprised by the meager results.

They encapsulated our calling as people of God in a broken world. We have just got to keep lifting one another up. When illness comes; we gotta lift one another. When disappointment comes; we gotta lift. When life beats down our brothers and sisters, when those who work for justice get discouraged, when we look out and see hunger and despair – we have got to keep lifting, because that is what it means to follow the One who lifted a cross.

There are a lot of folks bending low – some right near you…"We gotta lift 'um up y'all; we just gotta keep lift'n 'um up."

Words of Affirmation

It was an unlikely time and place for a moment of grace. I was sitting in the hall at the doctor's office, waiting to be ushered into an examining room, so feverish I could hardly keep my head up. The waves of coughing erupting from my chest sounded like a flock of geese. He had finished his appointment and was on his way out when he paused to tell me that something I said in a sermon had changed his morning routine .... She heard I was sick, and dropped me an e-mail to say she was thinking about me – and by the way, she said, something I have been reading made me think of you and some things you've said.

Simple little acts of remembrance, but they made a difference in how I remember what was otherwise a rather miserable 24 hours. Most of the work of God done in our world, the acts of support, kindness, and affirmation, happens in simple deeds of thoughtfulness. Is there someone to whom you could express appreciation today? By such simple things does the kingdom of God transform our world.

Epiphany, St. Matthews

When I was in seminary, all my classmates knew Epiphany Luther Church, in St. Matthews, S.C. It was a tiny congregation which depended on the seminary to send a student each week to be the preacher. Presiding at Epiphany was an odd experience. You arrived at the congregation a few minutes before 11:00. At the appointed hour, somebody would check his watch, walk up to the altar, flick his Bic to light the candles, and then nod to the seminarian to begin. When you stepped into the pulpit you saw about eight people (on a good Sunday) dispersed over a worship space which could seat 150. That made for a strange dynamic; if you made eye contact with someone, they felt like you were preaching directly to them. You had to be very careful how you said lines that were the least bit confrontational, lest someone feel singled out.

I don't know the history of that congregation. I never sensed any particular animosity among the faithful remnant who worshipped each week. But it was hard to feel much sense of community when the congregation was spread out, one or two to a pew, all around the nave.

I thought about Epiphany, St. Matthews this morning because Sunday's worship at Luther Memorial was the exact opposite. More than one person commented to me that, because it felt so intimate, they liked gathering in the smaller space of the picnic shelter for our Care of Creation themed worship. Okay, perhaps we gathered so tightly to be sure we did not get rained on, but the effect was that we could better see and hear one another. The sum was indeed greater than the total of the individual parts.

My point is a simple one, which I think needs to be made repeatedly: The life of faith is not an individual sport. We need one another. We are most joyful, effective, and what Jesus intended the church to be when we share our lives in worship, in service, and in small study and prayer groups. This week, think about one way in which you can build up a sense of community and common purpose in the congregation with which you identify. Sing a little louder. Drop a note to someone who is having a hard time. Invite someone to lunch. Greet a stranger after worship. The possibilities are many, but the goal is the same, to make the welcome of Christ tangible to all you meet.

Dronescape

Last week I attended the opening of a show by two talented members of Luther Memorial congregation, Donald and Joanna Sunshine. One of Donald's watercolors, entitled "Dronescape," continues to haunt me. I would not presume to say what the painting "means" or what it represents (assuming it is even intended to be representational), but I can tell you how it affected me. I associate landscapes and seascapes with natural beauty. Sometimes that beauty is savage and dangerous, but more often it is serene and peaceful. For me Donald's painting evoked the slums above Rio, the camps in Gaza, and the shacks of the poor which hang tenuously on eroded hillsides all around the world. Consider, the work said to me, another kind of "'scape," one where the sculpting power is not wind and water but the savage energies of war and technology.

Many mornings I wake up to news of a drone strike in some faraway place. But "drone strikes" had always been a rather abstract, bloodless idea for me. When I thought about them at all, they brought to mind men sitting in front of screens far from the muck of a battlefield who, at the end of the day, go home to their families in some suburb beyond the beltway. Donald's painting has got me pondering the consequences of drones in the real world – and I suspect that was at least part of the point.

The morality of drone strikes is not my point in this brief meditation. That is a topic with more facets than a fine diamond. If there is a political point to be made, the painting and its title do not need my commentary; they speak for themselves. Instead, I invite you to consider how often we are oblivious to the consequences of our actions. For good and ill we impact others daily and yet we are usually blissfully ignorant of how a word or gesture affects another. We launch multiple drones each day and then move on to the next item on the to-do list, seldom pondering what destruction we may have left behind.

I wonder, if we stopped to consider the consequences of our actions, how many of the things we have said and done would we take back? In my experience, few people are deliberately hurtful, but we are often thoughtless. Take a little time this week to notice how others are affected by interacting with you. Are you a blessing? What does the dronescape around your passing look like?

Ray

If you have not seen *Ray*, you have missed a great portrayal. As one critic said, Jamie Fox does not play Ray Charles, he becomes him. It's worth the price of admission just to see the acting. I mention this movie in Bread for the Journey because it points to an important truth about life. As I came out of *Ray* I was thinking that music was a mixed blessing for Ray Charles. Music was this blind boy's ticket out of grinding poverty, a source of dignity in the days of Jim Crow, and the language he used to express all that is human. At the same time music was a demanding mistress which strained his marriage, led him into drug dependency, and often caused him to treat friends with calculating coldness. His gift both gave and demanded a great deal.

It would be nice if life's decisions were all clearly labeled "smart" and "dumb," if each crossroads had an illuminated sign indicating "good choice" and "bad choice." But reality is messier than that. The project to which we give much time yields both a pay raise and children who miss their daddy or mom. The decision to decline the big promotion in order to coach soccer or stay home with a baby leaves us feeling unfulfilled. We take a stand based on conscience and discover it costs us a lot without really making much difference by worldly standards. Existence is a perpetual bazaar in which we trade our lives for things which turn out to be junk – or a pearl of great price.

At the end of *Ray* one senses that, on balance, Ray Charles has minimal regrets about his life. He made some choices, some of which were painful for himself and others, but in the end he seems to have exorcised the worst of the demons. I have no idea whether the movie is historically accurate or not, but it seems to me the lesson stands. We want to live each day with a clear awareness of what we are buying and what it is costing us, so that we can have few regrets. At the same time, let us never forget that, for the Christian, life is not beyond redemption when we discover we have paid too much for too little. Choices are seldom simple. We make mistakes. But confident of God's care we can begin again.

Pastoral Heart

One of my minor anxieties is that the day the Lord called me into ordained ministry, I wandered in front of the thunderbolt meant for my wife, Gail. I fantasize that Jesus started to correct the mistake, cocked his head, and said, "Oh what the heck, I'll use her as a teacher; let him give it a shot." In many ways Gail has a more pastoral heart than I do. For example, last Saturday night…

I was one of those who left the game with a quarter to go. No great anger, no disgusted displays of disproportionate investment in a mere football game. Actually it was just the opposite. I figured it was a rational, dispassionate decision: it was late. The game was no longer interesting or competitive. I had a long day coming up on Sunday. No need to be exhausted over a lost cause. So, over my beloved's objections, we left. I thought I was being eminently reasonable. You go to a game to be entertained and enjoy yourself. When the game is boring and painful there's no more reason to stay than there is to keep hitting your hand with a hammer.

Gail is much less interested in sports than I, but she understood there is more to going to a game than enjoying football. Part of being a fan is being there precisely when your team is doing lousy, when there is precious little reason to be proud. Being a fan is not just about what you get, but what you have the power to give. In retrospect I wish I had stayed to affirm those guys who gave the best effort they could on a night when a victory wasn't in the cards.

Each time we interact with someone there are two ways to look at the situation. We can focus on the task at hand: Is the checkout clerk working efficiently? Has the student planned the program well? Is this committee accomplishing anything worthwhile? Tasks are important, but they aren't necessarily the most important thing. We can also focus on how our words and actions are affecting other persons. Are they built up or torn down? Through us, do they experience the compassion of God or a sense of judgment? Do our actions lessen or increase the burdens others are bearing?

Having a pastoral heart has little to do with whether you are ordained or not. A "pastoral" heart is literally the heart of one who feeds others, a shepherd. A pastoral heart guides, nurtures, and protects. Whether our job is preaching sermons or producing widgets, we might focus beyond the tasks on our agenda in order to see the people whom we bolster or bruise by our actions. Such caring is calling for all God's people.

Lamott on Teens

You do not need to read this week's Bread for the Journey

unless you have a teenager, have a child who might become a teenager, care about a teenager, would like to make growing up less brutal and confusing for a teenager, or think our world would be better if we all cared about children struggling to become adults. Anne Lamott, in *Plan B: Further Thoughts on Faith*, on what young adults are looking for:

"I make Sam [her son] go [to church] because the youth group leaders know things I don't. They know what teenagers are looking for, and need – they need adults who have stayed alive and vital, adults they wouldn't mind growing up to be. And they need total acceptance of who they are, from adults they trust, and to be welcomed in whatever condition life has left them – needy, walled off. They want guides, adults who know how to act like adults, but with a kid's heart. They want people who will sit with them and talk about the big questions, even if they don't have the answers; adults who won't correct their feelings or pretend not to be afraid. They are looking for adventure, experience, pilgrimages, and thrills. And then they want a home they can return to, where things are stable and welcoming."

Twenty-one years as a campus pastor, and longer than that as a man trying to be a good father, convince me Lamott has nailed it. Can you be the adult she is talking about for a teenager this week?

And one final thing…thanks to all of you who serve as mentors in classrooms, on ball fields, and by being examples of Christian caring. You make a difference; never doubt it.

Gas and Katrina

He was bellowing about gas prices. Our daughter had some car trouble last week, and I was waiting at the service station to give her a lift. At the first sound of his cry (akin to a wounded warthog) I lifted my eyes from the newspaper photos of Hurricane Katrina's destruction to behold his brand new silver Cadillac sucking nourishment at the pump. He was well-dressed; his shoes alone cost more than you'd make working several shifts at minimum wage. This was not someone whose ability to work depended on affordable transportation. Yet you would have thought his first born child had just been snatched away in exchange for a few gallons of gas.

I confess I am always a bit mystified by folks who obsess about the cost of gas, who drive all around town to save a few pennies. Most of the world would kill to have our prices. But on this particular day his display was positively obscene. Bodies rotting in attics. Whole counties flattened. Families sick with worry after watching a loved one float away to an unknown fate. Virtually the whole population of New Orleans wading through sewage filled water. But his inalienable right to burn cheap gas had been violated, and the world was darn well going to know it.

I am thankful to that boorish fellow. Sometimes it takes an extreme example to remind us of what we do daily. I don't complain about gas prices, but I certainly take my wonderful life and family for granted. I can work myself into a fury when my internet connection goes down, my steak is tough, or the dishes sit too long in the sink (and whose fault is that). I blush writing these words. I unthinkingly take the most amazing outpouring of blessings in the history of humanity as my natural due. Lord, have mercy upon us. Christ, have mercy upon us. Lord, have mercy upon us.

Two texts for your reflection today:

> So teach us to number our days that we may get a

heart of wisdom. (Psalm 90:12)

Freely ye have received, freely give. (Matthew 10:8)

Edit Gently

My ongoing project these days is editing a study for young adults on the essentials of faith. Eight writers wrote on themes such as baptism, worship, and the church. My job is to make sure their work is clear and to give the multiple sessions a consistent look. These are smart people I'm editing. One publishes more in a week than I'll publish in a lifetime. So I agonize over the task. I think: "I don't understand this, but perhaps it's just me." "I'm inclined to cut this whole paragraph, but maybe doing that will destroy a progression of ideas I'm not seeing." "This is a wild tangent – or it could be a creative insight."

Because I take my own writing seriously, I realize I am laying unholy hands on somebody's pride and joy, dissecting her baby on my cold computer screen. I want to give the work the benefit of the doubt. I read and reread before I decide a sentence is unclear, too long, or superfluous. I make every effort to understand the writer's intent before deciding I need to make a change.

Unfortunately, I do not always do that in face-to-face encounters, particularly those involving a topic which evokes strong feelings. I only half listen as the other talks. My attention gets focused on framing a response to a position I'm not really hearing. My overwhelming temptation is to try to change someone before I have given him or her every consideration. The result of yielding to that temptation is usually contentious encounters which leave both of us feeling misunderstood and demeaned. My daily conversations would be infinitely more fruitful if I gave as much effort to understanding the person in front of me as I give to editing the manuscripts of those far away.

Luther reminds us that Christians are called to make every effort to understand fully and judge kindly. Explaining the commandment against bearing false witness, he writes, "We should fear and love God, and so we should not tell lies about our neighbor, nor betray, slander, or defame him, but should apologize for him, speak well of him, and interpret charitably all that he does." [*Small Catechism*] Today, as you meet people, remember you are holding their hearts in your hands. Listen well and edit gently.

Blackberry Ad

Last week on vacation I was riding the "L," the mass transit train system in Chicago. As you often do on such trips I browsed the placards posted overhead. There were ads for a local college, information about the route I was riding, and assorted "get rich in the comfort of your home in your spare time" schemes. But the one I most remember was an ad for a wireless telecommunications plan. It pictured a Blackberry with the caption, "Down time, prepare to meet your maker."

The irony, of course, is that the attitude that makes this product attractive and profitable (that one should be available at all times and all places) insures that there will never be any down time. The promise of the technology is illusory. Every minute gained in being able to deal with issues instantly is lost in the expectation that more tasks can be accomplished in the same amount of time. I get more things done in the same amount of time than I did before I owned a computer, but I do not have any more discretionary time for the pursuits which feed the soul.

Beyond the practical concerns, there is a religious issue in this ad; it makes a heretical claim. Is technology the "Lord and Giver of Life" (and time)? Our religious tradition emphatically says, "No." Time is God's gift to us to be used for a variety of pursuits. Yes, work is an important use of time, but we are not created solely for work. The Genesis narrative says we are first and foremost created to be in communion with God, to delight in the world in which God has placed us. One way to be in communion with God is indeed to be about work which improves the society in which we live, but be honest, is that what drives most of the appointments in your Daytimer or phone?

There are times we need to be instantly accessible to one another; I have a cell phone. But if we are feeling harried, we can't expect technology to solve the problem. We need to be clear about where time comes from and for what it is given – and then for a season, turn off the phone, stop checking e-mail, sign off Instant Messaging, and take time for the true "Lord and Giver of Life." If we can't do that, we do not have a time problem; we have an idolatry problem.

Bird Feeder

The birds finally came. We have three bird feeders on our deck, two filled with seed and one with sugar water for the hummingbirds. These are quality feeders, veritable four star restaurants for feathered folk. But for a long time they were ignored, except by ravenous squirrels (more on that below). Had it been left to me, the birds could just have taken potluck out in the woods, but Gail was committed. She changed the kind of seed in the feeders, adjusted the springs to make sure the doors were opening and closing correctly, and brewed innumerable batches of hummingbird cocktail when a feeder got slimy or ant-filled. And the birds finally came. I am no expert on birds, but I presume two things happened: the birds finally found the feeders and then decided they are safe.

The care we give one another is not so very different. Sometimes we have the very best of intentions. We reach out to friends or children, but they do not respond. All our efforts to be caring, supportive, and helpful are either ignored or met with surly antagonism. All that good seed just sits in the feeder; our care feels wasted. It's hard not to get discouraged. But endurance is one characteristic of genuine Christian care, as opposed to enlightened self-interest. Anyone can be "loving" when the object of our care is appreciative. It is when the extended hand hangs ignored that we prove our concern. We just keep filling the feeder until the other realizes there is good stuff to be found and feels safe enough to receive our gifts. As Paul admonishes us, "Let us not grow weary in doing what is right, for we will reap at harvest time, if we do not give up." (Galatians 6:9)

Now about those squirrels…It's a mystery to me why we have squirrels in our feeders. When, on those very rare occasions, I see that cold, dead-eyed look in Gail's face (like Clint Eastwood in *A Fistful of Dollars*), I don't hang around. But the squirrels do not seem aware of their mortal danger and show up every morning like the breakfast gang down at Hardee's. After many rounds involving hoses, squirt bottles, manic gestures, and even an ill-fated electrical anti-squirrel device, we have decided that if you are going to feed birds, you also have to feed the furry bandits.

Some folks are so afraid of being used that they are afraid

362

to be used – by Jesus Christ. There are a lot worse things than being too gullible and compassionate, chief of which is being so emotionally armored that you never touch and are touched by another person. Sometimes the squirrels do rob us blind, but isn't the sight of birds on the deck worth it?

Benedict and Leo

Some of the more attentive members of the congregation were surprised last Sunday when, during the children's sermon, I showed them a picture of the new pope, "Leo." Of course, Cardinal Joseph Ratzinger has taken the name "Benedict," but I know exactly why I accidentally called him Leo.

I admire St. Benedict as the father of a spirituality which balances work, prayer, and study. Benedictine communities are famous as places of hospitality where the monastic rule mandates "all guests who present themselves are to be welcomed as Christ." Benedict was a model of serious but gracious discipleship. In contrast to this spirit of gentleness, Pope Leo X excommunicated Martin Luther and tried to squelch the Reformation.

Before being elected to the papacy, Cardinal Ratzinger (whom some called "God's Rottweiler") was known for his narrow definition of orthodoxy and repression of progressive Roman Catholic theologians. I have opined to several folks that Ratzinger's style is more in keeping with the spirit of Leo than Benedict. That's why I inadvertently called him Leo during the children's time.

Some disagree with my opinion of Pope Benedict's track record. We can discuss that at another time, but my point here is something else: Because I repeatedly told myself and others that Ratzinger is more Leo than Benedict, it became "truth," until I unconsciously changed his name to suit my opinion. The image I projected took on a life of its own and became reality in spite of facts to the contrary. (I may think he acts like Leo, but the name is indisputably "Benedict.")

That's why it's important for us to be sure our actions are based on accurate and charitable perceptions rather than illusions. If I tell myself you are untrustworthy or malevolent I am likely to regard you with fear and treat you unfairly. If I brood about some imagined slight, the well of our relationship is poisoned. When nations make foreign policy based on illusion, people die; when people do it, friendships and marriages wither. So think of something about which you have a passionate opinion. Do the facts support your judgment or are you editing reality to conform it to your prejudice? Part of spiritual health is learning to let go of our favorite illusions. Part of Christian charity is assuming the best from others rather than the worst, for we usually evoke that which we assume.

Vacation Afterglow

Well, it's happened again. It's been a wonderful summer. I've attended a couple of helpful conferences, vacationed in Australia, and played enough golf at the beach to remember why that game is so frustrating. All that was great. Now I look down at my belt and realize I've picked up a couple of extra friends. It was good to break out of the spirit-deadening routine, but I also took a vacation from the healthy habits I was cultivating. It's hard to get in 10,000 steps when you are sitting in a car, hard to eat healthy when you are grabbing your in-laws' sausage gravy biscuits for breakfast instead of Go-Lean Crunch and skim milk.

I've also discovered that my devotional life often suffers in the summer. You would think it would be different; there is more free time, more flexibility in the schedule to do what is important. But freedom easily becomes license: "Just for today I'll skip devotions because I have a plane to catch." The next day it's an early tee time. Before you know it, devotions are not even part of the daily plan. I end my summer refreshed in some important ways, but also physically a little logy and spiritually diffuse.

Time to change some things. The point is not to feel guilty, to mutter that I really ought to do better. I know I feel healthier when I attend to a good routine. That's why I will get back in the groove. Few things are more useless than beating on ourselves for what we have failed to do. We do better to simply forget about the past and begin anew. That is what Jesus modeled; He held out the possibility that we need not be bound by old failings, that we can begin again from the moment we choose a new path.

So I am back to walking the dog each morning, laying off the empty calories (well, most of them), and taking the time to attend to what keeps me centered. If you need to make a new start, remember Paul's words, "Beloved, I do not consider that I have made it my own; but this one thing I do: forgetting what lies behind and straining forward to what lies ahead, I press on toward the goal for the prize of the heavenly call of God in Christ Jesus." (Phil 3:13)

Rein in Me

On Christ the King Sunday we sang a song at our "Alive in Christ" service with the recurring refrain, "Reign in me!

Reign in me!" I found myself thinking that we could just as easily be singing "Rein in me! Rein in me!", because that is what it takes for God to be sovereign in our lives. Somehow we have to rein in the attitude that "me" is the most important thing.

Nietzsche spoke of the spirit's "will to power," seeking to expand its sphere of influence at the expense of all around it. Luther described sin as the soul turned in on itself. Miss Elva identified the attitude as always needing to be "the biggest cock in the yard." Whatever language you use, highly philosophical or down home simple, the point is the same: We usually believe we are the center of the universe. We would seldom put it just that baldly; the belief may be unconscious, but it's true. Witness how aggravated we get when we are stuck in traffic, how annoyed we are when someone is a little slow in e-mailing the info we need, how testy we become when our children do not conform to the script we have written for them. We want the world to conform to our schedule and priorities. We can be gracious to others if it costs us nothing, but at crunch time it's me and mine.

Unless, of course, we are interested in following Jesus. Then we make a conscious decision to put His vision at the center of our lives. The goal is not pretending our hopes and desires are of no consequence; it's subjecting them to the bit and bridle of Christ. When a rider pulls hard on the reins she's not trying to crush the horse's spirit, but to control and direct it. The paradox is that when a spirit has no rein, it wanders, hurting both itself and others, but when it is controlled by Christ, it has a sense of direction which is wiser than it could have chosen on its own, and like a horse ridden by an experienced rider, it arrives safely home. Hymn writer George Matheson said it this way, "Make me a captive Lord, and then I shall be free./ Force me to render up my sword, and I shall conqueror be/ I sink in life's alarms when by myself I stand/ Imprison me within thine arms, and strong shall be my hand." – which is to say, "Rein in me."

Pulaski Globalization

Gail coordinates a feeding program for her school, and that involves an early Saturday morning trip to a Pulaski warehouse, once a month, to pick up a load of food. Making this month's run, I turned the corner onto Pulaski's all but deserted main street and watched the crossing gate come down. Three locomotives went by; this was going to be a long one. I turned off the engine and settled in to listen to "Weekend Edition."

Staring at the passing parade I realized that I was watching globalization come to Southwest Virginia. Most of the flatcars were carrying container shipping. China, Singapore, Korea, Great Britain, Japan, Germany, the Netherlands – that's just the countries of origin I could identify. Some of the writing looked Arabic to my untutored eye. Wherever they were from, it was abundantly clear "they weren't from around here."

Every morning you read about another legislative proposal to tighten up the borders, close the gaps in import security, and increase the scrutiny of folks who look or sound different from us. (By the way, who is "us"?) Surely we all want to feel reasonably safe. But it disturbs me when fear is in the driver's seat, when we act as though we can put up big walls, climb into our bunkers, and keep the suffering of the world hermetically sealed in pockets of misery far away.

367

Fearful isolationism is an economic absurdity; just check the labels on your clothes, car, and electronics – or the next train that blocks your way. More important, it is unfaithful and ignoble for Christians to view abundance, both material and political, as primarily a castle to be moated, rather than as a storehouse out of which to share with the wretched of the earth. Scripture is clear; when we are driven by fear and grasping, we lose touch with the God who gave us the blessings in the first place.

In Deuteronomy God gives Israel instructions for living in the Promised Land to which they have been delivered, "You shall love the stranger, for you were strangers in the land of Egypt."(10:19) Israel was infinitely more besieged in Canaan than we are today, yet God calls Israel to act out of a sense of gratitude rather than fear, hospitality rather than suspicion. The Christmas gifts have been unwrapped, but it is still worth remembering why we give presents: God did not choose to stay bunkered away from earthly anguish. Neither should we.

Niebuhr's Prayer

We pray for the wicked and cruel men, whose arrogance reveals to us what the sin of our own hearts is like when it has conceived and brought forth its final fruit. O God, who resists the proud and gives grace to the humble, bring down the mighty from their seats. – from a prayer by Reinhold Niebuhr

Anyone who has taken Psychology 101 knows the term "projection", the tendency to attribute to another that which I recognize, at some level, in myself. If I am wrestling with a demon, I accuse you of the vice. I view you through the filter of my own inner life. One of the ways we escape dealing with our dark side is to "project" it onto another. I thought about projection as I read Niebuhr's words during a devotional time, and they seemed particularly pointed when I put them in the context of today's bitter political climate.

It is all quite fine to condemn wickedness and arrogance in public life when we encounter them. There is rich biblical precedent for doing so, including the teachings of the Torah, the prophets, and our Lord. Ignorance, apathy, and blind obedience to authority are not Christian virtues. But as Niebuhr points out, wickedness exists, not just outside us, but as a home grown virus in every soul. Much of the virtue we are tempted to claim has more to do with a lack of opportunity to do great evil than with innate moral superiority. The difference between Enron's abuses and fudging on our taxes is one of degree not substance.

Confronting the abuse of the powerful is like seeing a malignant cell from our own bodies magnified so that we can get a good look at it, like viewing the time lapse photography of a noxious weed from seed to full flowering. Particularly in a democracy, we dare not forget the wickedness we find in others has a resonance in our souls. When I am honest with myself, in the privacy of prayer, I realize the arrogance, narrow-mindedness, intolerance, and callousness in the face of suffering I find so objectionable in another are precisely the spiritual cancers with which I struggle in my own life.

Niebuhr does what Jesus calls us to do, he prays for his enemies. When we do that we invite God's enlightenment and transformation into their lives. But just as important, we invite that same outpouring of God's presence into our lives. In praying for our enemies we acknowledge that at some fundamental level our soul is joined with the souls of those we find hardest to love. When we give ourselves over to bitterness and hate, we are condemned to be prisoners of the dark side made manifest in those we despise. Praying for our leaders, whether we admire them or not, is not just a nice thing to do; it is essential for our spiritual health. In praying for God's judgment and healing in the lives of others we begin to receive the same words of conviction and grace in our personal spiritual struggle.

This day ponder three things: Who evokes your enmity? How is that person like you? How might the life and teaching of Jesus Christ help you learn to love both that person and yourself?

Fear

One of my best friends is also a campus pastor. Over the years he has dealt with a lot of parental angst as mothers and fathers drop their precious treasures outside the residence halls and commend them to the not always tender mercies of the university. But it's different when it is your own pride and joy, and this fall it was his turn. It was his turn to pack up his daughter's room and put it into a space half the size, with twice the inhabitants; his turn to discover he really is old enough to have a college age child; his turn to experience the bittersweet relief of knowing she is successfully into the next stage of life and the gentle hollowness of realizing she does not need him like she did before.

Sometimes you know too much. As he carried a load into her dorm, a cadre of young men was hanging out of the adjoining residence hall yelling, "Thank you for sending us your daughters." That lighthearted jest must have brought to mind 20 years of tearful meetings with young women just like his precious Anna. He did not need an overly active imagination to be fearful, just a father's heart and a memory.

Fear. There seem to be so many reasons to have it: shaky economic news, the latest code orange alert, or your daughter going off to college. I find it interesting that Jesus seems relatively unconcerned about belief and unbelief, but he often admonishes those around him let go of their fear and trust God. Fear, not doubt, is the great crippler of life; it paralyzes us in the present and curtails our future. Jesus does not pretend threats to our health and well-being are illusions; he just asserts that God is bigger than those threats, real or imagined. He invites us to walk with serenity into the future, confident that if we rest in God's care, we will find strength and courage for whatever challenge waits.

Mustache

Now it all becomes clear! "Once a sign of great virility and hotness, the great majority of young America now assigns three distinct possibilities to the mustache wearer: porn star, cop, or homosexual." (*Roanoke Times*, 2/16/04) For some time now I have had the feeling my mojo is slipping. I enter a group and see those looks usually reserved for those who think competitive burping ought to be an Olympic sport. Now I understand. I am in trouble, not because of what comes out of my lips (a daily occurrence), but due to what hangs over them. I'd just like to know which of the three possibilities is the stopper for me in polite company…

Without a shred of defensiveness or the need to distance myself from any of the above attributes, I can honestly tell you that none of them applies to yours truly. In so far as I remember why I decided to grow a mustache over twenty-five years ago, I think it had something to with always being carded at the 7/11. Ever clueless, I had no idea what everyone was assuming about me from my little coffee strainer.

All humor aside, this bit of banal journalism reminds us how absurd it is to make judgments about others on evidence as flimsy as whether they wear a mustache, have a tattoo, prefer blue oxford shirts and khakis, follow NAS-CAR, or have a name which sounds Middle Eastern. Such fragments do not give us enough information to make judgments worth the breath to express them.

But the question is bigger than whether we can make informed judgments. Suppose my mustache were indeed a tip off to my occupation or sexual orientation. What would that mean for you as a Christian? Would you then be justified in shunning me? One thing abundantly clear from the gospel narratives is that Jesus hung out with a lot of disreputable characters and treated them with respect, if not always gentleness. Self-righteous religious leaders, lepers, arrogant rulers, hookers, crooked tax collectors, soldiers of an oppressive power, and often clueless disciples--he took them all seriously and engaged each one with deep concern.

The problem is not just that we sometimes make premature judgments (literally ones filled with prejudice). More important, as disciples of Jesus, we are called to follow the way of love and compassion at all times, even (especially) when we feel a certain distaste for another. Care toward the undeserving is what should set the people of God apart from those who merely render tit for tat. Think about the quick judgments you are prone to offer, and even if your negative perception were to prove accurate, is there a way you might deal with him or her which would reflect the attitude of

Him who always regarded human fallibility more with sorrow than contempt?

As for me, I am going to ask some mustached friends if there is anything they want to tell me...

Call the Midwife

I am willing to make the case that the PBS series, *Call the Midwife*, is one of the best television series of all time. The humanity of its characters, the pitch perfect writing, and its treatment of lives rooted in religion (neither romantic nor cynical) make this series about midwives in 1950s east London worth anyone's time....which is why I find it slightly incongruous that each episode is preceded by a big, black and white "MA" warning.

"Mature Audiences." That's the same warning that appears before slasher movies, the same warning that accompanies "slice and dice" television shows featuring serial killers, the same warning that goes on pornographically violent video games. And what is it that earns Call the Midwife the "MA"? Birth. That's all I can figure. Every week there is a least one scene in which a woman gives birth. We are not talking graphic pictures of genitalia, just tastefully photographed depictions of women engaged in the excruciating act of giving life to another. Murdered bodies, gun fights, seductions – these seem to be fine in prime time, but, for heaven's sake, let's protect the kids from seeing the reality of how we all come into the world. That might traumatize them forever...

Some years ago I heard one wag suggest that "we need to get sex out of the gutter and back in the church where it belongs." I took him to mean that the church too often treats sexuality as shameful, leaving the culture to define how we think about it. The inevitable result is that we end up thinking poorly about this primal force at the center of our lives. What should be beautiful becomes distorted. What should be celebrated becomes hidden and tawdry. Sexuality is one of God's good gifts to us and there is no reason why we should be ashamed of it or talk about it with a smirk.

I am not suggesting that every show is for every person, but I am suggesting that we sometimes get it exactly backwards, mindlessly accepting things which are contrary to the gospel and treating that which affirms life, sacrifice, and compassion as embarrassing. So, this week, a few questions: What would it mean to be truly mature in our thinking about sexuality; how do we get sex out the gutter and back where it can be affirmed and appropriately celebrated without shame? How do we raise up a people of faith who know how to use but not abuse this gift from our creator?

Books and Boundaries

I am one of those folks who always keep a book by the bed. It is seldom a professional book – you will not find systematic theology or *Ten Secrets to Effective Stewardship* on my bedside table – primarily because late at night I don't have the mental acuity to glean much from such books. No, it's usually a novel, picked explicitly to help me gear down at the end of the day. My first requirement of a book is that it be a good read; it must have characters or plot which keep me engaged. But I value one other thing.

I want my bedside book to take me to a place I have never been, cannot visit, or would prefer not to experience in person. That may be a physical place (the heart of India), a social place (the mean streets of New York), an historical place (medieval Europe), or a psychological place (inside the head of a detective on the trail of a killer). From even "mindless entertainment" I want something which expands my world. The power to take you across boundaries is one of the things which distinguish mediocre, good, and great writing.

One reason I read is to force myself across boundaries. It is dangerous to forget that everyone is not like me or that my reality is not yours. Compassion literally means to "feel with," but it is hard to feel with you if I do not know what the world looks like from your perspective. Most of us spend our days with folks just like us. We assume that the challenges of daily life are pretty much the same for all – but that is just not true. The girl who goes to school hungry, fresh from watching dad beating mom, with her gums throbbing because there no money for a dentist most assuredly has a different educational challenge than my children had. If we think twice, we know that. Yet we seldom alter our expectations.

So whether you read a book, listen to a news story which challenges your world view, go to a provocative movie, or volunteer somewhere that makes you terribly uncomfortable, go out of your way to see the world in a new way. Cross some barriers. That is part of what Christian discipleship is about, following Jesus to places we may have never been, would rather not see – but need to be.

Apology Inflation

I recently heard a radio story on what you might call "sorry" inflation. The researcher's starting point was that we are seeing more and more folks making very public apologies for everything from alcoholic binges to deliberating creating traffic jams on the George Washington Bridge. The interviewer gently opined, "But surely there are worse things than seeing an increase in people saying they're sorry."

Then the researcher got to the heart of the matter. The problem is that many of these apologies are attempts to quickly get beyond the reason for the apology, more public relations ploy and damage control than true contrition. "Real apologies should not get us beyond something, they should get us into something – namely a sincere effort to make things right." As with all inflation, the growth in the number of apologies has a way of devaluing them all.

"It is not enough to say, 'I'm sorry,' you have to do 'I'm sorry.'" I do not remember the first time I heard that statement. But it seems apropos to a discussion of apology inflation. A serious apology entails more than just remorse; it also implies a willingness to do everything within our power to make things right, to repair the damage that we have done by our words and deeds. If we are sometimes cynical about all the weeping apologies which flood the news, it is because we sense that the speakers have little desire to make fundamental changes in how they live. They are not sorry for what they have done, only that it is causing them a problem.

I am not suggesting that we wallow in guilt, but I am inviting us to think about our duty – no, let's say our opportunity – to take another person's pain seriously. Glib apologies are like a cheap paint job on a scratched car – a quick way to deal with a problem, but one which will not hold up over the long haul. To extend the metaphor, Christians are called to offer more than a cut-rate spray job which glosses over the ugliness; we are in the business of body work. As followers of Jesus we are about repairing the wreckage wherever we can. That can be hard work. It is a lot tougher to "do sorry" than to "say sorry," but it is also a lot more satisfying for both you and the other person.

Generous Listening

"Listening is the most generous gift you can give to another person." Ironically, I heard those words as I was walking around the neighborhood insulated from other people by my ear buds. My morning routine includes a long walk, usually listening to a podcast. This day a TED talk on our diminishing capacity to truly listen played on my iPod.

I smiled in recognition, realizing that I seldom really hear the people who may greet me on my daily rounds because I am focused on whatever is streaming into my ears. But then I lost track of the podcast because I started thinking about that one sentence. Listening is indeed a gift where demand greatly outstrips supply.

Think about your average interaction during the day. Do you really listen or are you just biding your time until you can make a response? Can you honestly say that when someone speaks to you they have your undivided attention? Sometimes we make it obvious that the person in front of us is not terribly important, such as when we check text messages or pick up a phone call in the middle of a face-to-face conversation (which, on the scale of sheer tackiness, are right next to chewing peas and mashed potatoes with your mouth open). Most of the time it is more subtle and unconscious. We just allow our thoughts to drift to the next item on the to-do list of our busy day.

Researchers tell us that one of the things widows and widowers most miss is simply the experience of being touched, not sex per se, just human contact. I suspect that most of us

377

have a comparable need to be heard, really heard. We yearn to get beyond superficialities and share who we are. We speak and we long to know that another person has understood our joy or our pain. The other does not have to have answers for our problems; connecting is what we crave.

The thing about listening is that it is both so easy and so hard. It costs us nothing except a little time and the willingness to give all our attention to this one person who is speaking to us. But that is terribly hard, isn't it? As any pastor or therapist will tell you, it is exhausting to be fully present for another person; listening is every bit as draining as writing a report or chasing kids around the playground. That is why "listening is the most generous gift you can give another person." When we listen we share ourselves. To fully listen is to say to another person, "Right now there is no more important person in the whole world than you; all that I am is at your disposal. In this moment I want nothing more than to understand what you are saying."

Listening, the gift we all have the capacity to give. It's free, but both costly and priceless.

Emma Goldman on Dancing

This quotation from Emma Goldman came across my desk last week: "If I can't dance, I don't want to be part of your revolution." I have no idea who Emma Goldman is, but I like her style.

Since "revolution" is a political term one naturally reflects on the toxic political climate which plagues our country these days. There was a time when leaders engaged in hyperbole to make their case, but you knew that they knew that is what they were doing – exaggerating for the sake of political theater. These days they really seem to believe the vitriol which they spew. They appear to be convinced we are one election away from the collapse of Western Civilization because their opponents hate God, country, and kittens. That contempt for those who see the world differently is dangerous and unworthy of anyone who claims Jesus as Lord. But politics is not my main point here. I am more interested in how her words apply to the church.

Few things are more off-putting than Christians who manifest conviction without joy. To use Goldman's image, it is quite possible for us to invite people into the revolutionary love of Christ and do it with a grimness which says there is no dancing allowed, no joy to be found in following Jesus. I literally experienced that kind of religion in my youth, the kind that banned dancing because it was too sensual (or as the old joke put it, banned sex because it looked too much like dancing). But there is a more subtle religious dourness which takes itself so seriously that it does not take others with kindness.

Discipleship is indeed serious business. Taking up the way of Jesus means offering God the one life we have. But the moment we find our faith making us bitter and judgmental, the moment we start looking at another with contempt because they do not seem to "get" the revolution which we think Christ is behind – then my friend, we need to think long and hard about whether we are truly on board with Jesus' revolution or just following our own angry agenda. Only the rabid want to join a revolution characterized by self-righteous rage.

The revolution of Jesus includes dancing. The gospels make that abundantly clear in their accounts of his ministry. St. Paul also gives us some good markers of what it looks like when Christ is guiding the movement of our hearts:

...the fruit of the Spirit is love, joy, peace, patience, kindness, generosity, faithfulness, 23gentleness, and self-control [Galatians 5:22-23a].

Difficult People

"How to deal with difficult people." I was at a continuing education event last week and that is what the speaker's slide proclaimed. The presentation was very good, and I understood what he was trying to offer us. All of us, both pastors and parishioners, need to find constructive ways to engage those with whom we have conflict. There are techniques for turning down the heat in an exchange: listening well, breathing deeply, and asking clarifying questions. These are helpful. I know what I am supposed to do – even if I am not particularly good at applying my knowledge. But as I sat there, I thought that there is one thing I need to do before I start applying any other techniques: try as hard as I can to avoid thinking of the other person as a "difficult person."

I suppose there is something primal within our DNA which inclines us to put people into simple categories of "friend" or "foe." When we were coming out of the caves, the ability to identify potential threats was important for survival; a correct assessment mobilized all sorts of biological responses which decreased the probability of being prey. But the moment we start thinking of someone else as a threat, as a "difficult" person, we can be pretty sure we are already shutting down some of our best skills for understanding. Some people do present difficulties, but that is different from tagging them as "difficult," as though that defines their core. Just as the best doctor does not think of Mr. Jones as the kidney in room 323, but as Mr. Jones who has a kidney problem, so we need to remember that others are always more than "difficult." Each person we encounter is a complex mix of joys and sorrows, gifts and challenges.

That thought was fresh on my mind as I opened Facebook and ran across a clip which included words something like this: "My name is Tom Jones and I love my church because it is where I experience God's grace. I am a gay man and I am not an 'issue;' I am a child of God." Once again I found myself thinking about how our labels easily dehumanize others and block us from relating to them with kindness, openness, and understanding.

The labels we put on one another have some limited utility, but more often they are signs of emotional and intellectual laziness. I easily think, "If you are a _____, then I do not have to take you seriously." This week, think about the labels you stick on people to avoid confronting the complexity of their humanity. You will probably experience some confusion; it is much simpler to deal with our created cardboard cutouts than real people. But you will also see the world a little more honestly – and perhaps with a bit more compassion.

Projections on a Painting

Hanging over my desk is a bright, minimally representational painting of eight figures in a row. If you were to walk into my office, knowing nothing about me, you might make a number of assumptions about me and the painting: that I am an anthropologist with a focus on Africa, that I like the colors in the painting, that I find the Masai people fascinating, that I bought the painting to support indigenous artists, that it is intended to make a political statement about colonialism, that it is a souvenir of a trip to Tanzania, that I have a deep understanding of West African art, that I want to cultivate seeing beauty beyond my own cultural context. Some of those things are true. Some are not. The best way for you to understand why that art is hanging there is to ask. "So tell me about that painting…"

Taking mental shortcuts and making assumptions about others based on minimal information is all but impossible to avoid. Our survival as a species required learning to make snap judgments about potential dangers. We are hardwired to make quick assessments, often unconsciously, even when it is not a matter of life and death. Still, it seems to me that we are often operating with a hair trigger these days, too quick to make judgments and assumptions about others' beliefs and intentions. Not only do we form opinions about another person based on inadequate knowledge, but we compound the problem by ascribing malevolence to any difference between their perceived beliefs and our own.

We dare not be glib about the dangers facing our society. Rule of law, willingness to compromise, the reality of truth as opposed to mere "spin," the sense that the communal good has a claim on me which may supersede my personal preference – all of these are very much in danger. But when we deal with those with whom we disagree we have to at least be sure we do disagree. We need to ask them to tell us about what they mean when they use a word or espouse a position. Sometimes we destroy the common ground on which we might meet by assuming it is not there.

Jesus did not agree with many with whom he dealt; much of the gospels is taken up with Him in conflict with those who opposed Him. No one would accuse Jesus of lacking conviction or courage. Yet He did a lot of listening to be sure that there really was conflict over what was truly important. Perhaps we should do the same.

Communion Wine

"Why can't communion wine taste better?" That is one of the questions taped to the door outside the confirmation class. Just as Luther posted 95 theses as the starting point for debate on the critical issues of his day, Pastor Stallings invited the students to post their own burning questions for discussion. To be sure the answer to this question does not have the weighty import of a statement on the nature of justification. Perhaps the author was not even serious in asking. Still it raises issues worth thinking about.

The short answer to the question is "because it is inexpensive." With wine, as with many things, you usually get what you pay for. Five dollars a bottle is not going to get you something you'd drink with a fine steak. Common sense and good stewardship suggest that you do not use the finest Bordeaux for the Eucharist, since nobody will taste more than a few drops on a dipped communion wafer. I suppose you could say we use cheap wine for the sake of authenticity; the wine in the upper room was probably nothing special. But that would be an after the fact justification. Really, it is an economic decision which makes sense when balancing a variety of spending priorities.

But my first Lutheran pastor and mentor would beg to disagree. In our very small student congregation, much of what we did was of necessity done on the cheap. But the communion wine we used was a moderately expensive sherry. David's feeling was that we should not give God second best. He did not want to associate the precious gift of grace received in the Supper with cheap wine. So we had sherry and fresh bread on the altar. The richness of the elements' taste was, in David's view, a sensory way to convey the richness of God's mercy. And I guess it worked because I can still remember the smells at those Eucharistic celebrations.

On one level, the quality of the wine is not terribly important. God can and does come to us in whatever wine we put in the chalice. That is what's crucially significant. God comes in the ordinary and makes it the channel of the extraordinary – whether we are talking about Mogen David Vin Ordinaire or our lives. So, I doubt if we will change the wine we use for weekly worship.

Still, a broader question remains: Do we tend to think that we can always give God second best? It is one thing to use inexpensive wine; it is quite another to offer God less than our best when it comes to how we deal with others, to where we put our resources, and to what we give our energy and creativity.

Some days I think David was right. Maybe if we modeled giving God our best at the table we would more often do it in our lives.

Not Superman

"I must look like hell." That was my initial thought after the third person solicitously sidled up to me and asked if I was doing okay. It had been one of those weeks which every pastor has from time to time: two deaths within a short period of time, serious illness of another person, a time crunch to get a few projects done before going out of town.

Throw in a high pollen count which made my eyes feel like sandpaper and a cranky computer, and sure, I've had easier weeks. But this is the stuff of being a pastor, certainly nothing which entitled me to special attention and care.

Then I started thinking that maybe it was not so much that I looked so bad, but that the folks around me were just that perceptive and thoughtful. Maybe my problem was less that I was run down than that I was unable to graciously receive what they were eager to offer. And maybe I was unable to practice what I preach to everyone who comes into my office stressed and exhausted: "Take time to refresh; the problems will be waiting when you return."

So for this week's Bread let me offer three things:

- A sincere thanks to those who care enough to care for me despite my superman delusions.
- An admonition to be realistic in what you expect of yourself.
- An invitation to appreciate those around you who carry you even when you do not realize you need to be carried. They are the ones who make "the body of Christ" a reality and not just a pious image.

Loaded for Bear

I was loaded for bear. I'm embarrassed to admit it, because in the great scheme of things it was not a big deal, but beginning that phone call I was prepared to deliver a jumbo load of righteous indignation onto someone's doorstep. "How can you design a system this way?" "Is this the way you treat your most loyal patrons?" "I have better things to do than…." Oh, I had rehearsed it all in my head and was ready to go to war!

She wasn't. She endured my opening salvo and simply said, "I am really sorry you had that problem, let me see what I can do to fix it." And she did. We've all talked to robo-responders, when we feel that they are just trying to get us off the phone. Maybe that was the case this time, but I do not think so. It felt like she genuinely wanted to make it right. As a result I felt my anger deflating like a cheap air mattress. A few observations:

Most aggravations just aren't worth the psychic energy we invest in them. This was about a few show tickets, not the fate of the free world. The "problem" was primarily my outsized indignation, not the online system I did not like. A sense of perspective is important, whether you are an artist attempting to accurately portray the world or somebody merely trying to live a reasonably happy life.

The writer in Proverbs was right, "A soft answer turns away wrath, but a harsh word stirs up anger." [15:1] Sometimes the best thing we can do when confronted by irrational anger and expectations is to lower the temperature of the exchange. It has nothing to do with right or wrong (Actually, I think I caused my own problem in this situation); it is about preferring resolution and reconciliation over winning.

Every day we are on both sides of the kind of exchange I've shared. Sometimes we are the aggrieved party; sometimes we have the chance to make it right for someone having a testy time. I am sure that young woman forgot about our conversation five minutes after we had it, yet her graciousness positively colored my whole morning – and prompts this Bread for the Journey. You never know how much banking the fires of your anger or being kind in the face of unreasonableness will improve the world far beyond the immediate encounter.

Lifting Prayer

It had been a typical hospital visit, like hundreds I have made over the years. Our conversation was pleasant, if not particularly profound. We talked a bit about the circumstances of her hospitalization, and her hopes for the coming days. As is often the case at the end of a pastoral call, I ended our visit with a prayer. Prayer seems a good way to gather up the conversational threads and weave them together before God. We held hands and I offered a prayer which was sincere but not terribly eloquent.

I let go of her hand, ready to leave – but she did not let go of mine. "Every time you pray for me," she said, "I want to pray for you." Then she offered her own prayer. She lifted up the needs of others we both knew to be in special need of care. She prayed for the ministry of our congregation. And she prayed for me. I cannot speak to the efficacy of my prayer for her, but I know I left that room empowered and strengthened for the rest of my day.

In Exodus 17 there is the story of a battle. The children of Israel confront the army of Amalek. When Moses raises his hands, holding the rod which parted the Red Sea, the tide goes for Israel. When he is overcome by fatigue and his arms droop, the Amalekites begin to prevail. So, the text says, Aaron and Hur station themselves on either side of Moses and hold his arms up until the battle is over. I am not so grandiose as to think of myself as Moses, but I certainly think of that woman in her hospital bed as Aaron, lifting up her pastor.

My point is two-fold. First, we all need someone who is willing to support us in times when we are weak; just as much, we need to be willing to receive what others have to offer. Second, there is never a time when we have nothing

387

to offer. That dear saint has spent much of her life giving to others, even from a hospital bed she found a way to keep giving. Lines from an old gospel hymn, "Hark, the Voice of Jesus Calling," capture her sentiment for service well:

If you cannot be a watchman,
Standing high on Zion's wall,
Pointing out the path to heaven,
Offering life and peace to all,
With your prayers and with your bounties,
You can do what God demands;
You can be like faithful Aaron,
Holding up the prophet's hands.

My prayer for you this day is that you will find a place to hold up someone's trembling hands.

Rumi Poem

In June, as part of my continuing education, I am planning to visit Turkey. This trip is not primarily the usual excursion which pastors take to sites of historical significance for the First Century church, places such as Antioch and Ephesus. We will see a little of that, but the primary focus of this particular trip is greater cultural understanding in a world often beset by stereotypes. So in preparation for this trip I have been reading Rumi, the great writer and Sufi mystic, who is often regarded as the greatest Turkish and Muslim poet. Here is one small sample of his work:

O pure people who wander the world,
amazed at the idols you see,
what you are searching for out there,
if you look within, you yourself are it.

Though written in the thirteenth century, this meditation seems to speak to the longing I sense all around me. The American soul often seems to be one part arrogance, one part despair. We are overawed by our technological wizardry, brimming with bravado rooted in all the scientific advances we have made. We feign an optimism that every problem has a solution amenable to human ingenuity. But beneath the bluster is what Thoreau called "quiet desperation," the realization that we easily sell our lives too cheaply. We slave at a job which fails to fulfill or we invest our energy in hot cars, new electronic gadgets, and perpetual partying which do not finally satisfy our longing for something which matters.

We are looking for ourselves, says the mystic, looking for the person God intended us to be. We are looking for that place where our need to be loved and our need to love merge, that place where desperation gives way to rest in the knowledge that we are profoundly valued – and thus have much to offer, not out of fear, but from gratitude.

Sometimes (not often, I grant you) people think preachers are fonts of wisdom. Yet I am often struck by the wisdom of those I serve. Not too long ago I was talking with a very gifted woman about the many stresses in her life, one of which is her job. "I am tempted to just quit," she said, "but I am pretty sure I would just carry the problems with me. I need to work on me." I think Rumi would smile at this dawning of insight. Would that we all had that much self-awareness...

Old Clothes

At the end of C. S. Lewis' *Screwtape Letters*, a fledgling Christian dies in the bombing blitz of World War II. Screwtape, a devil, describes what it was like for the man, saying it was a moment of absolute clarity, when what was hidden was suddenly obvious, when all the struggles of living by faith were swallowed up in the certitude of God's care. Death for the man, says Screwtape, was like suddenly shedding an old, dirty garment.

I thought about that chapter in the book this week because I happened to talk with three of my favorite Christians, all over 80 years of age, and they sounded a common theme. To paraphrase, each of them said, "At this point in my life, I see how little much of what divides Christians means. There is so little that I am willing to go to the wall for. My spiritual journey has been about slowly letting go of the unimportant elements of religion and focusing on the basics. Do you love God? Do you love your neighbor in tangible ways? If so, you are my brother or sister in faith." Growth for them has been about shedding the nonessential and shopworn.

These are not people who are tolerant because they have no opinions. They are not gracious because they adopt a "whatever" attitude toward anything which inspires strong feelings. On the contrary, they feel passionately about loving God and loving neighbor, and that is what gives them permission to slough off the things that do not matter. I like precision in theology and appreciate beauty in liturgy. I am perfectly willing to say that some expressions of the faith are more congruent with the life and witness of Jesus than others. But I wonder if I sometimes go to the wall over the wrong things, if I am passionate about things which prevent me from seeing the beauty of Christ in another.

Is there one thing which you can let go of this week, that you can shed like a parka on a summer day – a too rigid preference, a "righteous" resentment, a grudge that has been taking up emotional space for way too long – so that you can focus on what is worthy of total commitment?

Church Sign

Last week Gail and I drove up to Indianapolis to visit our son, Scott. We passed a church with one of those marquees displaying a pithy saying out front. This particular sign reminded passersby that "Exposure to the Son prevents burning."

My response to that sign was a like Roman candle, a series of reactions one right after another. First I smiled at the pun; I'm a sucker for word play. Then I frowned. This sort of "turn or burn" theology is not the core of the gospel proclamation, it does not work over the long haul (just how sincere is discipleship based on the thesis, "turn to a loving God or he will fry you"?), and its high visibility in our culture is a major reason that many dismiss the Christian faith as merely an appeal to ignorance and fear. But then, after a moment of wallowing in self-righteousness, I began to reflect on what that sign does.

Those words most assuredly do not represent my vision of what it means to follow Jesus, but they certainly communicate loud and clear a vision. In reading those six words I get a pretty good idea of what that community of faith believes about Jesus, why they think He matters, and what they want me to do. So, if I do not like their proclamation, what would I propose as an alternative?

You might say that Christian faith is too serious and complex to be reduced to placards and bumper sticker proclamations. That is certainly true. You can't communicate a whole tradition in one sentence. Nuanced ideas take more than six words to express. But still....if you had to sum up your theology in one short, easily repeatable phrase what would it be? Here are a few alternatives I like better than the one in front of that West Virginia church (none original with me); what's yours...

- Christians don't claim to be perfect just forgiven.
- God loves you just as you are...and too much to leave you that way.
- Be all you can be, follow the way of Jesus.
- Christian: claimed, called, sent for the sake of God's world.
- The love of Christ is free, but not cheap.

An All Saints Sermon

Last Sunday was All Saints Sunday, and I wrote a sermon for that day. But I wish my congregation could have seen the "sermon" I saw earlier in the week. I was privileged to preside at the interment of a retired pastor who had been in our area for a number of years before increasing dementia forced his children to move him to another community. I got much more than I gave.

The committal liturgy is a very brief service, consisting of a few scripture readings and prayers. The extended family gathered on a sunny hillside and I said my few words. As I stepped back from the casket, a halting but robust voice began, "Praise God from whom all blessings flow..." Immediately the whole family picked up the tune and the Doxology rang out across the cemetery, in the face of deep sorrow, a song of confident defiance. It was a bold proclamation of Paul's words, "We are afflicted in every way, but not crushed; perplexed, but not driven to despair; persecuted, but not forsaken; struck down, but not destroyed; always carrying in the body the death of Jesus, so that the life of Jesus may also be made visible in our bodies." Death does not have the final word their song proclaimed.

If you have been to a graveside service you know what comes next. There are some awkward words of consolation spoken to the family, and then folks begin to drift back to their cars. The American way of death usually spares everyone the grim reality of seeing burial. Not today. As soon as the last notes died away, the funeral home staff began to break down the sanitizing set. Up came the Astroturf which keeps you from seeing the mud of a grave. Down came the tent, the slipcovered chairs, and the apparatus for lowering the casket into the hole. Finally, all that remained was an open grave and, incongruously, a backhoe with a front bucket full of dirt brought from behind a grove of trees (the logic being, I suppose, that you would not want the grave's dirt next to the hole during the service – a little too much honesty). Then, with solemn dignity, the family took up shovels and began to fill the grave, one last sign of love, thanksgiving, and respect for the one they laid to rest. I watched in silence and pondered their confession of faith.

Here was no denial of death, no pretending that the pain is not real. Rather, there was an acknowledgement that ruin comes to all flesh – and a refusal to believe that this is the deepest truth. In the face of the great mystery we have the resources of the community and the promise of Christ. We lean on one another and rest in the faithfulness of God. We journey as far as we can with those we love – even to the messiness of a grave – and then commend them to God in hope.

Honesty, thanksgiving, and defiant hope. As I said, I wish

my people could have seen that sermon last week. It was a lot better than the one I wrote.

Flipping

For some reason my newspaper carrier has a hard time hitting my yard. I don't know why. It's a big, downwardly sloping yard into which I would think a blind man traveling at warp speed could fling a paper. But until recently I usually found my paper in the gutter of the street. Now I realize that this is a decidedly first world problem, but on a cold, dark, and rainy morning I would prefer to stay inside until I know the paper has arrived.

Lately I'm finding my paper right at the edge of the sidewalk. I wondered what had improved his aim until one morning I happened to look out the window just as a man and his four large dogs passed the house. Without missing a step he leaned over, flipped my paper into the yard, and continued down the street.

Such a small thing. I doubt if it even registers on his awareness. But each morning he gives me this little gift which starts my day off well. So, whoever you are, thank you.

If I am honest I am more likely to flip something besides a newspaper during the day – at least mentally. Some minor aggravation (like a paper in the gutter) is enough to make me wonder about the decline of Western Civilization and call down fire from heaven on the offending party. No doubt my blood pressure and the world would be a lot better if I learned to flip more newspapers instead of cursing someone's lousy aim.

There are lots of big problems we cannot solve by ourselves. And if we are not troubled by needless suffering in our country and world we just aren't paying attention. But we are not powerless. There are small bits of grace which we can offer if we will. Where can you flip a paper today?

Enough

At the gym where I work out there is a banner hanging over the free weights. It features a testosterone-poisoned eagle, wearing an American flag doo-rag and chomping on a cigar. On the banner is emblazoned, "Never Big Enough." Now, I suppose this is intended to motivate body builders to keep on keeping on when they want to quit. It does not have that effect on me, but then bulging muscles is not one of my main goals. Most days I would settle for decent wind and joints that don't ache. I understand that setting goals is important; aspiring to do and be better is what allows people, societies, and technologies to improve. I have no problem with striving to be better.

But every time I see that banner I imagine some young woman gazing into her mirror and seeing an invisible, "Never pretty enough." I picture her looking at any popular magazine and thinking, "Never slim enough." I imagine all the students I have met over the years who have internalized "not smart enough", "not popular enough," "not good" enough from their parents, teachers, and peers. The idea that nothing is ever good enough – particularly a person – is demonic.

It is empirically untrue to say that you can never reach the point of enough. You can drink enough water to hydrate properly. You can eat enough for optimum health. If you are spending 18 hours a day in the gym to get one more rep you have moved from dreaming to pathology. If you never see your friends or your family because "never enough" haunts your thoughts at work, you need to rethink "enough." Dwelling on "never enough" sets up expectations which, far from inspiring, crush the soul with a sense of failure. But more important, living by a creed of "never enough" causes us to lose a sense of perspective. Some things really are more important than others; you cannot have a "never enough" attitude toward everything. Every goal has a price and every priority embraced is another one left to languish.

The art, of course, is discerning when we have enough. When does accumulation of stuff become theft from the poor? When does obsession with a personal preference undermine the common good? When does the drive to excel in my chosen pursuit cause blindness to the needs of others?

Jesus said the great commandment is "…you shall love the Lord your God with all your heart, and with all your soul, and with all your mind, and with all your strength. The second is like this, 'You shall love your neighbor as yourself.'" Maybe that is the single aspiration about which we can never say "enough." If we focused on that one, maybe our other goals would find their proper place.

Disengaging and Bailing

What is the difference between disengaging and bailing? I periodically see folks post things like this on social media: "I will be off Facebook for a while because I am always upset." "I have turned off my phone's news alerts." "Know that if you insist on posting about politics I will unfriend you." I understand the impulse. Nobody likes to begin the day angry and tense because the morning headlines are discouraging, bearing witness to our almost limitless ability to hurt one another.

There is most assuredly a place for disengaging. The great spiritual traditions all agree that it is essential for us to periodically go apart from the trite and transitory in order to be fully present to God and discern what is most important. How that happens can range from becoming a monastic hermit, to taking a long hike, to engaging in daily devotions, to keeping an electronic Sabbath away from email. It is neither necessary nor wise to be constantly immersed in the problems of the world.

That being said, we need to acknowledge that disengaging is the luxury of people whose lives are minimally affected by the poverty and prejudice which are the taproot of all those things we find so distressing. When I get sick unto death of politics and turn off my alerts, I know that I will still have plenty to eat, my medical bills will get paid, and I do not have to worry about police stopping me for "driving while white." That is not true for many in our society. For them agitating for change is not a discretionary use of free time; it is a necessity if their lives and the lives of their children are going to get better.

The theology of Christian worship is that we are gathered to be sent, nourished in order to have strength to be Christ's presence in the world. Something comparable needs to be in our minds as we think about how aware we will choose to be. We disengage, not to escape, but to become renewed for faithful action.

Weight of Vengeance

Tim Gautreaux is my new favorite author. Based in southeast Louisiana he writes with a vivid sense of place and an ear for language which makes you chuckle just before you realize he has snuck in a profound insight. In his novel, *The Missing*, Gautreaux explores violence, guilt, and how we become whole.

Sam Simoneaux's parents and siblings were murdered by a vicious family clan taking revenge for an accidental death which they attribute to Sam's father. Raised deep in Cajun country by his Uncle Claude, Sam is haunted by his ignorance of exactly what happened and the sense that he needs to do something to avenge his family. After being away for many years he goes home to get some answers from his uncle:

His uncle took a deep breath… "If you lookin' to get back at these people, you can't do that. You can kill 'em dead with an axe and they won't even understand why you doin' it."

"What about justice?"

"Justice works if it puts a dollar back in your pocket."

"Punishment?"

His uncle turned toward the window as a tumble of thunder came out of the next parish. What I always told you?"

He looked down. "What people do wrong is its own punishment?"

Much of the novel is an exploration of that theological assertion. There are many ways faith can express itself, but among the hardest is trusting that in fullness of time evil will fall under its own weight. Maybe we believe the scales of justice can render the right verdict – but we suspect we need to put our finger in the pan just to be sure.

It is fine to long for restorative justice (what Claude means when he says, "Justice works if it puts a dollar back in your pocket."); where restitution can be made, it should be. But the quest for vengeance is very different; that is an animal which begins by consuming the one who unleashes it. Vengeance has a way of transforming those who seek it into the thing they hate.

Paul writes, "Beloved, never avenge yourselves, but leave room for the wrath of God; for it is written, 'Vengeance is mine, I will repay, says the Lord.'" Some hear Paul promising God's wrath. I am more inclined to see God as an adult taking a shotgun away from a toddler and saying, "You really don't know how to use this safely, so give it to me before you do something stupid."

Seeking justice but not vengeance is incredibly hard. When our emotions are enflamed it is all but impossible to be honest about what we want. Of course Jesus never said it was going to be easy. Nothing is more natural than giving tit for tat. The only problem is that it is a destructive path to a dead end. To be "people of the Way" is to choose another path which our Lord blazes.

Tolerance

Last week I visited my family in Lake Charles, Louisiana. Because of the way airline schedules work I knew I was going to have a lot of time on my hands, so I girded myself with a 900+ page tome, *A Column of Fire,* the latest installment in Ken Follett's Knightbridge series. The novel is set in mid to late 16th Century England, France, and Spain, during the reign of Elizabeth I. Follett aspires first and foremost to create a page-turner, but he also demonstrates how easily it was for good Christian men and women to slaughter, burn, impoverish, and behead each other to "preserve the true faith." By the end of the book you cannot help but see how religious tolerance is a tenuous and precious possession, hard won and easily lost.

It just so happened that as I was finishing the book in the airport terminal I overheard a gentleman (and I use the term about as loosely as it can be used) comment to his friend regarding the news footage from Syria playing overhead, "Yeah, they ain't nothing but a bunch of savages, killing each other for the hell of it." The juxtaposition of my book and his comment was disturbing.

We like to think we are soooo much more civilized that "those people" from other countries and religious traditions. But even a basic understanding of history says otherwise. The savagery of Aleppo has nothing on the St. Bartholomew's Day Massacre of 1572 (Take a second to look it up). We like to think that mindless religious and racial bigotry is a thing of the past, but there are plenty of folks who echo the naked ignorance of that fellow in the airport – and count it as standing up for their faith. Only a fool would think our own land is immune to the intolerance which has bloodied other times and places.

The apostle Paul wrote that right now "we see through a glass darkly [KJV]," which is to say, imperfectly. We do well to remember that when we feel tempted to judge the beliefs of others. A little holy humility is almost always appropriate. Hating for Christ is like committing arson because you love trees.

Sound of Silence

Seven of us were enjoying a nice meal at a local restaurant, celebrating my wife's retirement from teaching. The salad was good and the conversation lively as we awaited our entrees. With a slightly worried look our server approached the table and offered a sincere apology. "I am sorry it is so quiet in here. We have done everything we can to get Pandora to play, but nothing is working."

Has it come to this? Do we assume that every waking moment of our lives must be accompanied by some sound to beat back the terror of unfilled silence? Are we afraid to be together without the social lubrication of background noise? Sometimes we go to public places explicitly for the music which accompanies the food, a piano bar or a jazz club, for example. It would have been fine if soft violins had accompanied our meal that night. But it says something sad about our culture when a fine restaurant feels the need to apologize for offering the opportunity for table talk unaccompanied by music.

I have a friend whose great gift is making you feel incredibly interesting when you are with him. He once observed, "Good conversation needs plenty of white space." I think it is his attending to his own observation which makes him so good to be with. It is white space which is often lacking in our daily lives, those moments when we are neither actively giving nor receiving new data, but simply "being," fully present to another person and the world around us. White space is like a warm, tilled field in which understanding, like seeds, has room to grow.

There is an art to finding the sweet spot between constant stimulation and none, between sensory overload and boredom. Most of us could use more white space, both in our personal interactions and in our spiritual life. By cultivating times of silence we better attend to one another and create a vessel into which God can pour the word we need to hear.

Repaving and Milling

It's taking me a little bit longer to get from my house to the office these days. They are repaving Main Street. This is more than the relatively quick and painless process of laying down a new layer of asphalt. This time they are milling the road. Milling involves a machine ripping up the pavement and sending a wave of debris up a conveyer belt into a dump truck. As I understand it you can repave a street a limited number of times before you first have to mill it down to the roadbed. South Main will ultimately be much improved, but right now it makes for a painful commute.

By temperament I am more of a re-paver than a miller. I prefer to make the bare minimum of changes in my routine. When things are not quite as I would like in my life I make a few tweaks: I hit the gym an extra day each week, read some books to feed my mind, watch my diet a bit more closely, or make some calls to neglected friends. But this amounts to repaving my life, smoothing out the bumps and filling in the cracks. That is all well and good, but sometimes you need to mill.

By that I mean asking the most basic questions: Are my most important relationships in good shape? Am I using my gifts well? Does my job give me joy? Would I like my life to continue on this trajectory for the next five or ten years? You have to be willing to question your basic assumptions, to rip up what is safe and familiar in the hope of creating something even better. Milling your life, like milling a road, can be messy and disruptive in the short term. Yet it makes for greater integrity and fulfillment down the road.

Sometimes events force you to mill. I am realizing that as I contemplate the shape of my days after retirement. But a wise person asks those fundamental questions before he or she must. Doing so lays the foundation for a life well-lived and a journey which is paved with more than good intentions.

History Lesson

One of my friends recently lent me a book on the politics before, during, and after World War I (*The World Remade*, G. J. Meyer). As he handed it to me he added the caveat, "This was pretty disillusioning for me." I now see what he meant. I suppose I had an image of the United States and its president in that period as bit like the frontier sheriff in a classic Western: noble, reluctant to use violence, but righteous when forced to do so. The reality seems a bit more sordid. Truth was distorted, fortunes made in selling the war, and egos, not ideals, were more often the driving force of diplomacy.

One of the virtues of reading history is that it both recalibrates our moral gauge and helps us to see what is at stake in the present. When times are tough and it seems that chaos is lapping at the shores we are particularly prone to nostalgia. "If we could only get back to a simpler, more moral, more unified time..." We judge the present harshly because it does not measure up to the noble days of yore. The truth is that there never was a time when politics was not contentious, when greed did not exercise an outsized impact on public policy, when ambition did not color the noblest intentions. This is nothing new. If we understand that we are less prone to despair as we face our own challenges.

But realism is not the same as complacency. Clearer sight should not lead to glazed disengagement. As many have documented, the cost of World War 1 was horrific: Millions butchered for no purpose. The seeds of another war sown in its vindictive peace. Moral failing has profound consequences; we dare not forget that.

Knowing we have been here before reminds us that until the Kingdom of God comes on earth we can expect periodic revivals of this grim play. The Christian response to the ills of society is not to presume we can wield the tools of power more righteously than others. That is the stuff of hubris and Crusades. Rather, our calling is to bind up the wounded and keep challenging everything which wants to divide the world into "us" and "them." History should make us skeptical of "Christian politics;" that is usually a holy façade for decidedly unholy agendas. But each of us does well to ask how the example and priorities of Christ inform his or her politics.

Leonardo

I have been reading Walter Isaacson's wonderful biography, *Leonardo Da Vinci*. One cannot help but be awed (and not a little intimidated) by the breadth of Leonardo's interests: painting, engineering, anatomy, geology, optics, birds, and a host of other disciplines which have become their own fields of specialty today. In trying to explain Leonardo's greatness Isaacson repeatedly emphasizes that one of his distinguishing gifts was his incredible capacity to simply pay attention to what he saw. He noticed things that others did not see. He saw how important shadows and light reflection are in what we see, the way a bird's tail dips in flight, the connection between two muscles in the face. Because he noticed the specific, he could brilliantly convey the universal. Rather than taking as true the assumptions of others Leonardo had a passion for observation and experimentation.

That got me thinking about how much we could all

benefit from a similar attitude in our relationships. Too often we think we understand another person without taking time to pay attention to the individual who is in front of us. We assume motivations or attitudes because – well, because everybody says that is the way those people are. When we act on those assumptions we are blinded by our stereotypes and preconceived notions. We put up barriers where none need be. Instead of seeing the person in front of us, we construct a caricature.

Leonardo's greatest paintings are characterized by the blurring of lines; a technique called sfumato. Tones and colors shade gradually into one another. Leonardo's use of this style was rooted in his observation that in nature we do not really see the hard lines which many artists impose, that reality is softer, hazier, and more nuanced. When we are tempted to impose our own hard lines, we might do well to remember that life seldom presents us with absolutes of good and evil. When we appreciate the complexity of what others are dealing with we are much more likely to respond out of insight rather than prejudice – and that will probably mean with much more compassion.

In All Things God Works

As I approach retirement I find myself pondering the twists and turns which have brought me to this place in my life and career. I hope there are a few more chapters to be written, but this seems like a good time to reflect on the surprising strokes which have composed the book thus far. I am realizing how often the most significant turning points were preceded by bitter disappointment and what a tragedy it would have been had I gotten what I desperately wanted at the time.

For a whole year in college I pined away for Ruth, sure that we were meant for each other. She did not agree, thank heavens, for she could never have gone spiritually and intellectually where I needed to go. I was in agony. But without that year in the romantic wilderness I would never have found the one who has been my joy all these years.

When I applied to grad school I had my career mapped out. All I needed to start the journey was acceptance and money from a top-tier school. It did not happen. What I got was acceptance and money from a very good school which also had a great Lutheran campus pastor. He has been my friend and mentor to this day. That year I found a confessional home and a new calling. Oh, how I wanted Duke; how blessed I was to arrive at LSU.

I have only cried once over a job, the day they picked someone else to serve the campus ministry for which I was perfectly suited – or so I thought. It would have been a disaster. I see that now. The call to Blacksburg came within six months.

The only reason I share these incidents is to say that we do not know enough to despair. These days there is much to discourage anyone who cares about justice, mercy, the gospel, and basic human decency. Fear is rampant and the courage to stem it obviously lacking in those who govern. I would not for a moment minimize the suffering of those who bear the brunt of our corporate anxiety; we must do all we can, by the light that we have, to stand for the vulnerable.

Yet if the gospel narrative means anything it means that God is never absent from our world and is in the midst of even our most bitter disappointments, redeeming what we thought was hopeless. Our task is to decline to despair, work diligently, and hold fast to the promise of Romans 8:28, "And we know that in all things God works for the good of those who love Him, who have been called according to His purpose." (NIV)

Living on Purpose

I am sure the Holy Spirit must think I am terribly slow. The Spirit has to say the same thing multiple times, in different ways, to get my attention. For example, last week I came across a quotation from Thoreau, "Do not be too moral. You may cheat yourself out of too much life. Aim above morality. Be not simply good; be good for something." I nodded and moved on. No Damascus Road revelation.

Later in the week, at our synod assembly, I sat for parts of three days doodling with the pens and memo pads provided by Roanoke College for the delegates. Both were printed with the simple admonition, "Live on Purpose." [An aside: I tried to find the origin of that phrase; if you do the same you will discover it is like trying to trace the multiple headwaters of a river; at some point, clear provenance fades away like rivulets on the mountainside.] As I approach retirement Thoreau's words and that exhortation have a special relevance and urgency for me. A lot of my time has been spent over the years in work that I still find important; in a few weeks that big placeholder will be no more. There is a very personal word which the Sprit seems intent on delivering in these waning weeks: Find new ways to be a blessing.

I don't think, however, that this is a word just for me and others who are at the end of their paid work life and seeking new directions. Wherever you are on your journey I invite you to ponder these two quotations for yourself and see whether they call you to think and be in new ways. Nothing is easier than putting your life on automatic pilot, seeking to do well with what is expected yet never asking whether it is worth doing in the first place. One day bleeds into the next until you discover that you have been used by life instead of using the life you were given serve God and grace those around you. To live without a conscious choice to be a blessing is to risk finding yourself mumbling the words of Macbeth:

> Tomorrow, and tomorrow, and tomorrow,
> Creeps in this petty pace from day to day,
> To the last syllable of recorded time;
> And all our yesterdays have lighted fools
> The way to dusty death. Out, out, brief candle!
> Life's but a walking shadow, a poor player,
> That struts and frets his hour upon the stage,
> And then is heard no more. It is a tale
> Told by an idiot, full of sound and fury,
> Signifying nothing.

Live on purpose.

Losing the Soul

"What does it profit them if they gain the whole world, but lose or forfeit themselves?" (Luke 9:25)

You might be surprised to know that Evangelicals were once passionate defenders of religious liberty for all, crusaders in the cause of Abolition, and outspoken advocates of social reform, seeing the gospel as inextricably linked with justice. I say you might be surprised because the majority of Americans today (according to most polls) see White Evangelicals as racist, homophobic, anti-intellectual, angry, and selfish.

As one who was nurtured in Baptist congregations I take no delight in seeing how far the tradition of my birth has fallen. With all their faults, including some Jim Crow attitudes, I cannot imagine most of the people who taught me the faith giving an 80% approval rating to a serial philanderer who openly mocks the disabled, brags about groping women, lies daily, holds the poor in contempt, and values money above all else. If you need proof of the moral and theological bankruptcy of White Evangelicalism as a movement, consider that Jerry Falwell and Franklin Graham are this man's ardent supporters. Is it any wonder that people increasingly believe Christians have little interest in following Jesus when those who most vocally invoke His name hold His teaching and example in contempt?

Let me be clear, this is not a political rant. Yes, I think Trump's policies are mistaken and bad for the country and, ironically, the worst of all for his base. But that is not my primary point. Rather, I want to note how easy it is to be seduced by the scent of power, seduced to the point of sacrificing your core values to attain it. I used Evangelicals as my case study. I could easily frame this reflection around the tendency of Mainline Denominations to become a cipher for the latest trend, privileging novelty over depth, and sacrificing a clear confession of faith to gain acceptance in the wider, secular culture. The church is ever tempted to sell out to gain a seat in the inner circles.

You hear a lot these days about the supposed persecution of Christians. But persecution never has been, nor is it now, the greatest threat to the gospel. Persecution is easy to see; it gets your attention and gives you a clear danger to confront.

To speak of Christians in America as being persecuted is to trivialize the courage of real martyrs past and present. Evangelicals are just angry over lost privilege. How very sad that asking a group of Christians to share is what makes them apoplectic.

The greater threat has always been assimilation and acculturation, the seductive invitation to go along to get along, to pretend that the gospel does not call us to a distinctive way of living. In Matthew and Luke the devil offers Jesus a deal, "I will give you all the kingdoms of the world, just bow down and worship me," which is to say, "Be realistic, you gotta fight fire with fire, lose the suffering servant model, grab my kind of power and use it."

Jesus found the wisdom and courage to walk his distinctive path. I wonder if we can too.

Beingness and Busyness

There is something scary about purging your calendar. This morning I realized that my calendar had a lot or recurring events which I will not have after I retire in two weeks. Council meetings, study groups, committees, reminders of various sorts – in a few days they will not be part of my life. So I began going through them, clicking on "delete this and following events." Before my eyes my calendar got a lot emptier. I could have said "open;" that is how I expected to think about it, freedom to do just what I want. But as those deleted events disappeared from my calendar it also felt like a bit of my personhood was blinking out.

It is no great insight to note that much of our identity is tied up in our work. That is not necessarily even a bad thing; as the Genesis creation narrative teaches, part of our calling is to work productively in the garden of the world and be good stewards of our gifts. Still, there is nothing like deleting routine events to prompt reflection on the difference between busyness and "beingness." We easily mistake the former for the latter.

Beingness is that part of us which is most fully alive and joyous. It is what notices beauty and delights in those we love. It is what greets a new challenge with excitement because it offers an opportunity for one's passion and gifts to be used well. It is a sense that we are in the right place at the right time doing the right thing for ourselves and the world. Most of all, it is a sense that our daily pursuits are in sync with our calling from God to give and receive the wonder of life.

Cultivating beingness is hard work because it takes serious discernment and discipline. We often substitute mere busyness. We figure we must be doing the right thing because our schedules are so darn jammed. We do things, not because we think they are important, but because that is the routine path of least resistance.

Nobody gets to spend their day doing only what inspires and feeds the soul. But most of us would do well to ask whether each thing on the calendar is more beingness or busyness. Before I start repopulating my calendar with appointments, filling all that white space, I'm going to reflect on what gives life and what merely takes up time. You do not have to be retiring to do the same.

This is the last Bread for the Journey I will write as pastor of Luther Memorial. I may post occasionally on Facebook, but this is the last reflection which will go out as a broadcast email. Writers need readers, so thanks to all who have read,

responded to, affirmed – and occasionally critiqued my efforts.

Acknowledgements

Many people have participated in the birth of this book. The book's shortcomings are entirely on me, but I acknowledge here the very positive influences of others.